Tennessee Volunteer Heroes 2001

Tennessee Volunteer Heroes 2001

Introduction by Tennessee First Lady
Martha Sundquist

WRITE TOGETHER™ PUBLISHING
Nashville, Tennessee

© 2001 by the Council of Community Services. All rights reserved.

ISBN 1-930142-57-9

Publisher:
Paul Clere, Write Together Publishing

Book Design and Layout:
Charles King

Cover Art:
Red Grooms:

Contributing Authors and Editors:
Patricia Albrecht
Paul Clere
Fred Cole
Chuck Gilkey
Jennifer Gilligan
Charles King
Pam Pfeffer
Debbie Reaves
Debbie Runions
Sara Smith
Rachel Swann
Carroll Van West
Carol White
Marilyn Wade-Jordan

Red Grooms lives and works in New York City and Eastern Tennessee. He has exhibited regularly at Marlborough Gallery, New York, since 1974. In December 2000, he will exhibit new works at the Patrice Trigano Gallery in Paris. Red Grooms's Tennessee Fox Trot Carousel has been running at Riverfront Park in Nashville since November 1998. He was inducted into the American Academy of Arts and Letters in the spring of 2000.

Project Coordinators:
    Council of Community Services
        Stewart Clifton, Executive Director
        Sandra Poulton, Business Manager
    Tennessee Commission on National and Community Service
        Carol White, Executive Director
        Debbie Reaves, Heroes Coordinator
        Bruce Pittman, Project Launch Coordinator
        Susan Wilson, Media Coordinator

This book presents a wide variety of opinions from hundreds of individuals across Tennessee. The publisher and copyright holder of this book make no representations or claims as to the validity of these statements, and do not necessarily share the opinions presented.

Contents

About This Book / vi

Introduction and Dedication, by Tennessee First Lady Martha Sundquist / 1

A New Frontier of Service: Being the Davy Crocketts of Volunteerism / 5
    by Fred Cole

Volunteers in Tennessee History / 17

A Volunteer Life: Maggie Duffy / 29

Volunteer Heroes Sampler / 43

Tennessee Volunteer Heroes / 99

How to Get Connected to Volunteer in Tennessee / 227

    How Do I Choose Where To Volunteer? / 227
    Where Do I Go To Volunteer? / 228
    Can I Connect with Volunteer Opportunities On-Line? / 229
    National and Community Service Glossary / 235
    Directory of Volunteer Centers in Tennessee / 237
    Other Volunteer Mobilization Organizations / 238
    Directory of United Ways in Tennessee / 239

Acknowledgements: / 243

Project Sponsors / 249

Volunteer Heroes 2002 / 253

About This Book

To the reader:

This book, this celebration of the volunteer, is truly a labor of love and a gift to the citizens of Tennessee. Tennesseans are a proud, diverse, and spirited people with strong beliefs and rich traditions—paramount among these is volunteerism. The Tennessee River may divide our state into three regions, but our volunteer spirit unites us as a community. Within our borders, within every city, town, and county, the spark of caring and cooperation that earned Tennessee its nickname 189 years ago burns today as an eternal flame. That flame illuminates our souls and shines as a beacon of hope and humanity far beyond the borders of Tennessee, even far beyond the borders of our nation. Since the United Nations has declared 2001 the "International Year of the Volunteer," it is only fitting we pause to celebrate and to pay tribute to our Tennessee Volunteer Heroes.

Tennessee Volunteer Heroes 2001 is intended to introduce you to the history of Tennessee volunteerism and to offer a sampling of the millions of individuals and organizations perpetuating the legacy of our Tennessee heritage. It is also intended to inspire *you* to envision what would happen if every Tennessean were to volunteer for one day per month. Most importantly, this book is an open invitation for you, for all Tennesseans, for all citizens of our nation and all peoples of the world to make your visions a reality by doing just that—by volunteering one day per month.

I extend special thanks to Tennessee's First Lady, Martha Sundquist, for her leadership and support as Honorary Chair of the Tennessee Commission on National and Community Service and the Volunteer Tennessee initiative. Much appreciation and gratitude is also due renowned Tennessee artist Red Grooms for creating and donating the book cover inspired by the incredible volunteer life of Maggie Duffy. Finally, this book would not have been possible without the support, guidance, and dedication of the volunteer boards and staffs of the Tennessee Commission on National and Community Service and the Council of Community Services.

Please keep the flame burning bright for a new generation as you Volunteer Tennessee!

With best regards,

Paul Clere
Publisher

Introduction and Dedication

Tennessee Volunteer Heroes 2001 is a book to warm our hearts and inspire our souls. While no book can do justice to the gifts of caring from the estimated 3 million Tennesseans who volunteer, I believe this volume has captured the spirit of the Volunteer State.

Helping our neighbors is Tennessee's special heritage. As these stories show, when Tennesseans see a need, they reach out to help in more ways than can be imagined. Consider just a few of the people you'll meet. Consider 88 year old Red Cross volunteer Maggy Duffy (on the cover), known as the "Mother of Volunteerism" in Japan for her efforts there after World War II. Or Melissa Poe, who at age 9 started the world's largest youth environmental organization. Or nationally recognized "Daily Point of Light" Vernon Stewart who has delivered meals on wheels in Memphis in spite of illness, a car wreck, failing vision and car theft. Or AmeriCorps member Pam Gant who, in the course of her home health visits to low-income new moms, helped save the life of a new baby who had stopped breathing by administering CPR, calming the mother and calling for medical help. Or Lions International past President Austin Jennings of Woodbury, who led a massive campaign to eliminate preventable blindness. Or 81 year old Omie Street who takes two frail elderly neighbors to the doctor and grocery store when they need her. This is the indomitable spirit that moved Tennessee's pioneers, and it is emerging again in our times.

In July, 2000, I issued a call for nominations for *Tennessee Volunteer Heroes 2001* that was distributed through newspapers, radio, TV and mailings. In this first year for a first-time project sponsored by the Tennessee Commission on National & Community Service and the Council of Community Services, we know there are Tennessee heroes who did not hear of this effort or were too busy helping others to send in their forms. This book is dedicated to those mentioned in its pages, but, also, like the flame at the tomb of the unknown soldier, to the deserving but unsung heroes whose names we did not mention.

Nominations were reviewed by the Tennessee Commission on National and Community Service, who decided that all were worthy of inclusion. The profiles featured in the "Volunteer Hero Sampler" section were selected to give a sense of the diversity and richness of volunteer service across Tennessee. There is no way to measure the comparative merit of the many kinds of service Tennesseeans undertake daily to help their neighbors. The goal of this book was not to spur competition, but to celebrate the Volunteer State's own "thousand points of light."

I would like to express my thanks to several special volunteers whose support made Tennessee Volunteer Heroes 2001 possible: the Tennessee Commission on National & Community Service, the Council of Community Services, Write Together Publishing, BellSouth Pioneers, J.C. Penney, R.J. Young, WSMV Channel 4, Tennessee Cable Telecommunications Association, the Renaissance Center, Tennessee's Volunteer Centers, Ingram Industries Inc., history section writer Jennifer Gilligan and reviewer Dr. Carroll Van West, Hillsboro School students Jeremy Davis and Kyle Saccheri who designed the Volunteer Tennessee logo, college student coordinators Bruce Pittman and Susan Wilson, and the seniors at Scott's Hill Senior Center who prepared the call for nominations mailing. The Commission's volunteer steering committee of Debbie Reaves, Paul Clere, Sara Smith, Pam Pfeffer, Fred Cole, Sara Sellers, Lynn Stewart and Jim Hughson were volunteer heroes themselves, especially in the typing and proof-reading stages.

Beloved Tennessee artist Red Grooms delighted us all with his volunteer gift of cover art based on the likeness of volunteer hero Maggy Duffy. My deep thanks go to him.

May the stories within these pages bless you and inspire you, just as our Tennessee Volunteer Heroes have been blessed through their selfless service to others.

Martha Sundquist
Honorary Chair, Tennessee Commission on National & Community Service
Executive Residence, Nashville
October 2000

If every Tennessean were to volunteer for one day a month, we could…

educate and train all citizens in order to provide them with a better way of life.

—Norman Acres
Helenwood
Scott County

If every Tennessean were to volunteer for one day a month, we could…

prevent and reduce the teen smoking rate by 66% and possibly decrease the risk of chronic diseases by 50% through creating awareness among Tennesseans through one day volunteering for learning and teaching.

—Nasar U. Ahmed, PhD
Nashville
Davidson County

If every Tennessean were to volunteer for one day a month, we could…

drastically impact and improve the quality of life of all Tennesseans by being role models for young people and improving the society we live in.

—Melanie Alexander
Murfreesboro
Rutherford County

If every Tennessean were to volunteer for one day a month, we could…

raise the quality of life for every Tennessean EVERY day of EVERY month.

—Dr. N. Max Atnip
Cookeville
Putnam County

If every Tennessean were to volunteer for one day a month, we could…

stamp out welfare dependency completely. We could empower all individuals to take responsibility for their own actions. We could mentor, train, develop, empower, motivate and challenge all individuals to believe in themselves enough to use their own God-given talents to succeed. If just 31 people volunteer to teach a G.E.D. class, computer class, job readiness workshop or job placement assistance, we could serve clients everyday of the month and help more people. And ultimately, our economy, schools, businesses, neighborhoods and societies would become better places for all to live.

—Marene J. Austin
Memphis
Shelby County

If every Tennessean were to volunteer for one day a month, we could…

lend a helping hand to more people in need without putting a burden on just a few people. We would be able to make more visits to elderly and disabled persons to help with their daily needs. We could make a difference in our community by volunteering our time and energies to work with the local agencies that are short of staff. Serving as a volunteer in the community is rewarding in more ways than one.

—Margie Avery
Alamo
Crockett County

A New Frontier of Service: Being the Davy Crocketts of Volunteerism

A perspective on volunteerism, national and community service in Tennessee

I was born at a Naval Air Station in Beeville, Texas and lived as a toddler in San Antonio. When my parents divorced in 1962, I was five years old and the oldest of four children. My mother packed us into an old Rambler station wagon and we moved to a suburb of Chattanooga, Tennessee.

Before we left, my grandfather, whom I would never see again, gathered his grandchildren as he often had and took us down to the Alamo a short distance away. The Alamo is a shrine known and revered the world over, where one of the great battles for freedom and independence in American history was fought. It was at this old Spanish mission that I first learned of Tennessee. As we walked with my grandfather on the hallowed grounds of the historic mission, he told us about Davy Crockett and 28 other Tennesseans who died at the Alamo. He read to us the famous plea of Colonel William Travis for help in defending the fortress: "To the People of Texas and All Americans in the World… I shall never surrender or retreat… Victory or Death!"

All who defended the Alamo died in battle at the hands of Mexican General Antonio de Santa Anna and his forces. But it was the sacrifice of those Tennessee Volunteers and other defenders of the Alamo that rallied Texas revolutionary troops with the battle cry "Remember the Alamo!" and General Santa Anna was later defeated. Tennessee Volunteers helped win Texas her independence, which added more than a million square miles to the American nation at that time and paved the way for expansion to the Pacific.

To ease our childhood fears about moving from Texas to this unknown place called Tennessee, my grandfather charged us with this mission: "Texas is sending you to Tennessee to help pay back debt we owe the Volunteer State for helping us win our independence. Like Texans, Tennesseans never surrender or retreat. Do your best, fight for what you think is right, and help those less fortunate. Be Davy Crocketts of Volunteerism!" my grandfather said.

As young Tennessee boys in the years that followed, my brother and I were given coon skin caps and "Old Betsy" flintlock rifles as Christmas presents. We built our "Alamos" and pretended we were Davy Crockett and Tennessee Volunteers fighting to the death. In my teen years, I would come to more fully appreciate what my Grandpa Cole was conveying to me about Tennessee Volunteers on that sad day at the Alamo when we said goodbye forever. My grandfather wanted me to fully enjoy life, and he knew some of the more rewarding experiences in my life would come from volunteer and community service. So it has been that grandfather's admonitions have stirred within throughout my life—like a bugle call echoing across the distances of time and generation, calling me as a volunteer soldier to help fight the revolution of changing the world one child, one community, one state and one nation at a time.

Building Service Experiences and Memories

As an American young person makes the transition into life as an adult, I believe it is important for him or her to have a reservoir of volunteer service memories and, for Tennessee young people, a sense of the volunteer heritage of our state. The future of service would be very bright indeed if every young person today had as their ambition becoming a Davy Crockett of Volunteerism. We adults who have this high expectation of children and youth have an obligation and responsibility to ensure that opportunities for service learning are abundantly available. By doing so, we foster a service ethic that leads young people into a lifetime of service endeavors.

There is strong bipartisan support in Tennessee to set the example for making the expectation of national and community service real for all Americans. This moment in history is one of fantastic opportunity—an era when we have a chance to fully embrace big citizenship, to take the road of high and enlightened purpose, and it is up to us to decide where we go from here.

It is important that we, the people of Tennessee, volunteer for the front lines of battles of a new millennium—that we embrace the spirit of being "the Volunteer State." Why should we be any less fervent in fighting for our children and communities than Tennessee Volunteers of past? America's promise has been preserved for our benefit and enjoyment, and we have a sacred duty to preserve it for future generations.

The New Front Line

I believe we may be in an era where the greatest threats to our national security are building from *within*. As much as the foreign front has in times past, the domestic battle front now deserves serious attention of leaders in this country. We have monumental problems related to education, basic skills, workforce development, employment, housing, underdeveloped infrastructure, transportation, substance abuse, health care, and family breakdown.

It is well historically established that great but fallen nation states have decayed, crumbled and met their demise more from destructive forces emerging *within* their borders than from any foreign enemies. I fear, as the famous comic book philosopher Pogo concluded one day when pondering out in the Okefenokee Swamp: "We have met the enemy and he is us." And I am reminded of words the epic poet John Milton wrote in Paradise Lost: "Awaken, Arise or be forever fallen." If we don't awaken to our precious individual right to make a difference, and our responsibility to try and change the ugliness of the human condition around us right now, our future is not secure. It's going to take all of us working together, both those who need resources and those who have resources, to bring about the kind of change that will save us from ourselves.

All Americans should be prepared to give something back to the nation that has given, and continues to give them, so much. And those who hold positions of leadership and roles of formulating policy must emphasize, and perhaps demand, that an ethic of reciprocity and mutual responsibility undergird social public policy. Giving back to the community is something to which all Americans should be expected to commit themselves.

In my role as chairman of the Tennessee Commission on National and Community Service, I have had many opportunities to meet and speak with people at the grassroots level about the responsibility of individual citizens to give back in service to their communities. People are hungry for leadership, and waiting to be rallied for the battles of social change. When you ask folks to volunteer, when you send out a clarion call, they respond. There is a tremendous charitable force and spirit of concern. These people are doing the best they can while painfully aware we need to do more. Unless more volunteers and more resources gravitate to the cause of positive change and help fight the battles of community endeavor, it's going to be tough to advance. We need more help.

I believe that in plowing the ground that renews our civic landscape, there is a role for government. While government perhaps should not take the lead in fostering solutions to community problems, it should play a role in working with communities to foster an environment that will encourage the growth of strong citizenship and restoration of civic life. For example, closer collaborations between government and religious, charitable and nonprofit organizations could work to address the nation's problems. Troops on the front lines need support. Thankfully, in the last 6 years we have had a program of national service in this country that has clearly been monumentally beneficial in towns, cities and states across this nation.

But it has been a battle at times preserving this national resource. Some people have advanced the position that in the scope of national budget priorities, funding AmeriCorps and other Corporation for National Service programs should not be at the top of the list for spending of taxpayer dollars. Many argue that communities should organize, rally and address problems on their own, with no help from government. Ideally, if everybody met their obligation to "give back to the community," we could solve problems on our own. But everybody doesn't give back.

Making It Happen

The role of the Corporation for National Service, through such programs as AmeriCorps, Senior Corps and Learn and Serve, has been that of a facilitator and convener in communities. It has not become the huge bureaucracy and partisan organization some feared, but rather, quite the opposite. National service has been a catalyst in mobilizing volunteers, and in helping to make the community service given by the occasional or part-time volunteer more meaningful and effective.

The governors of this nation made it clear on September 20, 2000 how they feel about national service when 49 signed a letter urging Congress to extend the National and Community Service Amendments Act saying:

> "We have seen the progress of young people inspired by older students, the importance of trained hands helping after a disaster, and the pride of a senior sharing his or her time with a child in need of mentoring… As Governors, we recognize the value of national service as a tool in meeting important needs in our states. We do not want to lose this force for good in our communities, states, and country."

A new patriotism is emerging that is of a more local nature. We are engaged in a mobilization of all sectors of our society: business, non-profits, education, communities of faith, citizens young and old, civic organizations and government. The call to national service is one around which all Americans should rally. The underlying premise of national service—that service to one's community is an expectation of citizenship—is an American ideal. It doesn't belong to any one party or ideology.

Statistically Speaking

- an estimated 109 million American adults volunteered in 1998 (the latest statistics available), up from 93 million in 1995.

- In 1998, 56% percent of adults in this country volunteered an average of 3½ hours a week; giving a total of 19.9 billion hours. This is the equivalent of over nine million full-time employees.

    Who are America's volunteers?
- 62% of women say they volunteer
- as do 49 % of men,
- 43% percent of seniors aged 75 and over,
- 46% of Hispanics
- and 47% of African-Americans.

- 86% say they volunteer because they feel compassion for those in need.
- 72% percent volunteer because they have an interest in a particular activity or work.
- 70% volunteer to gain a new perspective on life around them.

- 9 out of 10 individuals volunteer when asked.

- 13 million teens, more than half of America's teen population (59%) volunteered in 1995 (the latest statistics available).
- Approximately one-third of young people in grades 7-12 identified "working for the good of my community and country" and "helping others or volunteering" as very important future goals.

(from *Giving and Volunteering in the United States,* 1999; Independent Sector.)

For adults looking to connect with children in their family or community, working together on volunteer and community service projects is meaningful and rewarding.

America's Corporate Involvement

There has been a great awakening of corporate America in support of volunteer efforts, community service organizations and events. There is, of course, tremendous debate about the obligation of business—in an era of great profits and great need—to give back generously to communities. From a financially puritan perspective, there is little or no obligation to have "contributions" as a line item in the company budget. But given that volunteerism and service is a booming interest among all Americans, the investment of corporate America in helping them advance pays dividends of monumental proportions. It's a meaningful way to reach customers and build loyalty as contributing members of communities whose collective purchases make or break their business.

Eighty-one percent of companies surveyed by the Points of Light Foundation in 1999 connect volunteering to their overall business strategies, compared with only 31 percent who did so in 1992. Respondents to the survey also unanimously agreed that corporate volunteering helps create healthier communities and improves a company's public image; ninety-seven percent said these programs improve employee teamwork. Everybody wins.

A Land of Contrasts

It's a good thing the picture of volunteerism and community service in America is improving. In surveying the landscape that is Tennessee, a sobering reality sinks painfully into the hearts and minds of most aware observers: In the midst of all the great natural beauty that graces our state is the tremendous ugliness of stories of people going without adequate housing, food, clothing, health care, transportation, education, employment and other fundamental and basic securities associated with being fully embraced by the promise of this nation.

Because of the 2000 presidential campaign, and Vice President Al Gore being from Tennessee, the media focused on life in the Volunteer State. There were, for example, numerous "quality of life" comparisons between Tennessee and Texas. *George* Magazine was in Campbell County, Sevier County, and several other Tennessee communities poking around, taking pictures and conducting interviews. And in their October 2000 issue, the world was reminded again that Tennessee children living in our cities and rural communities are going without the essentials of America's promise. For Tennessee, and for us all, it would be unconscionable to know of this ugliness in our midst, and do nothing to rid ourselves of it.

The future work of volunteerism and community service will be much along the same lines of what it has been in the past—that is, meeting individual and community need. Age and era may change, and become more technologically sophisticated and modern, but human and community need will remain constant, as will the demand for volunteers to meet these needs.

The Potential to Change

Turning the ugly side of Tennessee into individual stories of great beauty is both the challenge and reward of volunteering and community service. Volunteers are tremendous assets to work advanced by community nonprofit organizations, and often serve themselves as leaders in organizations focused on improving the quality and availability of needed resources. Given the important role of the volunteer in building a resource-rich environment, we wonder about what the effect would be in our communities if either of the two following phenomena occurred:

- If every Tennessean would volunteer for one day each month; or
- If every Tennessean who now volunteers didn't show up to volunteer tomorrow.

The potential effect in either direction is monumental. Without a doubt, there would be a social disaster of unparalleled magnitude if volunteers didn't show up. But if every Tennessean volunteered one full day each month, the quality of life in our state for all citizens and communities would radically change in truly positive ways.

As we advance volunteerism and national and community service in Tennessee and the nation in the new century, we have flags around which we can rally: America's Promise—The Alliance for Youth; 2001—International Year of the Volunteer; the Points of Light Foundation and Volunteer Centers; AmeriCorps, Learn and Serve America, Senior Corps, and the United Way. The great partnerships between these organizations and others that are emerging will be what revolutionizes the work we do—all the engines of giving back through community service ignited in a mighty push forward.

Since the Presidents' Summit for America's Future in April 1997, we have seen the vibrant rise of America's Promise—The Alliance for Youth in Tennessee and the nation. Communities of Promise in Tennessee have been models for the nation, and celebrated as such in national forums and marketing campaigns of which we are all proud. The reason for this is that we are learning more and more about how to sit down at the same table as collaborating partners focused on common goals. Sometimes, it is a difficult process just getting to the same table.

And when we do, it is sometimes a great challenge finding ways for moving forward in addressing compelling community and human needs together. But when we keep coming to the table of united effort we all win.

Volunteering in 2001

The year 2001 is very promising for the cause of volunteerism. The United Nations has named 2001 "International Year of the Volunteer," and as the Volunteer State, Tennessee is making big plans. We are ready for a cause that appeals to our better angels, and calls us to more than self-interest. Americans, and Tennesseans, respond to crusades, and the fight for our children and our communities is one for which there is a growing atmosphere of urgency. In 2001, International Year of the Volunteer, we expect that modern day Tennesseans will rally for the Volunteer cause; and they will do so with the moral equivalent of war, embracing the wartime spirit of unity and service which is the tradition of our state.

What It Means to America's Next Generation

I know it's an old cliché, but it is unavoidably the truth: "Our children are our future." As such, it is for us, as adults, to ensure our children are connected to the resources they need to secure both our future and theirs. If there was ever a time for us as adults to pay back for being helped along as children, that time is now. If there was ever a time for us to share the wealth we enjoy with groups and organizations serving those less fortunate, that time is now. If there was ever a day to give our time as volunteers supporting worthy human and community causes, that day is now. We have it within our power to change the world by changing the quality of life in one community or one life at a time. And as it relates to children and youth, we're going to give it our best effort for these reasons:

- Investing in volunteer, national and community service efforts will save taxpayer dollars of the future.
- Building children, youth and communities is cheaper than building prisons— moreover, it puts us on much higher ground morally.
- Ensuring that our children and youth have a healthy and smart start is preferable to paying their healthcare bill down the road.
- Connecting children to structured activities during non-school hours with volunteer adult supervision and participation is far better for both our young people and our communities than leaving them to televisions and the streets.
- Educating our children in such a way that they get marketable skills is clearly beneficial to both the young people and the community in terms of workforce development.
- Providing young people with opportunities to give back to their communities in service helps to make them better citizens and improves our communities.

General Powell has drawn us a portrait of the American landscape of national service as we move our country into a new millennium. "For some of our young people," he says, "preserving our democratic way of life means shouldering a rifle, or climbing into a cockpit, or weighing anchor and setting out to sea. For others it means helping a child to read, or helping that child to secure needed vaccinations or health care. Or it means building a park, or helping to bring peace to troubled neighborhoods, or helping communities recover from natural disasters, or reclaiming the environment."

There is more that brings us together than there is that separates us. We all have our "kingdoms" to nurture, protect, fund, showcase and work to build into efforts that make a meaningful difference for our communities and people. We have (I say this respectfully) big ambitions, and many wonderful things are being accomplished. But when we move beyond our own turf, and bring meaningful life to that seemingly worn-out word "collaboration," truly remarkable things happen. We can do more together than we can do alone. This has been validated by the progress we've made in recent years. My vision for the future of volunteerism, national and community service is that we as the people of Tennessee and as a nation, rally around the flag of common endeavor, and become individually, in our own ways, Davy Crocketts of Volunteerism.

Fred Cole
Chairman 1999-2000
Tennessee Commission on National and Community Service

> If every Tennessean were to volunteer for one day a month, we could…
>
> help those who need it, grow stronger, and be an example to others.
>
> —Amber Bailey
> La Follette
> Campbell County

> If every Tennessean were to volunteer for one day a month, we could…
>
> make a difference in thousands of lives and show the world what a difference can be made by one individual.
>
> —Odell Baker
> Germantown, Shelby County

Volunteers in Tennessee History

Volunteers. To some, this word conjures images of intense UT fans draped in orange, but for most Tennesseans, it is a word that defines the authentic culture of altruism and civic action that is the backbone of life in Tennessee. For years, Tennesseans have selflessly opened schools, championed civil rights, fought back floodwaters, cured yellow fever, built trails, fed the hungry, organized laborers, and nurtured communities through service.

We only know the names and stories of the most famous volunteers. We have heard of Andrew Jackson who called up thousands of "volunteer" troops for the War of 1812, or Diane Nash, who while at Fisk University, rallied thousands of student demonstrators in Freedom Rides and lunch counter sit-ins throughout the south.

But the silent, often unrecognized efforts of millions of others are part of the rich history of our state. You need only flip through a history book, or turn on a country or blues radio station to understand how profoundly Tennessee and its people have influenced the rest of the country. From its earliest moments to the present, volunteers have played critical roles in the social, cultural, political and everyday events that have helped shape Tennessee and inspired the nation.

Volunteers in a New Wilderness

Tennessee is a patchwork of people and culture. In fact, its early inhabitants from some five indigenous nations also produced some of the first documented volunteers. Cherokee, Shawnee, Chickasaw, Yuchi and Creek tribes spread across what is now modern Tennessee. The first interactions between these native peoples and Euro-American settlers were often tense and occasionally bloody. In many cases, volunteer guides and interpreters paved the road for peaceful coexistence and mutual benefit. Nanye'hi (Nancy Ward), a Cherokee noblewoman, was renowned for her valor during battles, but also learned to speak English and served as a translator, trade negotiator and peacemaker between natives and whites for dozens of years.

As more Euro-Americans settled the region, Tennessee became a gateway for western expansion. This push gave rise to a host of volunteer guides, explorers, surveyors and the famous "long hunters." As Tennessee settled and moved to statehood, these volunteers worked to establish the first vestiges of community life — churches, schools and civic organizations. These early volunteers in tribal nations and at Jonesborough, Fort Nashborough and other settlements established a strong foundation for Tennessee's volunteer legacy.

Soldiers of Service

As the state and its inhabitants grew and learned to live together, they came to view themselves as fierce patriots. Therefore, it is no wonder that Tennessee has played a pivotal role in every major military conflict since 1812. Prior to the twentieth century, soldiers themselves were volunteers. Tennessee is known as "The Volunteer State" because of the thousands of citizens who eagerly volunteered for military action between the War of 1812 and the Mexican War. In fact, in 1848, when Governor Brown called for 2,000 volunteers for the Mexican War, at least 30,000 Tennesseans responded.

In keeping with this tradition, citizens throughout the state have rallied to serve their state and country in times of greatest need. Consider Cynthia Dunn, who mustered dozens of women in the first all-female unit of the Confederate Homeguards. Or Dean Duke, who left his business to command troops stationed in Dahrain during Operation Desert Storm. One of Tennessee's most revered heroes, Sgt. Alvin C. York volunteered to use his Upper Cumberland sharpshooting talents despite conscientious objector views — in 1918, York and 8 other men captured some 132 prisoners in France, a success that led to his receipt of the Congressional Medal of Honor. Sometimes, men and women who volunteered in times of war were forced to combat prejudice or break new ground in order to serve their country. That was the case for Nashville native Cornelia Fort, who witnessed the bombing of Pearl Harbor during a flight lesson and then went on to serve as the first female aviator and flight instructor in World War II. It was also the case with Tom Martin, who left Vanderbilt Law school voluntarily and enlisted in the Marine Infantry during Vietnam. While on tour, Martin took a round of enemy fire in his spine and was permanently paralyzed. However, he returned to finish school and become active in volunteer initiatives to help returning Vietnam veterans in Tennessee find jobs.

Beyond serving as volunteer soldiers, many Tennesseans organized efforts to support service men and women. From 1917-1919, the Memphis Chapter of the National League for Women's Service retained over 1,000 volunteers who wrapped bandages, assembled first aid kits and collected donations for men on the Western Front. During World War II, citizens from around the state sold war bonds, donated tire rubber and other goods for the war effort. During the Vietnam and Gulf conflicts, school children from around the state wrote letters to soldiers and raised supplies for war refugees. The efforts go on today.

Tennesseans went beyond war to help build peace. Volunteers in the National Guard, Reserve Officers Training Corps and Civil Air Patrol help in peacetime while maintaining readiness for times of challenge. One of the finest examples of building the peace is the *Tennessee Volunteer Heroes 2001* cover feature volunteer Maggie Duffy, known as the "mother of volunteerism" in Japan, for her work to generate volunteerism as part of Red Cross relief efforts after World War II.

The Road to Freedom and Justice

In addition to Tennessee's role in regional and national military history, the state has served as a theater for major social and political movements over the last two hundred years. Volunteers throughout the state contributed to the abolition of slavery, the overthrow of Jim Crow laws, the passage of women's suffrage, and the organization of poor farmers, coal and textile workers. Volunteers in these efforts rallied against injustice and helped create local change that served as a catalyst for the rest of the nation.

Volunteers were the only soldiers behind early abolition and emancipation efforts. Pioneers like Quaker Elihu Embree published one of the first anti-slavery newspapers in the country, *The Emancipator*. His efforts and those of others allowed Scottish immigrant Frances Wright to establish the first colony for freed slaves in the south. Known as Nashoba, the settlement near Memphis gave freed slaves a formal education and access to doctors and trade skills. Although the colony was short-lived, it helped others understand that the battle to free enslaved African-Americans was one first of freedom and then of equality through education and political participation.

Even though the efforts of abolitionists like Embree and Wright led to slave emancipation in 1865, others carried the torch for social freedom in the face of the "separate but equal" Jim Crow south. Ida B. Wells, a school teacher, newspaper editor and volunteer from Memphis organized the first highly public anti-lynching campaign and later went on to be one of the founding members of the National Association for the Advancement of Colored People (NAACP). The 1950's and 1960's brought key reforms in political and civil rights for African-Americans through the help of vigilant citizens such as the Reverends Kelly Miller Smith and Jim Lawson, who organized desegregation demonstrations throughout Nashville, and Theotis Robinson, the first African-American student admitted to the University of Tennessee. During this time, black and white volunteers abounded across the state, fighting for equal pay, registering poor black sharecroppers to vote in Fayette and Haywood counties, integrating public buildings and lunch counters, and much more.

In many ways, the daily struggle for civil and political rights in the African-American community went hand in hand with the quest for women's suffrage and equality. In fact, many of the state's strongest abolitionists also volunteered around women's suffrage. Volunteers included women like Sue Shelton White of Henderson, who chaired the Tennessee Branch of the National Woman's Party in the early twentieth century. Her leadership spawned dozens of local chapters throughout the state and was instrumental in the ultimate ratification of the 19th Amendment in Tennessee. Beyond suffrage, female volunteers worked to create understanding and build bridges between black and white women. In Nashville, African-American businesswoman Frankie Pierce launched a series of small cross-racial coalitions that brought black and white women together around suffrage. Beyond that, Pierce started the first Tennessee Chapter of the Federation of Colored Women's Clubs—a social and civic club for African-American women that was instrumental in launching the schools, after-school clubs and employment training programs for children in black communities throughout middle Tennessee.

While many volunteers struggled to retain political rights for women and minorities, others valiantly fought to organize and support the state's rural poor. Throughout Tennessee, coal miners, textile workers and farmers struggled to makes ends meet. Volunteer organizations such as the Grange, and later the Tennessee Farmers Alliance, allowed farmers to pool resources to provide insurance and broker relationships with non-farmers. These organizations, fueled by volunteer members, created a safety net and provided a sense of community in Tennessee's most isolated counties. Beyond the farms, citizens rallied around mills and mines to support fair wages and safe conditions. Volunteers like Lucille Thornburgh walked out of the Cherokee Spinning Company in Knoxville to encourage businesses to work hand in hand with workers. Ultimately, Thornburgh lost her job, and was blacklisted in her community, but she continued to champion the causes of organized labor by studying at the British labor school, and later editing the *East Tennessee Labor News*. Her volunteer efforts and those of Myles Horton and Don West served as the backbone for fair wages and working conditions in East Tennessee and throughout the south.

The Altruism of Every Day

Clearly, volunteers have positively affected native-settler relations, war efforts and major socio-political movements, but perhaps the most enduring positive effect they have had is on day to day community life. Volunteers run the local PTA, the Red Cross, the VFW and American Legion, the civic clubs and the church administrative board. In early communities, volunteers organized and staffed the first hospitals, fire stations, and police stations. They built public parks, organized community gatherings and supported the development of the art and music that is native to Tennessee. Today, volunteers work through community organizations and federal programs like AmeriCorps. They run after-school recreation programs in Latin American Community Centers. They help Kurdish and Laotian immigrants learn English. They organize field trips in local senior centers. The establishment of social service agencies, civic clubs, churches and other service organizations are one of the key pieces of Tennessee's volunteer history.

Churches have long been key volunteer organizations in communities. In the days of circuit riding ministers, citizens served as deacons and elders. They visited shut-ins and provided services for widows and orphans. Beyond caring for local church members, religious volunteers were critical in the establishment of some of Tennessee's excellent colleges and universities, including Aquinas, Belmont, Bethel, Bryan, Carson-Newman, Christian Brothers, Cumberland, David Lipscomb, Fisk, King, Knoxville, Lambuth, Lane, Lee, LeMoyne-Owen, Lincoln Memorial, Martin, Maryville, Milligan, Rhodes, Southern Adventist, Tennessee Wesleyan, Trevecca Nazarene, Tusculum, Union, University of the South at Sewanee, Vanderbilt and others. Church volunteers raised money and donated land for many of these schools and continue to provide ongoing support. Outstanding volunteers such as Father Ryan, and Sister Katharine Drexel worked with African-American citizens to open many schools Nashville. Currently, many churches and faith-based volunteers play broader roles in communities. For example, in Knoxville, over ten faith communities provide tutoring and mentoring to children as part of Knoxville's Promise, an initiative designed to filter more services to at-risk youth. Tying Nashville Together (TNT) brings together 61 churches, synagogues and temples to work on broader issues such as school desegregation, community policing, economic development and affordable housing. Historically and today, faith communities and their volunteers have helped strengthen and improve neighborhoods throughout the state.

Community life hinges on the health and wellbeing of its citizens, particularly children. Throughout the years, the establishment of public schools, hospitals and community health programs was the role of volunteers. Large-scale efforts of philanthropist Julius Rosenwald (an executive at Sears Roebuck Corporation) established some of the only schools for African-American youth in rural Tennessee. In the 1930's, May Justus served as one of the first women to teach in remote sections of Cocke County. She went on to establish multiple schools in Appalachia and later taught at Highlander Center, a school established to teach core subjects, life skills and community organizing for the poor and disenfranchised. Winchester native Joseph Campbell championed for the education of blind children. Blind himself, he helped establish the first public school for blind children in the state— he became such a pioneer in special education that he later founded the Royal Normal School for the blind in London. The work of schools has long been the work of volunteers. Barbara Russell of Memphis pioneered the Adopt-a-School movement that continues to partner schools and businesses and parents to make the lives of children better.

Volunteers have also been critical links in improving public health and creating hospitals. In 1878, over 65 volunteer doctors and nurses lost their lives treating patients in the Memphis yellow fever epidemic. In the mid-1920's philanthropists provided funds through the Commonwealth Fund for the establishment of a Children's Health Department in Rutherford County. Dr. Henry Mustard, and a team of five public health nurse/educators worked for five years to involve parents, teacher and other community residents in preventative health care like basic hygiene, immunization and the development of proper indoor plumbing. Volunteers in the effort taught food preparation and led clinics for pregnant mothers and children. This landmark effort resulted in the establishment of a county health department and served as a model for other rural areas throughout the south. In the 1960's VISTA (Volunteers in Service to America) volunteers worked in public clinics in rural and urban areas to combat the health problems that go hand in hand with abject poverty. Modern volunteers are still critical to the promotion and support of public health. The Nashville Health Corps AmeriCorps members conduct home visits with low-income teen mothers in order to increase immunization rates and health of infants. Across town, the PENCIL Foundation and St. Thomas hospital operate a Science Scholars Program that allows Metro school students who are interested in pursuing medicine to volunteer and develop skills by volunteering at the hospital. Mothers Against Drunk Driving and other highway safety volunteers are grassroots advocates for health and safety issues.

Churches, schools and hospitals form the center of most neighborhoods and counties. However, Tennessee has a strong tradition of civic and volunteer clubs, nonprofits and associations that have strengthened communities and spawned some of the state's great leaders. For example, several women at the first Presbyterian Church of Nashville, including Ann Rodgers Grundy and her daughter Louise Grundy McGavock, founded the Women's Charitable Society in 1816. These volunteers provided key services such as clothing and food to those in need throughout the area. This club, one of the first female-initiated civic organizations, helped spawn clubs throughout the state, and eventually became one of a national network of the General Federation of Women's Clubs.

For many individuals, civic clubs and programs became a way to address issues they felt passionately about and to develop their own leadership. As a youngster,

Josephine Holloway was attracted to the ideals of Juliet Gordon Lowe, founder of the Girl Scouts and Girl Guides of America. As an African-American, she was barred membership into all-white troops, but, in 1923, she organized an unofficial group of girls in her native Nashville. In 1933, her efforts were recognized and her girls became the first African-American Girl Scout troop. Her dedication helped pave the way for the desegregation of children's clubs and programs throughout the south. And in 1991, Vanderbilt students Michael Magevney and Laura Mann founded Breakaway, the alternative spring break organization. Concerned by the actions of fellow students, they created an opportunity that allowed college students to donate their time to charitable causes during spring break. Hundreds of universities now participate in Breakaway, and over the years, the idea of "alternative spring break" has spread to churches, businesses and high schools around the world.

Often, civic clubs and nonprofits become leaders for efforts centered on community-wide improvement. Exchange Club of Nashville, a volunteer and philanthropic organization, is the largest chapter in the country and was instrumental in raising the funds to open Cheekwood Botanical Gardens to the public in 1960. Most Chambers of Commerce rely on volunteers to help recruit new jobs and address quality of life issues necessary to attract economic growth. Today, Fred Cole, a native of Campbell County, is working to rally his community around the issues of children as part of the national America's Promise initiative. In 1997, Cole formed Campbell County's Promise. This countywide collaboration brings stakeholders from the public, private and nonprofit sector together to meet the needs of at risk youth and teenagers. His efforts sparked similar initiatives in other East Tennessee counties.

Throughout the state, volunteers are working in rural counties and inner-city neighborhoods through museums, state parks, in political campaigns and homeless shelters. In fact, modern volunteers work not only in one civic organization, but build bridges between nonprofits, businesses, schools and other agencies to improve the world around them. Volunteers are creating new ventures and new organizations to sustain the ever-increasing number of students, working adults and retirees who volunteer each year.

Communities organized to engage volunteers and philanthropic efforts in a variety of ways. In many communities, United Ways and Volunteer Centers have emerged as key coordinating points. Since 1923, in Nashville, the Council of Community Services has provided information, planning and coordination services for Nashville's health and human services community. Its goal is to research, identify and find solutions to the emerging needs of the Nashville community. Hands On Memphis, Hands On Nashville and Nashville PULSE focus on making volunteering convenient for young adults and youth whose work and school schedules make traditional service difficult.

The Power of Volunteerism and National Service

Tennessee is also home to a rich history of national volunteer initiatives. Since the Civilian Conservation Corps enrolled 70,000 Tennesseans in the 1930's through the Peace Corps in 1961, national service in Tennessee has grown strong and followed a tide of national trends and support. VISTA or Volunteers in Service to America was established in Tennessee in the 1960's as part of the War on Poverty. Through this program, fulltime volunteers worked throughout the state on health, education and other initiatives to fight the impacts of economic disparity. Foster Grandparents, Retired Senior Volunteer programs and Senior Companions followed suit in the Volunteer State after key national legislation in the 1970's and 1980's. The success of these efforts paved the way for increased support and funding for service programs in public schools. This trend in "service-learning" has grown over the last 15 years, and was supported by national legislation in 1990. In Tennessee, this has meant increased effort to help teachers and other community educators learn about the educational value and community benefit of student service learning.

This strong foundation for national service and service-learning led to the passage of The National and Community Service Trust Act of 1993, which in turn spurred creation of the Tennessee Commission on National & Community Service. This bipartisan 25-member board, works throughout the state to promote volunteerism as a way of life, and administers funds that support national service programs in Tennessee. While many other states have had state offices of volunteerism since the 1970's, the commission is the first such office to be established in the Volunteer State. The Commission also works in turn with the Department of Education to provide expanded funding for service learning in schools and community-based organizations.

One significant result of this legislation is the creation of a full-time, year-round youth service volunteer corps called AmeriCorps. Since 1994, this new domestic Peace Corps has spawned more than 15 youth service initiatives throughout Tennessee that meet community-identified needs in education, environment, public safety, health and housing. Nationally, more than 100,000 people have given a year of their lives in service to their communities through AmeriCorps.

National service and traditional volunteerism in churches, schools and civic clubs are often combined in Tennessee with dramatic results. Consider the Emerald Youth Foundation in Knoxville, which engages child care professionals, AmeriCorps Members as coordinators, and church member volunteers who come together to provide a wonderful, caring after-school tutoring and mentoring program for hundreds of inner city young people.

This marriage of traditional altruism with full-time effort is an important step in the evolution of the service tradition in Tennessee. For years, Tennesseans have addressed hunger, health, homelessness and education through a range of short-term and part-time programs. By working hand in hand with existing schools, community agencies, local governments and volunteer programs, full-time AmeriCorps and VISTA members are creating long-term solutions to community problems. Every day in Tennessee, these national service programs work side by side with museum docents, candy stripers, Lions club members, ministers and others to increase the power and strength of neighborhoods and people in the Volunteer State. In the end, the public, private and governmental alliances developed through volunteerism and national service may reshape the way we address issues and solve problems in all of Tennessee's communities.

A Work in Progress

Tennessee's volunteers paved the way to the west, built bridges for the Civilian Conservation Corps, mobilized underpaid coal miners, desegregated lunch counters, and immunized children. Beyond the confines of Tennessee, its volunteers have braved battles, established schools, taught nonviolence and shaped the path of history. Today, volunteers work in schools, hospitals, parks, community centers, synagogues, senior centers, prisons and museums. Tennessee's volunteers are lawyers, farmers, AmeriCorps members, garbage collectors, welfare mothers, business owners, and students. They are inventors of kindness, champions of justice, but more than that they are upholding a legacy. It's the legacy of Tennessee's volunteers — the state's brightest and most enduring heroes.

If every Tennessean were to volunteer for one day a month, we could...
build a better community for you, me and many generations to come. The state of Tennessee needs healing, we (the people) are the medicine to repair broken wounds. Building better homes or repairing them, befriending those children in need of help, teaching the underprivileged, and helping the old or sick are just some ways we can make this state a better place. Finally, it would help people who are able to volunteer feel better about both their state and their state of mind.
—Douglas Baron
Germantown
Shelby County

If every Tennessean were to volunteer for one day a month, we could...
help those in need and meet some of the finest people in the world. Show that we are truly Tennessee volunteers by giving of some of our time, efforts and skills to see that Tennessee becomes the number one state in the United States, in services.
—Bernard Barton
Rickman
Overton County

A Volunteer Life: Maggie Duffy

"As soon as I saw the children, I knew I would stay." — Maggie Duffy

If Margaret Gooch Duffy had acted on her hesitation to go to Japan in post-war 1947, it is possible— very possible— that Japan would not have become one of Tennessee's largest foreign direct investors. Fortunately, Maggie overcame her feelings and went to Japan. She fell in love with the Japanese children, their culture, and their spirit, and she offered them solutions to their post-war problems in such a caring, creative, and powerful way that understanding all the effects of her service is as complex in some ways as understanding the delicate, complex and powerful art of origami.

Early Years and Education

In 1917, when she was five years old, Maggie lived in rural Spring Hill, Tennessee. She remembers using slim wooden needles to knit washcloths out of string for the soldiers wounded in the battles of World War I. By her mother's example, Maggie learned how to volunteer and how to give back.

Her parents, Kit and Azile Gooch, along with their children and parents, moved to Brentwood, Tennessee, several miles outside Nashville, a few years later. She and her family became members of Glen Leven Presbyterian Church (where she has been a member for 80 years now). Maggie was fortunate to attend Peabody Demonstration School for ten years (now the University School of Nashville) and Belmont College (now Belmont University). Maggie's father was the first coal broker in Nashville.

Maggie's first job after graduation from Belmont was with the Davidson County Welfare Commission (later the Federal Emergency Relief Administration) in 1932, during the height of the Great Depression. Here, as a social worker, Maggie had a caseload of over 500 clients. For seven years, this job was "my best education. Working with the welfare department, I met a cross-section of humanity in great depths of struggle and pain." Meanwhile, Maggie fostered a desire to complete a degree in Education and Psychology, though "I was very scared to go back to school," she says.

Eventually Maggie managed to create a work-study program for herself that supported her through school. She took classes from 8 a.m. to noon each day, and worked from 2 p.m. to 10 p.m. with the Traveler's Aid Society, until she graduated from what is now the Peabody College at Vanderbilt University, in 1940.

While earning her degree and working with the Welfare Commission, Maggie was loaned to the American Red Cross as a caseworker during the devastating flood of the Cumberland River in 1937. "My caseload was all underwater," she remarks. Maggie learned how the Red Cross made it possible to give immediate relief to those in need. In 1941, when she was asked to join the American Red Cross as the Director of the Home Service Department, her acceptance was immediate. Her decision to accept is one that neither she, nor the Red Cross, has ever regretted. This introduced her to the full-blown world of volunteering— something that has been a focal point of her life to this day. Maggie recalls, "I received expert mentoring from Ruth E. Moor, an efficient twenty-six year Chapter CEO."

World War II and Australia

During World War II, Maggie was assigned to the American Red Cross's National Headquarters for overseas duty. In September 1943, she was sent to Sydney, Australia, where she worked in the American Red Cross's field director's office for two years. "Back in '43 I was one of a group of 65 Red Cross workers who zigzagged across the Pacific Ocean to Sydney on a troop-ship with 15,000 GIs. It took 20 days— two meals of dried army food a day! This was the first ship to cross the Pacific without an escort. Every morning before sunrise, the crew and passengers would stand on deck wearing life jackets on the lookout for enemy ships." Maggie laughs, recalling how all the women wore mounds of lipstick so that their lips wouldn't burn so easily. In the afternoon, on board the ship, she and other women would enlist performers to sing, dance or play an instrument as they skimmed across a shining blue Pacific.

When the war ended, Maggie was sent to war-torn Manila (chief city of the Philippines) to help with Prisoners of War (POWs). Manila was the clearing depot for thousands of American POWs brought there for debriefing while awaiting transportation to the United States. Red Cross Chapters across the United States collected mail from POW families, which was flown to Manila and then delivered to the POWs by the Red Cross staff in the processing center. "Many POW's had not heard from home, had never seen pictures of their children during their three to four years in prison, and the taste of freedom was overwhelming." Maggie helped POWs work through their debriefings, helped reestablish communication between the POWs and their loved ones, and listened to them by the hour as they shared their memories of home. "The records of 'Sentimental Journey' and 'Rum and Coca Cola' were played 24 hours a day and were worn to shreds. Many had beriberi [a vitamin deficiency characterized by impairment of the nerves and heart] and other illnesses, but nothing could destroy their dreams of returning to freedom after years of deprivation with no word from home."

In 1946, Maggie had a second assignment in Manila, where she helped the Filipino Red Cross as the country prepared for its independence. Maggie was ready to leave the humidity of Manila when a call came from Tokyo to fill an assignment requested by General MacArthur's headquarters. She was asked to become one of seven members of an American Red Cross Advisory Team loaned to MacArthur's headquarters to help the Japanese Red Cross Society restore their programs in order to serve the people of devastated Japan.

Beginning in Japan

"The American Red Cross asked me to join the group to become responsible for introducing the concept volunteerism, a cornerstone of democracy. Few people realize that General MacArthur's goal of introducing democracy to Japan was probably the greatest experiment in Human Relations in the history of the world."

Maggie's initial hesitation toward going to Japan was based on a fear of not knowing much about the culture or customs. She speaks of MacArthur with great admiration and respect. "He was an expert on the Japanese. Here was a 2,000-year-old feudal system he believed could be changed by the democratic principles of a country less than 200 years old."

Though hesitant, Maggie agreed to take on the assignment. In order for her mission to be a success, Maggie knew she needed the willingness and help of the staff of the Japanese Red Cross. They became mentors and close friends, and their friendship continues today.

The Japanese Red Cross was founded May 1, 1877. On May 21, 1881, Clara Barton founded the American Red Cross. Both societies, in accordance with the Geneva Convention of 1864, began their assistance to the disabled in times of international conflict during the 1890's.

From 1906 to the present, the two Red Cross Societies have supported and helped each other in times of disaster. One of the worst disasters 1923 was the earthquake and fires in Tokyo/Yokohama that caused the loss of over 200,000 lives. The American Red Cross sent food, clothing, funds and medical supplies, including medicinal whiskey. Three years later, a hurricane demolished part of Florida, and Japan, familiar with typhoons, sent generous aid through its Red Cross.

It was with intense anticipation that Maggie boarded a flight in September 1947. When she arrived in Yokohama and traveled by Jeep along the bombed-out roadsides she was shocked beyond belief. "The Japanese people were desperately struggling to keep alive. There was an awesome scarcity of everything—food, utilities, transportation, and housing, clothing… in fact, all necessities. As soon as I saw the children in their tattered clothes, waving and smiling, there was no thought of going home. I stayed. Children were getting less than 800 calories a day when they needed 2,000. Local governments had almost no funds. Schools were still struggling to revive and survive. It was a country in shambles that would not give up, and the Americans were there to help them."

Just as Maggie had been told of Japanese Military atrocities, the Japanese people had been told that Americans would kill, rape, steal and plunder. Fortunately, American GIs paved the way to good will, carrying out General MacArthur's edict of being friends and advisors to help Japan recover. The Japanese people were shocked when the GIs arrived with candy, smiles, gum and cigarettes. Gradually the personal defenses of the beleaguered Japanese people were lowered and disappeared. Their gratitude and graciousness extended to Maggie and all Americans.

An unexpected interlude for Maggie was an invitation to tea with General MacArthur's wife, Jean Faircloth. Maggie's mother had studied at Soule College in Murfreesboro while Jean was there. Maggie learned that Jean was a close friend of her cousin, and learned how devoted Jean was to her husband's vision. "MacArthur knew that the concept of volunteering could be helpful in demonstrating democracy." MacArthur also realized it was necessary to maintain the great dignity of His Majesty the Emperor, and this was accomplished with great creativity and sensitivity.

Spreading the Word— *Hoshidan*

"The most important part of our job was to assist our counterpart Japanese Red Cross staff to develop services that would meet the dire health needs of the Japanese people in this beautiful but devastated land, as opposed to copying programs of the American Red Cross. My special assignment was that of introducing volunteerism, for which there was no word at that time in the Japanese language. So the society and the Health and Welfare Sector made a new one— *Hoshidan*, meaning *service groups*." It was not an exact match, but it sufficed.

Maggie was already familiar with the fact that volunteerism was very difficult to explain. "You have to do it to understand it, or be helped by someone offering it to you." In order to express the ideals of volunteerism, Maggie needed a skilled interpreter. "In early 1948, we were fortunate to find a well-educated lady just repatriated from China who was fluent in English and understood the concept of volunteerism." Knowing very little about the Red Cross, Sachiko Hashimoto accepted Maggie's request to attend the first national meeting of the Volunteer Service Groups. "Delegates came from all prefectural Chapters. It was a bitter, cold January in Tokyo. We could see our breath inside the old National Headquarters building. No heat. Only men attended, several from each prefecture Red Cross Chapter."

One man said, "At a time like this we need to receive help rather than give service to others." Then Sachiko, a stranger in their midst, raised her hand and shared from her heart the story of how she had left China. "The trains from Peking were not for people. They were open coal wagons, forty people in each wagon. Each family was given a 2 meter square tablecloth. One tablecloth alone was of little use, but by sewing the cloths together we made a roof over the wagon to shelter all of us from the cold, wind, and rain. As for a toilet, there was none except an oil can but nobody would have used it if it hadn't been for the tablecloths sewn together to make a screen for privacy."

Maggie's heart misses the spirit and dedication of Sachiko, who became a devoted leader in the Junior Red Cross and a dear friend. She adds, "Sachiko became a leading figure in the World Red Cross family and was the first woman and first Asian to receive the Henry Dunant Medal for excellence from the International Red Cross in Geneva."

For nearly two years, Maggie visited nearly all of the prefectures in Japan. Many illustrations were given and many programs were directed to show what individual volunteers could do to help others in need. At first only men attended the Chapter meetings. Gradually, women came and they seemed to grasp the idea of volunteerism. Finally, breakthroughs began with simple volunteer services undertaken by individuals— visiting the elderly, repairing clothes for orphans, cleaning streets, and maintaining parks.

The Mother of Volunteerism and The Father of Democracy

With a Saxon heritage and sensitivity to the sun, Maggie's hair, white since her teen years, now stays mostly hidden under her trademark color-coordinated scarf. "One day, at a Volunteer meeting in a school auditorium, there was smothered laughter in the audience. I was puzzled and wondered what could be so funny. My interpreter, Ota-san, finally told me that the people thought I looked like George Washington and in truth there was a likeness— my white hair and page boy style was offset by a military-like Red Cross uniform and hat. So, thereafter, my resemblance to 'George,' called by the Japanese, the 'Father of Democracy,' was always mentioned during introductions and this became a great icebreaker to open meetings." George Washington's portrait hung in every school and many public buildings. Few people realize what a rarity it was for the Japanese to see not only an Anglo-American woman, but also one so young sporting white hair.

After meetings, Maggie was impressed when, during informal gatherings, the Japanese always offered to share what little rice and vegetables they had with their American advisors. Maggie learned the Japanese custom of light entertainment after work. The Japanese managed to find refreshments including saki and beer then everyone performed a dance, read Haiku, executed a karate stance or sang. "I learned a Japanese children's song *Sho-Sho-Sho-Jogi* that Sachiko taught me." Loosely translated, it's about a well-fed badger who sits on the steps of a temple after supper beating his fat tummy like a drum. "These informal gatherings were filled with laughter and fun and usually we'd end up with the well known *Coal Miner's Dance*. These evenings did much, if not more than anything else to build relationships and friendships and even helped to explain volunteerism." The memory of these important, informal moments, in light of the tragic circumstances the Japanese people were working to overcome, have found a very special place in Maggie's heart.

Maggie credits the outstanding support and intellect of the Japanese Red Cross with much of the success she and her American Red Cross colleagues were able to have. Her assignment to the Japanese Red Cross was brief, but its effect has reached beyond the barriers of geography and time.

Maggie directed more volunteer services in Tokyo when the Korean War broke out in 1950. More than 2,000 volunteers were organized by Mrs. Kestor L. Hastings, the American Red Cross's Chair of Volunteers, to assist with many duties formerly performed by American servicemen who were fighting on the Korean Front. These volunteers came from the families of the American and United Nations servicemen, and from embassies of other countries.

Service and Family

After a short stint in the U.S., Maggie was sent to Europe in 1954 as an American Red Cross Director to work with the Chair of Volunteers to promote volunteer programs on 100 military installations. These programs helped meet the needs of American families living at the installations in Europe, England, North Africa, Turkey, Greece and Saudi Arabia.

In mid-1958, Maggie was back in the states and working for the Eastern Area Headquarters of the American Red Cross in Alexandria, Virginia. Eugene Duffy spotted Maggie in a local deli. Maggie laughs at his boldness. He finagled her phone number from the deli owner and called her up. "I'm Gene Duffy. I just saw you in the deli. I just bought a new air-conditioned Pontiac— would you like to go for a drive with me?" Maggie didn't know him, but her curiosity about driving in an air-conditioned car was what eventually landed her in the front seat. "I said 'Yes,'" she chuckles. Eugene, a chemical engineer, worked with early computers briefly as his hobby at Fort Belvoir, Virginia. "He was a wonderful dancer and a prize jitterbugger with professor good looks." A year later, with Gene's grown daughter and young family in attendance, Maggie Gooch became his bride, and a mother and grandmother, all in ten minutes. They honeymooned at the Waldorf Astoria and flew home above Fourth of July fireworks across the Potomac. They lived happily for many years on the seventeenth floor of their apartment complex near the nation's capital, celebrating their anniversary with friends at an annual "Picnic in the Sky on the Fourth of July."

"Those were wonderful times," Maggie remembers.

During 1974, to the great sadness of his loved ones, Gene's health failed and he passed away.

About 1975, while Maggie Duffy contemplated retirement from the American Red Cross in Washington, DC, Nissan Industrial Equipment Company became the first Japanese company to locate in Tennessee. Within three years, six additional Japanese companies opened offices throughout Tennessee. In 1977, Toshiba Corporation purchased 107 acres in Lebanon, Tennessee, marking a major expansion in television manufacturing. In the year 2000, more than 130 Japanese Operations in the State employ roughly 35,000 Tennesseans, and equals approximately $700,000,000 in investments.

Maggie moved to the National Headquarters of the American Red Cross, where she served as National Director of Volunteer Personnel until her retirement in 1977. She was not out of work for long before she returned to the Red Cross as a volunteer. Maggie returned to National Headquarters in 1988 to serve as volunteer liaison with the Embassy of Japan to promote the involvement of Japanese citizens living in the U.S. in Red Cross Chapter activities.

Back Home

In 1991, in order to be near her younger sister, Jane Ambrose, and brother, Chris Gooch, Maggie moved back to Brentwood, Tennessee, where she lived with her sister. She counts herself fortunate to have had a chance to spend time with her brother and sister after this move. Both passed away within several years.

Maggie became active again in 1991 with her Red Cross home base— the Nashville Area Chapter. Always one to use her skills in a situation where they are needed, she became the liaison with the Nashville Japanese Community and began the Japanese Initiative in Nashville. By her efforts and love, Maggie is greatly responsible for the involvement of hundreds of Japanese volunteers who have served in numerous volunteer Chapter activities since 1992.

From 1991 to 2000, hundreds of Japanese volunteers have supported the Chapter with their volunteer service and finances. They are an integral part of Chapter programs and are members of the Red Cross family working side by side with the American Red Cross volunteers.

Maggie easily befriends and welcomes the wives of Japanese officials in local Japanese-owned companies. She has a strong link with the Middle Tennessee Japanese Ladies Society and the U.S.-Japan Center for Studies and Cooperation of Vanderbilt University. Maggie is also affiliated with the recently organized Tennessee-Japan Society.

Sally Slayden-Berry, Director of the Nashville Chapter of Volunteer Services, has been working for more than five years with Maggie. "When I watch her, I know she's got 60 years experience, but she never skips a beat. She's always thinking of how to better a volunteer program, how to always be inclusive…. I took Maggie to a National Red Cross Convention this past year. She knew everybody. *Everybody!* It's pretty rewarding and amazing that we have her here in Tennessee." In 1999, with a committee of ten volunteers, Sally and Maggie produced a handbook on the *Administration of Volunteers,* a policies and procedures manual that is the most complete in the Nashville Chapter's history.

Many Japanese and American people consider Maggie an international treasure. The Japanese dubbed Maggie the *Mother of Volunteerism* when they presented her the highest award one can receive in Japan; in 1991, Maggie was honored by His Majesty the Emperor of Japan who conferred the *Order of the Precious Crown Butterfly* upon her for "the contributions in promoting volunteerism in Japan and in strengthening the friendship between the people of Japan and the United States through various activities of the American Red Cross."

Maggie has received numerous domestic awards including the *Clara Barton Award* in 1994, the *Distinguished Alumna Award* from University School of Nashville, in 1996, and the *Brotherhood-Sisterhood Award* from the Council of Christians and Jews in 1997. In May of 2000, for consistent and cumulative goodwill, for its involvement of the Japan Society Ladies Group, and for its involvement with Japanese volunteers, the Nashville Chapter of the American Red Cross was presented with the *National American Red Cross Diversity Model Award* at the National Red Cross Convention. Accepting the award, appropriately, was Maggie Duffy along with her friend (and fellow volunteer) Yuko Wada, wife of a former executive at Bridgestone-Firestone.

Recently, at an awards ceremony, a seventy-year-old visiting Japanese businessman approached Maggie. He told her he had been a teenager when the first Americans arrived in Japan and that he had never forgotten the kindness the Americans showered on post-war Japan. "He was profuse with gratitude," Maggie says. "He intends for me to revisit Japan in 2001." Maggie's kindness is infectious, memorable and timeless.

At age 88, Maggie Duffy still volunteers at least four days a week in the American Red Cross Office of Volunteer Resources, the personnel office for all volunteers. When necessary, Maggie gives more time for special projects. She jokes, "If you reach 88 years old in Japan, it's considered a magical number and you stand a good chance of going on." From all appearances, the Japanese are right. Nothing appears to obstruct her passion or vibrant good health. Maggie looks considerably younger than her 88 years. Her eyes are bright as she fiddles with a hearing aid that whines and fades— a cure and curse she has grown to accept like so many other modern technological contrivances designed to make life easier.

Regarding the current trend in how some interpersonal relationships are developing in the world, Maggie is concerned and surprised. "We need to guard against losing our humanity and personal touch in such a mechanized and technological era." She points out that setting a good example by volunteering is "one of the best things that parents can do with their kids. It is a great legacy."

Maggie has left a legacy deeply rooted in decades of national and international service. She is convinced our country would shut down without volunteers. Though she has outlived many of her family and many of her friends, she is fortunate that four nephews and their families live nearby. Maggie is also close to her family in Washington, DC and West Virginia, including her daughter and son-in-law, three grandchildren, and two great-grandchildren whom she communicates with and visits frequently.

A candle remains in Maggie's heart at the altar of her late friend Sachiko Hashimoto, who so simply stated, "My concept of service is to offer what little time, money, power, or wisdom each one owns for the sake of others as well as for one's self." Maggie is profoundly happy that *Hoshidan* is now a part of the Japanese vocabulary and part of their lives.

In an address to the International Youth Forum held in Japan during a conference celebrating volunteers for the Japanese Red Cross in 1998, Maggie modestly thanked the people of Japan for allowing her do what came naturally to her. Today, in a family of 175 Red Cross Societies, the Japanese Society is among the strongest and gives more aid to the emerging and developing societies than any other. Her hope for them is universal. "What's happened in Japan in fifty years is a miracle and I am deeply grateful to have been a small part." After telling her audience about her life, and the partners and volunteers she worked with during

Tennessee Volunteer Heroes 2001

her time in Japan, she said. "Let these accomplishments inspire you to continue helping with compassion, dignity and lots and lots of love."

"Volunteers are the lifeline of humanity! They keep us linked together around the world. Many world leaders believe that our bilateral treaty with Japan is the most important in the world." — Maggie Duffy

If every Tennessean were to volunteer for one day a month, we could…

make a difference in more children's lives. The Lord blessed me with the gift of giving to others and I cannot imagine how my life would be without the pleasure of seeing how even the smallest of acts impacts the lives of others.

—Viola G. Batts
Memphis, Shelby County

If every Tennessean were to volunteer for one day a month, we could…

educate that EVERY PERSON HAS the "ability to respond." They will then develop "response-ability." Our purpose for being is to work beyond ourselves toward attacking the myriad of problems among human beings, while eradicating drug dependency, taking pride in neighborhoods, assisting each other through illness, helping each other to cope with tragedies, working with mental disabilities and strengthening the weakness of human nature.

—Mickey (Mary K.) Beazley
Brentwood
Williamson County

If every Tennessean were to volunteer for one day a month, we could…

see Tennessee come together as a team and community. We would be able to help more people including troubled teens, and abused children and women. We could give hope to these Tennesseans. The people the volunteers help will someday be able to volunteer to help others. When we see a homeless person on the street or a mother that does not have food for her children and no means to get it, this is our community.

—Diane Beets
Knoxville
Knox County

If every Tennessean were to volunteer for one day a month, we could…

accomplish much-needed tasks for individuals who are homeless, elderly, poor but trying to work, children needing food and mentoring in reading and mathematics, collecting food items for those in need, and collecting clothes for poor adults and children.

—Ann Bell
Memphis
Shelby County

If every Tennessean were to volunteer for one day a month, we could…
significantly impact such problems as poverty and illiteracy, provide important opportunities for today's youth, and give comfort and assistance to the sick and infirm. Thousands in our communities would benefit from such an achievement and people everywhere would truly know why Tennessee is the Volunteer State.

—Ray R. Bell
Franklin, Williamson County

If every Tennessean were to volunteer for one day a month, we could…
bring comfort to those in sorrow, help those in pain and sickness, and provide for the needy. As you are helping others you are making the world a better place. By taking a little time for others, you are making your life much better and happy.

—Betty Belote
Gallatin, Sumner County

If every Tennessean were to volunteer for one day a month, we could…
teach and visually illustrate an entirely new lifestyle— a lifestyle of service that rewards! What other job allows caring to be uppermost, not downgraded? Volunteers don't just love people in general; they see individuals, one-on-one, and touch them in meaningful ways. Volunteers don't *have* to work, they do it for the sheer joy of it! They truly restore 'truth in advertising' because they model the *real* thing!

—Louise Bentley
Jackson
Madison County

If every Tennessean were to volunteer for one day a month, we could…

see a reduction in crime, conflicts, suicide, depression and loneliness.

—Connie Berry
Holladay, Benton County

If every Tennessean were to volunteer for one day a month, we could…
accomplish the "impossible." We could become all that God intended us to be. When you take your eyes off yourself, you find that your challenges are not so significant. You become a "giver" instead of a "taker." And when many do their part, it lightens the load for everyone.

—Becca Bolding
Germantown
Shelby County

If every Tennessean were to volunteer for one day a month, we could…
transform our communities into thriving and wholesome living environments where there would be plentiful adult mentors in every school, parent role models, children who would not be lacking attention, parish nursing programs in every school and we would be better equipped to promote parenting skills and intact families.

—Rae Young Bond
Chattanooga
Hamilton County

Volunteer Heroes Sampler

Professor Ann Bell

In the early 1940's, Ann Bell graduated from Randolph-Macon Woman's College in Lynchburg, Virginia. Dr. L.W. Diggs, Associate Professor of Medicine at the University of Tennessee College of Medicine, a hematologist who contributed prolifically to studies of patients with sickle cell anemia, offered Ann a position as a teaching assistant. Ann accepted the position, and completed her master's Degree at University of Memphis, on her way to completing her doctorate. As Ann became an accomplished specialist in hematology, she made many contributions to the Memphis Community.

Ann takes pride in her work with the Patient Assistance Programs at the Church Health Center, a non-profit health care ministry treating over 22,000 uninsured patients annually within the Shelby County area. Its programs are designed to assist patients with incomes near the poverty level. If a patient falls within certain financial guidelines, pharmaceutical companies provide needed medication at no cost. Making this program work is a very labor-intensive process, and Ann assists each week by filling out the paperwork necessary for enrolling patients in the program. The nurses and administration are very grateful for her help. When the drugs arrive, she labels them with the patients' names and shelves them. The medical conditions afflicting the patients in these programs range across the entire field of medicine. Without this program, many of the patients would not receive the care they need. Ann has been essential in the growth of the prescription program, which has a turnover that exceeds $35,000 per month in medicines.

"I volunteer," she says, "because I like to help people." For many years, she has also been a volunteer at Idlewild Presbyterian Church, in charge of the Food

Pantry for families in need. She helps to serve dinner to the homeless one night a month, and she is a church librarian.

When Professor Ann retired in 1991, she continued to offer assistance to Dr. Diggs, who was well past 90. He was then Emeritus Professor of Clinical Laboratory Sciences and Emeritus Assistant Professor in the Department of Medicine. He needed a curator for his photographs, slides, books and papers on sickle cell disease. Professor Ann made five sets of books of photographs of tissues from sickle cell disease patients for St. Jude's Children's Research Hospital, UT Library, the National Library of Science and Medicine in Washington, DC, UT Hematology Oncology Division and the Sickle Cell Repository in Mobile, Alabama. "I feel like I am contributing to the community," she says of these projects.

Professor Ann continues to teach medical students and works on teaching material (blood smears and kodachromes), as she has for more than forty years. She has received numerous awards from medical students locally and nationally. Since her retirement, she has worked without pay. "Volunteering keep me young, keeps me active. My heart is on others instead of myself." She points out that, despite all her efforts, and although students and people call her "Doctor," she never had the time to complete her degree. Professor Bell will always be remembered by the thousands she has helped, however, as one of the finest experts in community medical service.

BellSouth Pioneers

BellSouth Pioneers are proud of their history as members of the Telephone Pioneers of America, which was founded in 1911. Throughout the nine-state region served by BellSouth, the Pioneers' 94,000 members (current and former employees of BellSouth and their families) contribute millions of hours of community service each year.

In Tennessee alone, over 10,000 employees and retirees contribute over one million hours of community service each year. Volunteer activities focus on education and efforts to ensure that the youth of Tennessee are better equipped to lead productive, successful lives.

BellSouth Pioneers also perform countless other projects such as environmental activities, building Habitat for Humanity houses, sewing Hug-a-Bears to give to children who are victims of crime or accidents, managing health screening projects, and accomplishing many other services aimed at improving the quality of life in our state.

One project that is most rewarding for BellSouth Pioneer volunteers is Camp Bluebird, which offers a unique experience for adult cancer patients. In pristine natural surroundings, campers are provided a creative, educational atmosphere of support. The 3-day, 2-night camp is held in the spring and again in the fall. The camp provides patients a time for listening and learning, sharing and caring. It is an ideal atmosphere for providing family support, management of cancer treatments and their side effects, nutritional information, and creative outlets through arts and crafts. Camps are held in East, Middle and West Tennessee, and offer opportunities for cancer patients across the state to participate.

BellSouth is proud to be a sponsor of *Tennessee Volunteer Heroes 2001*, which honors several outstanding individuals who have given of their time and talent over the years to support many worthwhile efforts that require volunteer assistance to succeed. As we look to the past with pride, we can look forward to the new millennium with excitement. BellSouth salutes those who make a difference every day.

Robin Brewer

Seven years ago, a member of Robin Brewer's family was a victim of domestic violence. When Robin saw how the court system further victimized her loved one, Robin got mad. Robin got involved. "I was just a housewife, but I was determined to get into the court system, see who was accountable and educate them." What began as an intensely personal agenda turned into a program that has helped hundreds of women.

Now, seven years later, Robin, as a founding member of The Domestic Violence Coalition of Greater Chattanooga, Inc. (DVC), continues to serve as chair of its Monitoring Evaluation and Enforcement Committee. Through the DVC, Robin has created monitoring, enforcement and advocacy programs to helped abused victims. She has a remarkable passion and empathy for victims and children.

Robin teaches training classes for volunteers who wish to become DVC monitors. A monitor becomes a "court watcher." Monitors have forms that ask questions like: Does the victim have an attorney? Did the perpetrator have an attorney? How did the judge respond? What went on in the courtroom? Through studying the answers to these questions, Robin trains her monitors to spot the "gaps" in care.

Frequently, Robin goes to court with victims as an advocate. She gets referrals from all parts of the justice system, helps victims to get protective orders, and meets with judges to keep them updated about changes in the Coalition.

Robin is proud of the many private donations, and community funds that come to the coalition for education. Major corporations have donated goods and attorneys and legal service providers have donated their time.

The Domestic Violence Coalition is partnered with the Nationwide ADT Alarm Program. Counselors and police officers recommend clients to Robin, who then helps coordinate the installation of a panic button, which victims wear around their necks.

Robin works with nine municipal police jurisdictions, the Chattanooga Police Department and the Hamilton County Sheriff's Department. Her reputation and opinions have helped solve many of the human problems that go unaddressed in our communities. Robin also heads up Law Enforcement Appreciation Day events and works on Special Events Committees to raise public awareness about domestic violence.

Sometimes it is thankless work. Many times, victims choose to return to their perpetrators. But it is the people like Judy, whom Robin met for the first time in Court three years ago, that help to reinforce her commitment. Judy was living in an abusive relationship, and had multiple sclerosis. Robin helped Judy through the court system. A month later, Judy was forced to retire from her job.

"Not knowing what to do," Robin remembers, "Judy became an advocate, and she has helped us tremendously ever since. I've come to know and really like her and know she's in for the long haul." Robin adds, "If more people were concerned about the human rights of others we could reduce violent crime to a negligible level."

Kenneth Caldwell

Sometimes, the greatest heartache can transform itself into the greatest healing. When fifteen-year old Kenneth Caldwell lived in Dayton, Ohio, his cousin Leroy lived with him. Leroy was like Ken's older sibling. Leroy was expert at auto painting and detailing. "At that time, I wanted to paint cars, to mix and prime like my big brother," Kenneth remembers. Unfortunately, Leroy got involved in drugs and alcohol. The combination turned deadly when Leroy's contacts in the subculture turned bad and he was murdered. Kenneth felt like his dream had died, too.

Perhaps one saving grace was the fact that Kenneth's mother owned a private childcare center. As early as the 6th grade, Kenneth knew what it was like to be a "big brother" to the many toddlers his mother cared for. He credits her with showing him how to care for younger people— to volunteer the gift of himself. Quite naturally, the babies loved him.

An older peer helped also Kenneth. "As a kid growing up in rough neighborhoods, an older gentleman, Mr. Lewis, would take my friends and me to different social programs. He was a retired baker who would drive up in an old bread truck. He's one of the main people who inspired me to want to give back."

Kenneth's mother moved back to her hometown of Humboldt, Tennessee, thirteen miles north of Jackson, and Kenneth moved his family to be closer to her. Kenneth found that "…in Jackson, crime was on the rise. There were a lot of activities for kids but no one was motivated. I took it upon myself to encourage the kids at the Jackson Halfway House as a way for them to turn their lives around." Kenneth's focus is on the kids. "If we can capture their attention and educate them to be positive citizens, informing them about health issues and the value of education, then right there— that will deter violence."

While working with the Office of Minority Health's Teen Violence Alternative Program in connection with the Boys & Girls Club, Kenneth has written grants for the deterrence of violence. Kenneth also founded the Books & Ball Program, which emphasizes the importance of education for those children participating in sports. Kenneth stresses that athletes should strive to be the best they can be inside the classroom. "Across the country we have superb athletes who lack knowledge and 'book sense.' An athlete has a short shelf life, but the smarts keep one going."

Kenneth instills, "principles before pleasure" to high school boys who want to play basketball and still want an Associate's Degree. Kenneth speaks fondly of one young man, TJ, who was thirteen when they first met. "He was very defiant, rude and attracted to gangs. TJ's self-esteem was poor and he knew nothing outside of the violence he saw and experienced while living in the projects." Today Kenneth is proud to see TJ leading a youth choir at church, his grades have improved, he plays football and he has repeatedly been recognized by his peers as the Boys & Girls Club Teen Member of the Month. TJ says he owes his turnaround to Kenneth, but Kenneth sees it differently. "I owe it to TJ for being willing to change."

Today, representatives from area colleges seek out the wisdom and expertise of Kenneth. In 1998, Humboldt's Chapter of Alpha Kappa Alpha, the oldest African American Sorority in America, awarded Kenneth the Outstanding Male Role Model of the Year. A year later, the Mayor of Jackson presented Kenneth with an Individual Excellence Award for outstanding work with youth and for the prevention of drugs and sexual abuse among teenagers. Kenneth reminds child development authorities "we don't always have to walk in here as a professional. All we have to do is walk in here and be a kid."

Kenneth believes that, no matter how many negative influences might be around an individual, he or she can learn courage and strength of character. "There used to be a time when I had to beg these kids to join… and now, they just come on their own!"

This kind of response proves how much difference the care and interest of even one individual can make in another person's life. Now, when thinking back about Leroy, Kenneth smiles, "I guess I am a painter. I can take damaged goods and turn them into works of beauty."

Suzanne Mandel Cohn

"Tikkum Olam"— the repair of the world, is a cornerstone of Jewish faith that Suzanne Mandel Cohn weaves into all areas of her life. Though no one person can finish such an enterprise, those of the Jewish faith feel obligated to begin it, and Suzanne has taken this commitment to heart and invested it into her community.

Seventeen years ago, Suzanne was a founding board member of Chattanooga Area Food Bank, part of Second Harvest. Food items that have short shelf-dates, while still useful, are shipped in from around the country and local restaurants supply their menu items at day's end. The Food Bank, with a dedicated staff and loyal volunteers, helps non-profit agencies to meet their goal of feeding the hungry.

Ten years ago, Suzanne began a similar food drive at her Mizpah Congregation. As part of the traditional Yom Kipper fasting, she offers bags to the congregation members the week before, on Rosh Hashanah. For those wishing to participate, they return their bags on Yom Kippur morning, filled with food or a check. A Food Bank truck assists by waiting in the parking lot of Mizpah for collection.

As coordinator for her Temple's participation in the Interfaith Hospitality Network, Suzanne helps her congregation feed and spend time with families in Mizpah's partnership with a local Methodist Church, caring for temporarily homeless families in the community.

Suzanne is always looking for ways to brighten the lives of others and to get as many people as possible to join in her mission. Suzanne found her niche in 1993, when she started the K.O.O.L (Knit out of Love) project for Hospice of Chattanooga. "I love this program," she says. Suzanne has recruited more than a hundred volunteers to knit and crochet afghans for donation to clients under Hospice Care. Many of the knitters are homebound, and this gives them an opportunity to do volunteer work from home. Sue makes her rounds to the homes and churches to collect the warm fuzzy afghans. She catalogs each one with a list of its maker, a description, and she totals the number of afghans donated to date by each knitter. She then packages the afghans and encloses a hospice card that reads: "Hoping that the hours of love and talent put into this afghan will give you a great deal of warmth." The family keeps the afghan to remind them of their loved one. Over 1,000 afghans have been delivered—true gifts from the heart.

For her enterprises, Suzanne was recognized with the J.C. Penney Golden Rule Award in 1994, and the local Hospice Volunteer Award in 1993. Also, she received the East Brainerd Sertoma Club Service to Mankind Award in 1998.

Suzanne believes that if every Tennessean were to volunteer for one day a month, we could "excite individuals to answer community needs. Through their volunteering, they would learn how to solve problems creatively for others in need. They would meet talented and interesting folks and they would enrich their own lives as well."

By following her heart, Suzanne has truly found the way toward *Tikkum Olam*.

Charles Davis

All his life, Charles Davis has aimed high. Charles grew up in the inner city of Nashville. Since there were no social supportive services available to him as a child and teenager, Charles relied on his ingenuity and his academic and athletic prowess. Being 6'6" tall was the perfect asset for a guy who loved basketball. His first vehicle towards success was receiving a full athletic scholarship to Vanderbilt University at the age of sixteen in 1981, but Charles's heart was still in his neighborhood.

What Charles always wanted was "a program where kids could go to expand their goals and career options." In 1982, Charles incorporated a non-profit organization bearing his name (The Charles Davis Foundation) that is "dedicated to empowering Nashville's youth and their families to reach their full potential through PEACE— Positive Educational, Athletic, Cultural and Economic development."

While playing collegiate basketball, Charles expanded his education in business. During the 80's, he was drafted to professional leagues and played pro basketball with the Washington Wizards, Milwaukee Bucks, San Antonio Spurs and Chicago Bulls. By 1993, Charles Davis was known internationally as a professional basketball player in Italy and Japan.

In 1994, Charles returned to his home court to coach Vanderbilt Basketball until 1996. Simultaneously, he founded three businesses in the areas of real estate, distribution, and fiber optics.

Charles believes that is "vitally important to empower today's youth to realize their full potential." Nine years ago, Charles began raising funds to get certified teachers involved with his foundation and programming. He sought the support of businesses and recognized the value and importance of business partnerships. PEACE has created programs for after-school enrichment, a "PEACEmaker" program for parents and kids that meets two Saturdays a month, summer camp activities, sports, heath and fitness, a variety of arts instruction and nature education and activities.

Partnering is a cornerstone for the success of PEACE. Some of the boards Charles has served on include the YMCA, Martha O'Brien Center, Bethlehem Center, Boys & Girls Clubs and the Children's Theater.

The Charles Davis Foundation has adopted a school in the Nashville Metropolitan County. His PEACE program is currently in thirteen schools with mentoring programs that allow college students from Vanderbilt, Meharry, Fisk, TSU and Belmont to mentor students. Mentors work with children from pre-K through high school. High school students, sharing the values they've learned from being mentored, are carrying on the service ethic and are mentoring children in the lower grades.

The greatest challenge for the foundation is the constant need to raise capital to meet the demand for services. Charles's impeccable taste and commitment to excellence carries over into his foundation. "We are successful because we are constantly critiquing our programs so that our relationships within the community continue to be good role models."

"When a kid tells me they are a peacemaker, or when a parent shares what a difference PEACE has made in their child's life, or when I hear about the good remarks written on someone's report card, or when I hear about the increased participation of a student in an after-school program— that is my greatest reward." Charles says. He believes that PEACE's year-round consistency offering solutions to kids at risk is part of its success.

Charles sees more and more of his students returning as mentors and teachers in his programs. He's even seeing the children of his first students returning. A PEACE is easy to implement, and he'd like to see it expand into more urban and suburban areas. "Where there is a need, we can make a difference and give back to the future." Charles Davis has taken a long shot and scored.

Patrick J. Doyle, Ed.D.

Patrick Doyle's first exposure to the importance of conservation, he recalls, was during the World War II. As a child, he remembers the radio messages urging everyone to conserve as part of the war effort. At ages seven and five, Patrick and his younger brother Bob would take the aluminum foil from gum and cigarette packages they found and form it into balls. Every so often, someone would come around and collect it along with the grease that his mother had saved from her cooking. The aluminum would be used to make airplane parts and the grease would be used in the production of explosives.

After the war, Patrick and his brother went door to door to collect newspapers they would sell at the scrap yard for a dollar per hundred pounds. Twenty-two cents each bought the boys a movie, a coke, and a candy bar. And so it began.

While the Middle Tennessee State University (MTSU) Biology Club recycling program started out strictly as a newspaper recycling program in 1972, it was expanded to include aluminum cans in 1987, and, since 1990, it includes office paper. Patrick has helped shape the recycling habits of Murfreesboro/Rutherford County Citizens and MTSU students, faculty, and staff. His efforts have resulted in the collection and recycling of an impressive tally:

10.4 million pounds of newspaper

1.3 million pounds of office paper

206,000 pounds of aluminum cans

300,000 pounds of mixed paper

100,000 pounds of corrugated cardboard.

How does this mountain of trash help the environment? The 10.4 million pounds of recycled newspapers alone saved nearly 96,000 trees. Each aluminum can recycled represents enough energy saved to power a television for three hours and will prevent three ounces of acid rain and 40 pounds of carbon dioxide from entering the environment. And this recycling effort has saved 18,450 cubic yards of landfill space.

MTSU sees the merits of this professor's work. Patrick receives release time to administer this campus-wide program. He presides over three pickup trucks, two of which have been donated by local Murfreesboro auto dealers, and a cadre of diligent workers. "The best kind of people come from the community. They have brought over 10 million pounds of newspaper from their homes and workplaces since the program has begun." Dr. Doyle believes every citizen of Rutherford County who has contributed to the recycling program is a volunteer.

With approximately $400,000 raised through the recycling efforts program, 32 scholarships have been established and some 350 students have received financial assistance and recognition for their outstanding academic achievements. The MTSU Recycling Program has served as a model for programs throughout Tennessee as well as in Kentucky, New York, Kansas, and Iowa.

Patrick's efforts at promoting an awareness of environmental issues and recycling earned him the Conservation Award from the Daughters of the American Revolution and the recycling program that he directs at MTSU has twice been recognized by the Tennessee State Legislature through Joint Resolutions. The Tennessee Department of the Environment and Conservation honored him with a Lifetime Achievement Award and twice he's received the MTSU Outstanding Public Service Award. In 1999, he was named a Point of Light by the Points of Light Foundation and was selected from 365 recipients to receive one of 20 President's Service Awards from President Clinton. This award is considered the nation's highest award for volunteer work.

Dr. Doyle enjoys teaching freshman biology, history and philosophy of biology, and environmental problems. "Environmental ethics is part of every course. Field trips allow some students to see first-hand the problems associated with burning coal and nuclear fission." Patrick works on environmental issues when they arise. "If people consider air and water pollution, and the depletion of non-renewable resources as a battle, then everyone can be part of the war effort against them by recycling what they can. Maybe we will see a bottle bill passed and curbside recycling for every community in Tennessee." Until then, Patrick urges, "there's never any lack of things to be done."

Emerald Youth Foundation Volunteers
Clark Reyes, Chastity Morris, Nancy Surber, and M. Chris Douglass

Have you ever wished you could take a year or two of your life and give back to the community through an organization that meant a lot to you? That's just what Nancy Surber, Chris Douglass, Clark Reyes and Chastity Morris have been able to do through AmeriCorps at Emerald Youth Foundation, an urban youth program in Knoxville. Three of the four were youth participants in this Christian after-school program and then went on to become peer models for the children who follow now. All are service heroes, especially inspirational because their lives could have gone in radically different directions.

Clark, a Filipino immigrant, grew up in urban Knoxville and developed a passion for giving back. Since he completed his service as to AmeriCorps, Clark has begun taking classes at Pellissippi State and working five days a week as the head of the library of the Boys & Girls Club. At first, only five or six children came to this program; now he has 15-20 kids asking him for advice and waiting to listen. Clark is a compassionate mentor. His service at Emerald Youth Foundation provided the training and experience needed to know how to relate to the children. Who better than he knows what these kids are going through? In his second month with the Boys and Girls Club, the staff and kids have shown their confidence by voting him "staff member of the month."

"I don't think I could have gotten through my AmeriCorps term without Clark," said Chastity, a young single mom who has been balancing parenting, college, and service. "Sometimes, I felt the kids at Emerald Youth Foundation expected me to give up on them. He challenged me to be a constant and accountable friend to them, even through difficult times."

Each of the four volunteers served more than 3,400 hours over two years as AmeriCorps Members in the Emerald program, mentoring young people and coordinating traditional church volunteers who could only give a few hours a week. The partnership of the faith-based program staff, high-energy AmeriCorps members and traditional church volunteers has caused a dramatic strengthening and expansion of the Emerald Foundation program.

Nancy Surber's experience with service has affected her life so profoundly that she has changed her major from graphic design to child development. "Volunteering changed my feelings towards the kids I helped."

In the Emerald Youth Foundation after-school program, Nancy loved the games on the playground, where she grew to know the kids better. "I enjoy spending time with the children and learning about their lives. Some of the experiences these children go through I could never imagine facing as a child."

Chris Douglas has been a positive role model for dozens of inner-city children. Because of the relationships Chris has built with the children, he has changed his major from physical therapy and computer science to primary education. "Once you fall in love with the kids, the ball starts rolling. You take yourself out of the picture and it brings out the best in those kids."

Now, once a month and on school breaks on his own time, Chris is thrilled to join Clark, Nancy and Chastity in service. "They are all so dedicated," he says. "They go above and beyond the hours required. These three are examples of why the AmeriCorps program flourished."

Maggie Joy Flynn

An early encounter with volunteering taught Maggie Joy Flynn how powerful a difference she could make in the lives of others. As a college student, Maggie volunteered in a home for autistic children, working consistently with one boy. Despite months of intervention, he made no visible progress and had never spoken. It wasn't clear if he really understood anything they had done. Then, suddenly, Maggie had a broken leg and was unable to work with him for a few days. The first night she missed, the boy had an outburst like never before. And, miraculously, he spoke— calling over and over for Maggie.

Maggie moved to this country as a 13-year-old who was "rail thin and in a cast" because of polio and who "had a funny accent" because she came from Australia. She felt alienated for quite a long time. Today she promotes acceptance of others through her involvement with the Mayor's Diversity Program in Jackson and through the Optimist Club.

Always desiring to help in as many places as possible, Maggie is a well-rounded volunteer. She serves the United Way as part of its allocations committee, ensuring that funds are utilized as intended and where they are most needed. For fun, she helps with the National Association of Intercollegiate Athletics women's basketball championship. This national event is held in Jackson every year and is run entirely by volunteer power. She began supporting the Jackson Symphony Orchestra even before she lived in Tennessee, buying tickets before she knew her moving date!

Health care is another of Maggie's passions. She works with the Kiwanis Center for Child Development, the American Heart Association, and the American Cancer Society. Even though she had been an active volunteer with many causes for most of her life, experiencing her own cancer heightened her sense of gratefulness and her passion to help others. She says, the conviction and humility clear in her voice, "I'm so thankful to be alive. Every minute of every day is so incredibly precious. I do this because I'm able to." She is truly grateful to be "helping others help others" and firmly believes in the power of human potential. "We've got an enormous, generous world. There is so much to be done, so much disease, so many in need. If each of us could do something, it would be fantastic for the cause and also because you learn something about yourself when you volunteer."

After forty-two years of volunteering, what are the most important things

Maggie Joy Flynn has learned about herself? "That I am very, very blessed. Although there have been many hardships in my life, compared to what other people have been through, my life has been a walk in the park. I've also learned that I'm flawed but that it doesn't matter."

Linda Gilbert

McMinnville native Linda Gilbert sees herself simply as a "giver," but she is much more. She is an energy vortex who attracts other givers. She is a catalyst who can compel and propel those around her to volunteer time, money, talents, and whatever material goods they have to contribute to her service projects.

"I just try to be open to the opportunities and possibilities I see around me," Gilbert says, modestly. "Service projects bring together lots of very caring, compassionate, and joyful people. I am surrounded by people like that— the givers. I love to bring these people together."

Some of the projects that Gilbert has spearheaded are the *USA Today* magazine's "Make a Difference Day," "National Youth Service Day" sponsored by Youth Service America, "Trailblazing at Taft" within Tennessee's Taft Youth Development Center, and therapeutic humor workshops for teachers, health professionals, teens, and seniors.

Gilbert specializes in interdisciplinary, intergenerational projects that supply heavy doses of humor. For three years, she organized "National Youth Service Day" programs that official media sites in Tennessee, and for four years she spearheaded "Make a Difference Day" projects In her region.

"For those projects, churches, community organizations, civic clubs, businesses, individuals, schools students and seniors came together to provide workshops and services for low income, elderly, disabled or otherwise marginalized people," the volunteer coordinator remembers.

One of her nursing home projects received an Honorable Mention. The fourth year's "Make a Difference Day" project benefited Taft Youth Development Center, Tennessee's toughest juvenile facility. The project was a regional winner and the boys got to see their story featured in *USA Today* magazine.

"I started volunteering at Taft about 1997," Gilbert explains. "This is a group of people who have been pretty well forgotten by the general public. Taft is a perfect place for volunteers to reach inside to try to touch the students' lives in a positive way."

Gilbert's passion and dedication have prompted many in the last two years to reach into Taft. Nursery owners of McMinnville donated teaching time and trees, plants and shrubs so that the boys might learn horticulture. Extension Agents brought in petting animals to teach kindness and a gentle touch. Playwrights, singers, storytellers, jazz and blues musicians and bagpipe players have performed and interacted with the boys behind the prison walls.

"My biggest passion right now is getting the old swimming pool turned into a theater," Gilbert says. "I have all kinds of theater, dance and orchestra groups that want to set up programs with the boys. They want to teach them how to operate sound and lighting systems, and help them learn how to express themselves.

"A lot of people want to help and volunteer and be of service and contribute, and they're looking for ways to do that," Gilbert concludes. "Bringing attention to a volunteer project touches people's hearts. Then they are drawn to contribute whatever they have to give. Volunteering can make a real difference in everyone's lives."

Tennessee Volunteer Heroes 2001

Mary Lou Goins

It all started with a public service announcement. Mary Lou Goins, as the sole office staff member for a small radio station, had to prepare an announcement about area 4-H Club happenings. The public service announcement was so powerful, she became involved in 4-H herself.

Now, "Mama Lou," as she is known, can walk anywhere across the state and see a child she's helped. Serving at every level within 4-H, Lou's joy has been "to see that a child has potential, to help the child see that potential and to develop it, especially when there has been little parental involvement." She has shepherded many state-level winners, but quickly points out that having kids "doing the best they can is the most important." She loves "seeing their faces, helping them know they could do it."

Feeling "compelled by God to help, to love, to care, and to share," Lou uses every creative instinct she has to guide and improve the lives of children. She has been found teaching creation to 3 year olds by "sitting under a blanket with a flashlight" at the First Baptist Church in Woodbury. With the Cannon County Dixie Youth baseball and softball programs, she has been scorekeeper, coach, concessions manager, and clean-up crew. Through her work with the Cannon County Child Protection Council, she has done everything from forming clown teams, where performances are used to teach kids to say no to drugs, alcohol and tobacco, to teaching at hands-on Science Day Camps, to starting a pregnancy prevention program that has now been replicated in 22 other counties!

"If you're a part of the community, you shouldn't be sitting on the sidelines, waiting to be served. I don't like sitting on the sidelines," Lou insists, convincingly. "I may grow physically tired from giving, but I never tire of the joy. When you're working with youth, the clock is irrelevant. Each of us has to find our own little niche of what we can do to give back instead of just being takers."

And she has given back, indeed. Lou has been volunteering for 29 years, but community service took on another layer of meaning when she entered public political service. The first woman in Woodbury to run for, and be elected alderperson and, later, vice-mayor, she was greatly honored when the *Daily News Journal* headline read "Woodbury has a mother."

"If you preach it, you had better do it," Lou stresses. She is tapping even more of her own potential by returning to college to earn an accounting degree. "You can do this," she tells herself— that's another public service announcement!

Mollie Gross

Two years ago, when Mollie Gross was just eleven years old, she followed her grandmother, Glen, into Pine Oaks Assisted Living facility. It was expected that Glen would be there temporarily, but fate had other plans. "My grandmother helped me to grow up. I see her almost everyday and I talk to her." Today, Mollie comes to Pine Oaks an average of three days a week and stays three to five hours at a time. When her hectic schedule permits, she comes more frequently and during school breaks, it is not unusual to see Mollie for this same amount of time seven days a week.

Although she has a much older brother, Mollie has grown up like an only child of parents devoted to volunteering as well. This and her academic accomplishments make Mollie unique. She is an accomplished ballerina with the Johnson City Ballet Company, studies flute at the Suzuki School, sings in a junior choir, is a member of the youth group of the local First United Methodist Church, and is the president of her school class. With so much time needed for school and rehearsals, the staff of Pine Oaks is amazed at her dependable contributions.

"After I saw my grandmother, I met other people. Sometimes I just go into a resident's room and talk to them or give someone a hug to make them feel better." Mollie spends time with the residents, assisting them with activities of daily living. She brightens their days by performing flute concerts, has danced and even taught the "Hula" at the annual Luau. Mollie is equally gifted in assisting the residents with craft activities and is always there to lead a lost guest back down a lonely hall to find their room.

Mollie especially likes hearing and learning from the older residents. "They tell me stories about how they've grown up. One lady friend of my grandmother's went to UT and told me her experiences and what to expect. She especially told me to 'Watch out for those boys!'"

Since many of the residents suffer from Alzheimer's Disease, Mollie has learned some needed skills. When asked how she deals with the residents she has grown close to who show signs of deterioration, Mollie's comment conveys wisdom. "I have days when I wonder what the Alzheimer patients are going to do. They want to go home. They cry for their mother to come and pick them up. Some think I am their daughter and want to go home with me. It takes a lot of patience." Sometimes, Mollie's heart breaks for the people she works with, but her enthusiasm for joyful expression is the compass that leads her back.

Pine Oaks commends Mollie for the many student volunteers she has recruited to join her in care giving to those suffering. "It's going to be hard at first," she tells her friends, "just be patient. When you see how much they enjoy seeing you, you'll want to come back."

Mollie believes volunteering has helped her to be "a better 12 and 13 year-old." It's easy to see that this young lady is well on her way to being successful in whatever she undertakes, especially since she already understands so much about what is truly important. Anyone in her presence is lucky to be touched by her.

Virginia Holland

Virginia was born and raised in Waverly, Tennessee. On her fifth birthday, Virginia's father was killed in a freak accident while working for the city of Waverly. Virginia's mother had other children and the only way to help them through their grief was to take them to the American Legion Hall. That's where Virginia learned to dance. She did two-step, waltz, square and buck dancing. Those steps got her through her grief.

As a young woman, married with children, Virginia moved to Ohio. There, she had a series of nervous difficulties and spent valuable time in a Cincinnati mental hospital. With counseling, she rehabilitated by doing needlework and crafts. It was there that a man with the Salvation Army saw her spark and invited her to help attend to the clients in an adult daycare. Virginia visited, she listened, and she made the people smile.

Once she no longer needed professional care, Virginia returned the kindnesses bestowed on her by volunteering her time to other patients. She took them to symphonies, to art programs and shopping. Some were handicapped, so with those she would hold a hand and watch a movie. "I guess the staff saw something in me," she says, modestly.

"I love to dance. I used to put on little magic shows and make them laugh." Virginia's good sense of humor and love of entertainment were her tickets to greater emotional freedom.

When she moved back to Waverly ten years ago, Virginia volunteered at the Humphreys County Chamber of Commerce. She enjoys the interaction with her co-workers and gets satisfaction from the many clerical duties she assists with.

For years, before her retirement in June of 2000, Virginia added her special touch to the lives of Alzheimer's patients at the Waverly Health Care Clinic. She enjoyed interacting with the patients, and found joy even in grinding food to feed those critically close to the end of their lives.

Virginia is devoted to her community. "A few years ago we had a dream. We wondered how we could keep our kids in our county. We decided we wanted our own College." Virginia sold tee shirts and books to help raise awareness. Three million dollars later, with the help of the community, Humphreys County has bought and paid for the Humphreys County Center for Higher Education. For all her hard work, Virginia has received numerous awards and recognitions.

Virginia recently finished writing her life's story; *Growing Up in a Small Town,* and her story is serialized in the local newspaper bi-weekly.

She plans to begin doing volunteer work for the Blood Mobile soon. "Having someone to take care of helped me. If it hadn't been for them, I might still be on medication. I have always said if people would volunteer their time to hospitals and nursing homes, we'd have a better place to live." By Virginia's example, she has found it, in Waverly.

Mai Bell Hurley

Nearly fifty years ago, after a short career as a newspaper reporter, Mai Bell married and began a family. Because she had familial support and the opportunity to devote time to others, Mai Bell was able to start volunteering in her home town of Chattanooga.

Today, councilwoman Mai Bell Hurley is a passionate advocate for early childhood development and strong pre-school education. "If kids don't have age-appropriate vocabulary or aren't read to from the cradle, they suffer. This issue cuts across all socioeconomic and racial lines. Some very well-educated people are so busy that they don't take the time to read to their children and those children suffer this deficit for the rest of their lives."

Mai Bell has worked on organizational efforts to create educational programs in pre-schools, adolescent tutoring and parenting classes. At the United Way of Greater Chattanooga, Mai Bell is the Volunteer Chair of the program "Invest in Children," an initiative similar to Nashville's "Success By Six." She led the development of Families First, a Welfare Reform Model that brought her to the attention of the State of Tennessee's Advisory Council for Families First, where she worked with Bob Corker during Governor Sundquist's first term, helping to develop the Tennessee Department of Children's Services.

As a member of the City Council of Chattanooga, Mai Bell never imagined that she would be instrumental in the cultural renaissance of downtown Chattanooga. Her leadership has been important for several major projects including the Tennessee Aquarium; the Parent's Place, Books for Babes and the Westside Medical Home.

Mai Bell and quickly applauds businesses that encourage employees to schedule volunteer time into their work schedule. Understanding that "time is money" she sees this release time as an invaluable contribution. She also appreciates the people in management positions who find time to volunteer, like a young lawyer she knows who artfully juggles a chair on a volunteer board, legal work and the mothering of her own small children.

"If you're really building a community planning effort then you have to work on many fronts at once. I believe the most important is the education of children and the quality of life this ensures for our broader community of citizens."

Mai Bell believes that "our country was built on volunteer and philanthropic endeavors and they are part of the fabric of our civilization." Volunteerism continues to give birth to a supportive atmosphere for those in need. "If you're able to think of other people, you're less likely to think about yourself," she chuckles.

Martha Ingram, Orrin Ingram, John Ingram, David Ingram, and Robin Ingram Patton

No chronicle of volunteerism in Tennessee would be complete without noting the contributions of the Ingram family. In addition to contributing hundreds of millions of dollars back into Tennessee communities, the family has actively served as volunteers for an extensive variety of causes and has established a business culture in which associates (employees) are encouraged and supported in their volunteering. This support includes corporate matching of contributions and paid release time for employees to perform community service.

While the late Bronson Ingram created Ingram Industries, he and his wife Martha also raised a family and instilled in them this standard: "To whom much is given, much is expected." Bronson and Martha gave generously from their financial successes in their marine barge, product distribution, and insurance companies. They also maintained a long-standing tradition of supporting the Middle Tennessee community.

One of the Ingram family's greatest legacies to Nashville is the Vanderbilt Ingram Scholars Program, which provides scholarships to students based on a combination of their academic and community service successes. Bronson believed that once scholarship recipients established careers of their own, they would carry the community service values they had fostered into daily service and would perpetuate the gifts of service to their communities. Highly civic-minded, Bronson was active in Nashville's Chamber of Commerce and supported education as one of the founding members of "Inroads," which provides minority students with work-related opportunities to supplement their education. Bronson was one of the founders of the PENCIL Foundation in Nashville. He was a dear friend to the community, and is missed.

Martha Ingram's volunteer efforts are rooted in the arts. Desiring that her children and others in Tennessee have exposure to the arts and humanities,

Martha spearheaded a first-of-its-kind statewide public-private initiative that resulted in the creation of the Tennessee Performing Arts Center. Annually, tens of thousands of children from across the state now view performances through the center's Humanities Outreach Tennessee (HOT) program. Additionally, Martha served as Chair of the Tennessee Bicentennial Celebration. She has also been instrumental in the renaissance of the Nashville Symphony and supported it during a period of bankruptcy. In 2000, the Symphony earned a prestigious invitation to perform at Carnegie Hall.

All of the Ingram children have followed their parents' lead in giving back to the community. Orrin served as Chair of the United Way of Davidson County in 2000. His focus is on supporting health and human service programs in the community. He believes that as we "give time, leadership skills, and leverage business contacts, it inspires others to get involved and creates a venue for community involvement." Through his contributions of time and funds, Orrin supports the Vanderbilt Cancer Center. Since his dad died of cancer, he and the rest of the Ingram family have a personal commitment to supporting those engaged in finding a cure.

John Ingram heads the company's book distribution businesses. He remembers growing up with the understanding that "advantages obligated the family to give back to the community." This "obligation" was not understood as a burden, but was seen as a cherished opportunity that made his family happy and proud. John has a personal interest in the special educational needs of children with learning differences and in supporting sports programming at Vanderbilt University. Vanderbilt athletic scholarships have provided many with the chance for an excellent education. John is proud that Ingram Book Company partners with La Vergne High School through the Partners in Education Program. Daily, students are bussed to the Book Company to work with mentors and to participate in various school-to-work initiatives. The company's campus serves as an extension of the school's campus. Much of the company's involvement is designed to integrate severely disabled students into the community and the workplace. This program and a student leadership program in the partnership have been recognized nationally for excellence and are being replicated in other communities.

Younger brother David supports the community through his personal and his company's corporate support of United Way programming. David and his wife Sarah are regular volunteers for Chukkers for Charity, a polo match that benefits the Rochelle Center and Saddle Up! Both agencies support with children with disabilities. As with other Ingram-owned companies, Ingram Entertainment (which David runs) provides matching funds and incentives for employee involvement with community initiatives.

Sister, Robin Ingram Patton, devotes her volunteer efforts to animal rights groups. She is a leading activist with the Humane Society and with the Nashville Zoo. Additionally, Robin supports education and, in particular, programs targeting the educational opportunities for young girls.

Personal involvement by Ingram family members has led to the three most successful fundraising walks in Middle Tennessee. Two of the walks supported AIDS education and research and the third benefited the Juvenile Diabetes Foundation.

John believes that by engaging individuals and the private sector to get involved in community service "we could significantly reduce our dependency on government service to meet the needs of those less fortunate than we are."

Martha quotes the late, great Albert Schweitzer: "To be truly happy you have to serve. It is really the only road to happiness."

JC Penney Volunteers: Supporting America's Communities

James Cash Penney, founder of the J.C. Penney Company, left a legacy of partnership and community responsibility, hard work and moral principle, which the Company continues to affirm today. The legacy lives not only in the Company's business integrity and fair dealing, but also in its dedication of financial and human resources to help meet today's social needs.

JCPenney employs 290,000 associates (employees) in approximately 4,500 operating units nationwide— JCPenney stores, catalog sales and fulfillment centers, JCPenney Direct Marketing Services, Eckerd Drugstores, and other business offices. The units are located in all 50 states, Puerto Rico, and Mexico. In Tennessee, there are 26 stores located in Maryville, Chattanooga (2), Cleveland, Columbia, Dyersburg, Goodlettsville, Greeneville, Jackson, Johnson City, Kingsport, Clarksville, Knoxville (2), McMinnville, Morristown, Oak Ridge, Paris, Cookeville, Antioch, Memphis, Franklin, Tullahoma, Murfreesboro, Union City and Bartlett.

A healthy social environment is important for JCPenney associates, their families, and their friends. A healthy social environment is also one where business can grow and prosper. For these reasons, JCPenney reinvests its money, and— equally important— its people, skills and know-how, in communities across the nation.

JCPenney associates, encouraged by the Company, actively participate in community affairs. All across the country, thousands of JCPenney associates volunteer to work with charitable groups, parent-teacher organizations, chambers of commerce and a host of other civic and community service organizations.

This support is augmented by financial support to civic and charitable organizations, which in 1999 totaled $27.6 million— $24.5 million in cash and $3.1 million in in-kind donations. More than half those financial contributions were given by stores and other facilities to support organizations in their local communities. The remainder was contributed to national organizations serving a variety of community needs.

To target its resources for greatest effect, the Company concentrates its community support and involvement on five programs:

- support for the United Way
- improvement of pre-kindergarten through 12th grade education, primarily through the JCPenney Afterschool Program
- promotion of volunteerism, primarily through Golden Rule Awards and James Cash Penney Awards for Community Service
- Susan G. Komen Race for the Cure
- March of Dimes

JCPenney supports volunteerism through encouraging associate participation in volunteer activities and through its two major award programs. Through the two award programs, JCPenney makes charitable contributions to award-winning volunteers' non-profit organizations (more than $1.8 million in 1999 to local charities).

The James Cash Penney Awards for Community Service honor JCPenney and Eckerd active and retired associates who volunteer in their communities. In 1999, associates who applied volunteered more than 190,000 hours to service agencies, the equivalent of $2.8 million in non-profit salaries.

The JCPenney Golden Rule Awards, established in 1982, honor community volunteers from outside the Company, recognizing volunteers in four categories: adult, group, youth and education. In 1999, nearly 1,000 Golden Rule Award winners and 20,000 nominees were cited in 210 communities in 45 states. Local nominations are solicited annually in the four categories. A panel of judges, normally community leaders and high-profile individuals, selects a number of winners and finalists, and cash contributions are awarded to each winner's volunteer organization. Local winners automatically become eligible for JCPenney National Golden Rule Awards and the opportunity to win an additional $10,000 for their volunteer organization.

The JCPenney National Volunteer Awards were initiated in 1987 to focus attention on volunteering nationally. Annually, seven volunteers are recognized on behalf of the James Cash Penney Award for Community Service and the national Golden Rule Award programs. Three National James Cash Penney Award winners are selected in the categories of Active Associate, Retired Associate, and Education. Each recipient receives a crystal award and a $10,000 contribution for his or her nonprofit organization. In addition, four National Golden Rule Award winners are selected from thousands of local Golden Rule Award winners from across the country. Adult, Group, and Education winners receive a crystal award and a $10,000 contribution for their nonprofit organization. A Youth winner, 18 years or younger, receives a crystal award, a $5,000 contribution for his or her nonprofit organization, and a $5,000 scholarship.

Austin P. Jennings

Austin Jennings is an entrepreneur, historian, publisher of multiple newspapers and stalwart example of community spirit. "I've lived in Woodbury since I was born. Living in a small community, it's hard not to have that volunteer spirit. That's just what people do," Jennings says. "I grew up during the Depression and people helped each other as a way of life."

Jennings remembers the first time he volunteered. He was seventeen years old and a senior in high school. "It was toward the end of World War II," he remembers. "I volunteered for the U.S. Army Air corps. I lied about my age, had a friend sign my parent's signature, and wound up in the aviation cadet program, learning how to fly airplanes."

Tennessee Volunteer Heroes 2001

In the course of his lifetime, Jennings has been a jeweler and diamond dealer, director of several banks, and the founder of Research Marketing, Inc. He is a husband, father, grandfather and great-grandfather. He pretends to be retired.

"I quit working for a living several years ago. Since then, I've been working outside the business in community activities— either locally or on a larger scale," he tells us. "I've never been a workaholic. I've never been one to try to make all the money I could. I make enough to live on and then give my time to the community."

The Woodbury native has been involved in so many volunteer efforts over the years that he has a hard time narrowing down to his favorites. "In 1964, Dr. J. F. Adams, a friend and community leader died. We wanted to create a memorial for him," he explains. "We wanted the memorial to be a gift in his name to the community. So we created a county library at no cost to the county. I'm very proud of the Cannon County Library. We have the highest circulation of books per capita of any small library in the state."

Jennings is also founder and president of the Cannon County Historical Society. Since its beginning in 1976, the association has published eleven books of historic value to the county. "Most recently, my wife and I were involved in creating a 544-page history in which we preserved for posterity about 2,000 old pictures of families, places, things and events in Cannon County."

As a member of the Lions Club, Jennings has been instrumental in creating programs to help children see. As World President of Lions Clubs International in 1988-89, he created a project called SightFirst designed to eliminate preventable and reversible blindness in the world.

Closer to home, the retired businessman headed Operation KidSight, a program to establish Tennessee Lions Eye Center at Vanderbilt Children's Hospital to provide the only exclusively pediatric ophthalmology center in the South.

"We've now screened about 30,000 kids and we've found that about five percent do have a potential eye problem that if it's not treated in a timely way will create a lifetime of eye trouble— even blindness," he says. Helping to prevent these problems is "a very gratifying project," he remarks.

Jennings says that though he has traveled the world promoting his favorite volunteer projects at his own expense, it has never been a sacrifice. "On the contrary, I've gained so much… in opportunities… in seeing things happen that wouldn't have happened otherwise. What I have gained, I could have never received by doing anything other than what I've done."

Paul LeBlanc

After raising ten children, after thirty-two years of active and reserve service in the United States Navy, after getting an Associate's Degree in Accounting and Management and after working as a warehouse foreman for Service Merchandise, Paul LeBlanc has earned a little time off. What Paul does with his time off is share it with an elementary school full of kids.

Paul was born and raised in Massachusetts. He joined the Navy during World War II and was assigned to flight crews. "I just tried to be a nice guy," he says, laughing. The Navy transferred him to Washington, DC for four years and then to the Memphis Naval Base. While working there, Paul volunteered with Family Services. "When someone in the division died or needed help, we offered them support and assistance."

Since his retirement, Paul also volunteers hosting tours for international and domestic visitors who want to see the Memphis Belle, the first Army Airforce Fighter to complete twenty-five missions in England and Germany. It is parked on Mud Island in the middle of the Mississippi River. The area around the Memphis Belle is jazzed up with musicians and award-winning barbecue. Paul is proud to be a part of the celebration of history, and proud of his military past. "I miss the guys. I miss my comrades," he says.

About eight years ago, Paul's grandson invited him to his school. Kate Bond Elementary wasn't far from Paul's house and he agreed to visit. What started out as a promise to one child for one day has turned into hundreds of promises made to the children and adults who have grown to depend upon and love him. Twice each week, Paul volunteers in the school library checking books in and out for the students. He is a faithful custodian of stories both on the shelf and in his heart. Paul shelves, cleans, and processes newly received books. His contributions allow the librarian and assistant to work more directly with the students. Shortly after his grandson asked Paul to come to school, his family moved. "When the school found out my grandson was leaving, they asked me if I was going to stay." The answer was yes, and the staff and children admire him even more for it.

"I treat all the kids fairly, no favorites." At a time when male role models are especially needed, Paul provides a smile and pleasant conversation to students in need. With just a look, (and the experience of raising his own children) Paul can calm any disorder. His sense of humor has endeared him to the teachers, administrative staff, and of course, the kids. "If I don't go to school, I'll just go to Tunica," he jokes. "School keeps me out of trouble."

A single widower since the death of his beloved wife in 1979, just six years after his retirement, Paul says, "volunteering never got in my way." Even during the death of one of his sons from cancer, and Paul's own health challenges, he has continued to volunteer. "I enjoy working with the teachers and students so much that I haven't missed a day of volunteering, even for chemotherapy treatments."

Paul believes that if more people volunteered, we could "Make Tennessee a better place to live in, ease racial tensions, and help assist those who need help the most— the young, the old, and the ill." His hearty good nature and deep inclination to help others follows him like a ray of sunshine on a brisk school morning. "I can't quit if I wanted to."

Lucille Shattuck Lewis

"When books are celebrated as magical and extraordinary," says Lu Lewis, "they become the most important things in your classroom."

Lu Lewis's heart is with children. She is viewed by her peers and the Chattanooga community as an expert in early childhood education. Though Lu is retired after thirty-five years of teaching kindergarten and first grade, she is still a principle force in keeping children's education a focal point in the community of Chattanooga.

Lu began her volunteer work with the Chattanooga Association on the Education of Young Children. What started out as a pre-school council devoted to professional development for private child care workers quickly grew to include public school educators and later anyone involved with kids and education. Lu has also worked on the Early Childhood Advisory Committee for the Tennessee Department of Education and was part of the founding board of the Creative Discovery Museum of Chattanooga, of which she was the Director.

Through these programs, Lu has helped design professional development and is proud that the Chattanooga Association for the Education of Young Children presents the "Lu Lewis Award" annually. "This goes to a classroom teacher. Not the author or the supervisor but the teacher that cheers her kids on, who helps shape their young lives and inspires them in the simplest ways, everyday."

Lu is also an avid storyteller. Like her friend and peer Mai Bell Hurley, Lu believes that reading to your children is one the of the most important "gifts" you can give them. Currently, Lu leads the Books for Babes effort for United Way of Greater Chattanooga/Invest in Children. Books for Babes provides a book a month for children 0-6 years of age in the Chattanooga/Hamilton County area as a community Success by Six strategy for early childhood education.

Throughout her career, Lu has served on Chattanooga boards that made sure the children of the community had a place to go and something to be involved in. Lu's involvement in hands-on, interactive activities for children include: "Artstrataganza" in Miller Park, where children are given the opportunity to participate in the arts through activities such as making tee shirt impressions, murals, creating collages, wood working, puppet shows and music; "Christmas on the River;" "Farm Day;" and "Week of the Young Child."

Lu is convinced if more people volunteered we could "energize Tennessee! There is a place for each of us to volunteer: building, tutoring, answering phones, cleaning up an area, or reading to a child. Try one… you can't stop at just one!"

Clint Mathis, Jr.

"On any day, in any part of the three Tennessee Metros, you can drive ten minutes in any direction, and you will find an elderly person who has food needs that are either not met or met occasionally," Clint Mathis says. His passion is to eliminate hunger among Tennessee's elderly population. The first through third Saturdays of every month, Clint volunteers at the Mississippi Christian Boulevard Church to make over 800 food deliveries to elderly citizens as part of the Manna Outreach Ministry. Since 1992, Clint has chaired the steering committee that coordinates the purchasing of the food, recruitment of the many volunteers, packaging of the food in bushel baskets and large paper bags, and, ultimately, delivery of the food to the homes of the elderly recipients. The recipients are all sixty years or older, have a need, and have been referred by senior citizen groups, members of churches or members of the community. In 1995, the steering committee set a goal to serve 1,000 recipients and Clint is proud to say that by the end of 2000, they will come close to meeting that goal.

The Manna Outreach Ministry is a labor of love. Seven years ago, during a BellSouth conversion, Clint, a BellSouth employee, was in the middle of changing a telephone central office and addressing the subsequent problems that occurred. It allowed him only about three hours sleep during a twenty-eight hour period one Friday through Saturday. He had a choice to make on Saturday morning, to go home and sleep or to check and see if there was a shortage of delivery volunteers. He stopped at his church on the way home and discovered they were short of drivers, so Clint made deliveries. His last delivery was to an elderly lady who sat alone on her steps looking ill. After unpacking her food he asked her how she was. "I ran out of food yesterday, and I can't take my medicine without food."

Clint is convinced that "hunger among senior citizens can be eliminated" and he remains devoted to that cause. His actions have resulted in the start of a second Manna Outreach in Houston, Texas. "The financial resources required to meet this challenge," he remarks, "are minuscule when compared with the amount of volunteer hours that are needed." Volunteers can be the nets for others to fall into so that "no one falls through the crack."

During the week, Clint is responsible for all BellSouth Central Offices in West Tennessee. As a BellSouth Pioneer, he serves as BellSouth's liaison for Junior Achievement, which has a program where volunteers from the business community go into schools for an hour each week for five weeks or nine weeks. He has spent classroom time with students in grades 1-8. Recently, because he was so well received by the students, Clint was asked to come back again and work with a class of fifth graders.

Because of his labors of love assisting seniors and children, Clint is a real Tennessee Volunteer Hero.

Scott M. Niswonger

Niswonger is a Germanic name that means "white swan." Scott M. Niswonger was likely never an ugly duckling, but he's accomplished a great deal as a volunteer and has become a white swan of a Tennessee Volunteer Hero.

As a "kid from a cornfield in northwestern Ohio" Scott's dream was to be a pilot. At age twelve, he worked odd jobs, saved money and began flight lessons. By age eighteen, he had a commercial flying license and went on to Purdue University where he earned a degree in Professional Pilot Technology.

Scott worked his way up from Pilot, to the President of the Magnavox Company, to become Vice President of the Flying Tigers. Trips for Magnavox landed him in Greeneville, Tennessee, which became his adopted home. Simultaneously, Scott spread his wings and became Founder and CEO of General Aviation, Inc., an all-cargo transport service that included a large number of charter aircraft and trucking groups. Demands for his services evolved into two publicly traded transportation and logistics companies, Landair Corporation and Forward Air Corporation. "I tell young people that it's only in America that you get to try," Scott says. "It has been a lot of hard work building the business, and now we employ over 2,500 between the U.S. and Canada."

Scott is easy to talk to and modest. He gets excited about his "pet projects," which are mostly centered in and near Greeneville. These are community service efforts aimed at improving schools and buildings, providing scholarships, and helping people in need.

Scott uses his resources where they are needed the most. Phillip Jennings, who was paralyzed in a high school football game, is grateful for the handicapped-accessible home Scott donated to him. "I just spoke with Phillip," Scott says, excitedly. "We were at South Greene H.S. and he was just beginning to get movement in his right arm." Scott is thrilled for what this means to a young man with a positive attitude who has risen above his quadriplegia.

Scott is eager to talk about something he and his friends collaborated on for seven years: "We took on a community project which was the restoration of a Civil War Era hotel." Their vision was the catalyst for the donation and restoration of twelve historic buildings downtown. Scott's expertise has helped to make Greeneville a renaissance community. Profit generated by the historic properties gets recycled into other philanthropic efforts. Today, in the second oldest town in Tennessee, the revitalized buildings and General Morgan Inn serve as a conference center and a tourism hub.

Scott's enthusiasm for education and Tusculum College is infectious. He is especially proud of the additional classroom space and a new Commons his volunteering and contributions have helped to create. "Freshmen coming in participate in the civic arts," he explains. "Everyone is expected to give of their time either to local governments, education, nursing homes, or wherever their passion may be. Tusculum places a huge emphasis on citizenship and entrepreneurship, producing business majors, teachers, pre-med and pre-law students."

Still holding onto the spirit of a twelve-year-old who wants to fly, Scott has volunteered the gifts he has cultivated, has flown high and wide, and glides through life with the natural grace of a white swan.

Melissa Poe

It all began with a beloved actor, a television program, and a nine-year-old girl with the audacious faith of a child.

"On August 4, 1989, I was watching *Highway to Heaven* ," recalls Melissa Poe. "The show depicted what the world might look like in twenty or thirty years if people didn't start paying attention to the pollution problem. It scared me because it was showing a future that was supposed to be mine. What I was seeing, I wanted to prevent."

At the end of the program Michael Landon, the multi-talented actor, writer, producer, and star of the show said, "It's not too late. People who care will do something." Melissa took him at his word, and she began to think what she could do to create a healthy, beautiful world for her future.

"I thought the best way to prevent something was to get a lot of people involved," said Melissa. "At first, I tried to think how I might do that by myself, but then I thought there's no way that TV is going to interview me or I'm going to get in the newspaper. So then I thought, 'Who's always in the newspaper and whenever he talks, people listen?' The President, of course. So that night, I wrote a letter to President Bush asking him to help me stop pollution."

Poe expected a return letter in a day or two. As days turned into weeks, Melissa became impatient. She decided that it couldn't hurt to write other political leaders, so she began a letter writing campaign. After three weeks, the little girl decided she should make the letter bigger in order to catch the President's eye. She began to write it on large pieces of cardboard.

It was then that Melissa's mother explained to her the concept of billboards. The determined child called billboard companies asking that they post her letter to the President. Her first went up in Nashville, free of charge. "Then it occurred to me that the President doesn't live in Nashville, so if I wanted to make sure he saw it, maybe I needed to put one up in Washington," says Melissa. The second billboard went up in D.C., also free of charge. By April of the following year, Melissa had 250 complimentary billboards across the country asking President Bush to create a program to stop pollution.

Melissa Poe finally received a letter from President Bush in November, twelve weeks after she had sent hers to him, ten weeks after she had begun her letter writing campaign. "The letter I got back was a form letter saying 'Stay in school and don't do drugs,'" she sighs. "I was convinced he had never personally seen my letter. I decided I couldn't wait for the President to help. I thought that maybe it was my responsibility to make a program to take care of the environment. So I created Kids for a Clean Environment, Kids FACE®."

With her characteristic chutzpah, Melissa wrote "The Today Show" and asked to be on the morning news show to tell kids across America about her program. In January of 1990, her request was fulfilled and Kids FACE took off.

Today, Kids for a Clean Environment, is the world's largest youth environmental organization with more than 2,000 club chapters and 300,000 members across the United States and in twenty-two foreign countries.

And it all started with a little girl in Tennessee who believed she could save the environment and her future— even without the help of the President.

Barbara Russell

When a Memphis mom decided to get more involved in the lives of her children by volunteering at their school, she ended up getting involved in ways that have positively affected thousands of other children in Memphis and across the nation. Barbara Russell is known nationally as the Godmother of Adopt-a-School. "I wasn't the first to do this, but as a volunteer I wanted to be available and help support my kids in their education."

During the late 60's and early 70's Barbara retired from business to become a more available parent for her four growing sons. Court-ordered desegregation lost 35,000 students to private schools by the late 70's in Memphis. Barbara stayed in the city while many of her friends moved out.

As a concerned parent, Barbara noticed "there was a need for all kids." Barbara recognized that the "human element in the classroom is the most important learning tool." Since faculty and staff were overextended in the Memphis public school system, Barbara set out to recruit business partners in the community who would adopt a school. Barbara saw that the need to integrate the schools meant incorporating the greater community at large. Her initial volunteer projects were with the Parent Teacher Association.

In 1975, Barbara was asked to help promote community involvement in 45 of Memphis's schools. Barbara used a concise outline for Adopt-a-School into the business community. She gave speeches at Partners in Education conferences asking businesses to sign a contract with their partner schools that highlighted their full commitment to work with their school. "The greatest challenge is to match the school's need to the company's mission. The pay-off for companies is free advertising along with hands-on connection to students who might eventually work their way into that company. Companies offer scholarships, mentoring, even down to basic school supplies. Children exercise their scholastic aptitude and gain a working knowledge of the business world by working as interns writing papers on the business and getting to know its employees. The bottom line is always mutually beneficial."

The results have been staggering. Today, over 164 schools in the Memphis area have business partnerships. When President Reagan invited Barbara Russell to the White House in 1983 he declared 1983-84 to be the National Year of Partnership as part of the challenge to help convince businesses to volunteer in schools.

Public benefactors include businesses, civic groups, faith communities, military installations, government agencies and higher education institutions. There are hundreds of examples of innovative ways in which sponsors have helped their schools. By commending students, appreciating educators, hosting awareness events, and offering their own employees release time, the many rivulets of service join into a mighty river. When the owner of Guardsmark Security Co., Ira Lipman, was honored with a needlepoint banner on his 40th birthday he was so moved that he asked the kids what they would like most in the world. One child wanted to learn how to speak French and another wanted to be a ballerina. Lipman followed up and the school has a French and ballet teacher.

The personal triumphs are endless. While walking in her own community of Memphis one day, Barbara and a businessman were confronted by a young man who thrust his hand forward with enthusiasm. "I just wanted you to know, because of you, I am going to college. I just wanted to say 'thank-you!'" Barbara never found out what specific program enabled that student to go to school, but it doesn't matter; the end result is victory for the Adopt-a-School program.

Barbara's motherly instinct to help her own children naturally grew outward and adopted the needs of all kids. She believes that "volunteering can turn the world around— across the country."

Kathryn Shanks

When she was eleven years old, Kathryn Shanks volunteered for the Rocky Mount Museum, where she received the Frances C. Charles Youth Volunteer Award in 1998. For her outstanding volunteer work, Kathryn also won the J.C. Penney Golden Rule Youth Award in 2000.

She began volunteering for the museum after applying for a scholarship for a summer camp program offered by Rocky Mount. Although she was not awarded the scholarship, Kathryn was offered the chance to volunteer at the Museum.

Thousands of visitors who pass through this small eastern Tennessee museum are transported back to 1791. They are welcomed by Kathryn, dressed in historic costume as Eliza Cobb, granddaughter of the builder of Rocky Mount. In this capacity, she gives tours, plays her fiddle and helps with school tours. She also instructs visitors in period craft projects. When she takes off her costume, Kathryn helps out with odd jobs around the museum and consults with the Director of Education on details for special days, school group visits, and offers suggestions to improve Rocky Mount's public programming so that the historic site can stay true to its intentions.

Kathryn has proven her reliability to the Museum by getting rides from co-workers and from her parents. In an era when many individuals complain about our young people and their lack of responsibility, Kathryn Shanks sets standards for her peers in terms of community commitment. Her parents also model such strength of character; both are committed volunteers.

Home schooling has its advantages for Kathryn. Community service with her family to help clean signs for the National Storytelling Center has allowed the family entrance to the national festival. Kathryn's musical education is further supported when she plays the fiddle with the performance band Celtic Air.

When Kathryn's mother volunteered for the Bays Mountain Park Association, she brought along her daughters. That is when Kathryn began volunteering, at age eight. The center is devoted to educating the public about the need for restoration and preservation of wildlife and specific habitats. After three years of volunteering, Kathryn, her mom, and a core group of volunteers became the surrogate family for a couple of gray wolf puppies. For three months, they helped raise puppies that were then introduced into the park's existing wolf pack.

In 2000, Kathryn was an American Ambassador to the British Isles in the People to People Student Ambassador Program. Kathryn feels that "volunteering not only helps the recipient, it helps build community and personal well-being."

Ida Starkey

"The truth is… I always wanted to be a nurse but I couldn't stand the sight of blood so this is the next best thing." Ida Starkey, eighty-five years of age, drives herself to Nashville Metropolitan Bordeaux Hospital seven days a week and cares for the patients from 5:00 a.m. until well after 6:00 p.m. Her first patient is her invalid sister. Ida helps care for her sister then begins to make her rounds.

Ida's basic daily task is the distribution of donated personal items, (toiletries and clothing) to individual patients, and to nursing units for general cares. Recently, when a nurse's station was understaffed, Ida pitched in. Weekly, Ida manages the in-house transportation of an average of 110 patients from three different buildings to and from Sunday morning church services, and then again for 40 patients so they can attend Thursday Bible study class. She maintains inventory records of donated items, shops for patients on request, helps them with correspondence courses and distributes a monthly calendar to each.

The hospital becomes home to many of its more than five hundred occupants. At one time, Ida knew well over five hundred patients by name. She is their Florence Nightingale; her smile is their sunshine and her listening is their comfort. Her message is strong for those who will hear. "We have so many retired people with time on their hands, and so many people here who could use their help."

Through her own network of friends from her Church of Christ Sunday School class, Ida has brought many new volunteers to her cause and has begun a program of monthly birthday parties for the patients. At Christmas, the volunteer work is doubled. Ida helps with the organization and distribution of gifts received from Churches of Christ throughout Nashville. If a gift arrives unidentified, that gift must be opened, identified, rewrapped and assigned to an individual. Not many people know that such a small gesture requires so much extra time, but it is important to Ida and the hospital that the quality of life for these patients is as "normal" as possible, despite their handicaps.

"I love what I do," she says, and it is obvious she means it.

Floyd Stewart, Jr. a quadriplegic who made his way out of the institution owes much of what he has accomplished today to Ida's inspiration. "What can I say about Miss Starkey? She was almost like a mom to me. She knew I was trying with every breath to work my way out of the nursing home where we met. She was a great helping hand," he says, with love in his voice.

Ida knows Floyd well. He was someone with whom she could share stories about her family life. "Oh, Floyd is one of my buddies, a great fellow. I really miss him."

Floyd was proud to mention that Ida Starkey was a recipient of the Mary Catherine Strobel award. Ida has also received the 1981 Volunteer of the Year award by the Tennessee Health Care Association, the JCPenney Golden Rule Award for outstanding volunteer service, in 1990, and the NAAP (National Association of Activity Professionals) Volunteer of the Year award in 1993. Ida also received personal letter of recognition and congratulations from President George Bush in 1991.

Marie Slaton, one of her former co-workers, who later became a patient, writes, "Loneliness can be a big problem, particularly to those recently admitted to a nursing facility. It was Mrs. Starkey who came and sat and talked for long periods of time. She had time to listen to some of my frustrations, and that in itself lessened those frustrations."

For over sixty-six years, while working at an administrative position with the Genesco Corporation, while nursing her invalid husband, and sister, and even through a recent bout of pneumonia, Ida has given generously of her time and attention to helping others feel better. "I don't think I would have done as good a job as a nurse as I've been a volunteer." Ida feels blessed. "I just love what I do."

Floyd Stewart, Jr.

Floyd Stewart, Jr. was injured in an automobile accident January 15, 1984, on the birthday of Dr. Martin Luther King. His car hit a patch of ice and he lost control, hitting a tree. Floyd's neck was broken. He was thirty-five years old, married, and had four children. Instead of death, God blessed him with quadriplegia. A year later, he entered MTSU as a freshman majoring in psychology. In 1986, as a result of two bouts with pneumonia, kidney infections, the onset of adult diabetes and other surgeries, Floyd had to move to the Bordeaux Nursing Home.

Floyd's paralyzed body was in the way, but his vision of returning to school for a degree is what kept him going. That and being surrounded by supportive family and friends and meeting volunteers like Ida Starkey. "Ida has a heart as big as Tennessee. She took me under her wing like a mother hen." Floyd's fondness for her is evident. He met her at the Bordeaux Nursing Home and she became a key figure in Floyd's vision to live independently.

"My disability has changed my life in many ways. The lack of basic supports resulted in my being placed in a nursing home for about five and a half years. Initially, I had no idea how to regain my independence but I knew there had to be some way to overcome disability, reenter the community and go back to work."

Ida helped Floyd become a volunteer at the Technology Access Center, where the director introduced Floyd to the executive director of People First of Tennessee and the Volunteers in Service to America (VISTA) program. "I learned how I could live at the nursing home, work in VISTA and receive a small stipend," he remarks.

VISTA is now a branch of AmeriCorps. Floyd was assigned to People First of Tennessee, an advocacy organization for individuals who have mental retardation as a disabling condition. "I spent two of the most productive, gratifying years of my life as a VISTA with People First."

From there, Floyd has been the Treasurer for the Consortium on Disability Issues and is a former Tennessee Commission on National and Community Service Board

Member. Currently, he is an Independent Living Advocate for the Center of Independent Living in Middle Tennessee. In this capacity, Floyd works with peer counselors training them to help at organizations like the Multiple Sclerosis Society.

Now, as a VISTA Supervisor, Floyd's schedule includes public speaking and a vigorous effort to provide testimony to policymakers to support an appropriate level of services for individuals with disabilities. Floyd is on the Advisory Committee on Long Term Care. One of his duties is to work with area agencies on aging and to get a new long-term program up and running. Another responsibility is to advise people with disabilities of their rights and to help them locate resources.

Today, Floyd's grandchildren visit with him at an 'accessible home' he's purchased while working at the Center for Independent Living. He is proud to share that in 1998, the Peabody College presented him with the "Changing Lives Award" on Dr. Martin Luther King Day, eleven years to the day of his accident. It was there that someone he didn't remember came out of the audience. "Floyd, you gave me information three years ago to help my son and I just came back to see you receive this award."

Floyd is a trailblazer and a real Tennessee Volunteer Hero.

Vernon Stewart

Vernon Stewart became a volunteer for the first time in 1983— the day after his retirement as a senior warehouseman. "I thought, 'what am I going to do, sit in a rocking chair for the rest of my life or go out and do something different from what I've been doing all of my life?'" Stewart remembers. "People die in rocking chairs. I decided I'd just as soon get out and get mixed up in it. Keeps me in the swing of things."

Stewart considered many volunteer options available to him in the Memphis area and settled on meal delivery for the Metropolitan Inter-Faith Association (MIFA). MIFA feeds 3,000 people each weekday. Of that number, 1,500 are frail, homebound seniors.

"I felt that delivering meals was something I could handle," laughs Stewart. "We call our seniors 'clients,' but they are more than clients— they are my friends. I try to make everybody laugh and I crack a few jokes now and then. I see if they need repairs to their homes. If they don't have air conditioning, I see to it that they get a fan. I'm not just delivering meals. I'm trying to be as helpful as I can. It's the greatest job in the world to be able to make somebody's day a little happier."

At the Metropolitan Inter-Faith Association Stewart's dedication is legendary. He has been a volunteer 18 of the program's 25 years. A rough estimate of service that Vern Stewart has given MIFA alone would be more than 12,000 hours. When you consider that for eight of those years, Stewart was almost totally blind, the strength of commitment is astounding.

"A few years ago Vern's eyesight became so poor that he was unable to drive," says agency director Margaret Craddock. "During that time, Vern became a 'running' partner for other MIFA volunteer drivers. He would ride a city bus to MIFA, which entailed quite a walk to the bus stop and a bus ride of more than twenty-five miles. With a supreme effort, treatment and specially designed glasses, Vern was eventually regain his driving status and was joyous to be on his own again."

The seventy-six year old Stewart looks forward to continuing his volunteer work for the rest of his life. "In these later years, I really have found what I was looking for to do. I would have never dreamed that it would have been charity work," he says with a softening of his voice.

"I'm going to continue until I drop dead. Someone's going to find me somewhere when I'm 95 years old, lying dead in the middle of the street with some food in my hand," he laughs. "I just hope that one gets delivered! I don't want anything to be incomplete."

The Tennessee Cable Industry

For more than 30 years, Tennessee Cable Telecommunications Association (TCTA) and its member cable operators have been an active part of their communities. TCTA represents over 95% of the cable operators in Tennessee and their 1.3 million subscribers. From donating Public Service Announcement time on cable channels to sponsoring key community events, the cable industry places a priority on giving in the communities where its employees and customers live and work.

The cornerstone of the cable industry's commitment to its communities is a strong belief that business involvement in education is critical to the future growth and prosperity of the communities it serves. TCTA members strongly believe that local schools are the groundwork for the future, and gladly provide assistance in a number of ways, including donating cable service, televisions, and high-speed internet connections to schools and public libraries, and providing free technology workshops to teachers across the state.

In addition to the sponsorship support and donations provided by the cable industry in the community, TCTA's members give generously of their time and talents to support meaningful community efforts. Each year, employees volunteer their efforts to provide support for community initiatives and organizations across the state in a variety of ways. From United Way to Habitat for Humanity, the cable industry remains committed to building prosperity in the communities they serve.

William J. Vaughn

Blame it on the coal. In 1926, Nashville was a cloud of black smoke. William J. Vaughn ("Billy Jim") searched for a place to belong, a home for his ideals, and a place to share and learn with other boys around his age. He didn't quite know what it would look like or where it would be, all he knew was that he couldn't find it in Nashville. His parents told Billy Jim that to escape their chronic headaches they needed to move out to the country. The family found a new home in Brentwood, Tennessee. They attended Brentwood Methodist Church, where Billy Jim's prayer was answered— founder Curtis B. Haley invited Billy Jim to join Boy Scouts Troop 1.

And so, seventy-five years ago, Billy Jim joined the Boy Scouts. Since then, he has "loved every day of it." He believes that "if a boy learns something good he will always stay with it." In 1935, one of Billy Jim's best friends asked him to take over Troop 1 from Mr. Haley. With a heart for the boys and a deep desire to help the underprivileged, Billy Jim accepted.

Since then, Billy Jim has known three, "soon to be four", generations of scouts. Frequently men will come up to him and thank Billy Jim for the words of wisdom and time he took when he listened while they were young. "I don't know what I said— we never do— we never know how what we say helps other people."

Billy Jim recalls one boy who stands out. "He would be about sixty now," he observes. One day, a little lost boy of eleven wandered into Troop 1. The boy lived in a one-room house in Brentwood. When Billy Jim asked the boy what he wanted to learn from the scout's handbook, he got a memorable and energetic response.

"I want to learn everything, cover to cover and learn it well."

Billy Jim watched out for the boy. The boy kept up his studies and sports and graduated from Franklin High School, then won a scholarship to Vanderbilt. That boy earned his degree and now owns six companies throughout Georgia.

Billy Jim has also volunteered for the American Red Cross, Junior Achievement, and Nashville Rotary Club and has taught Sunday school for 54 years at the same church where Troop 1 meets. Billy Jim retired in 1977 from the United Methodist Publishing House for a short time, then went to work for "a brave lady," Jane Jones, who owned a small temporary agency. Today that temp agency is Randstad and Billy Jim still handles Public Relations for the company. "I think people have to do something worthwhile to satisfy themselves."

Billy is proud of the scouting program. He looks forward to the candlelight service every Thursday after the meeting and what goes up in smoke. "Boys will share deep matters of the heart and offer a prayer." This is how the merit of strong character is perpetuated. "You can know everything in the world, but if you don't pass it on, it's not worth a thing."

Deborah White

Deborah teaches Leadership at ETSU. Her philosophy is that service and leadership are inextricably linked and "that everyone will serve as a leader in some capacity. Leadership is not an exclusive club. Knowing oneself, understanding groups, and believing one can act upon shared beliefs results in leadership."

As a Girl Scout in her youth, Deborah did a lot of service at nursing homes for the elderly. "I remember I truly looked forward to going. It was my favorite thing to be a part of." From Girl Scouts to college projects with youth organizations to recording books for the blind, service commitments grew to become major in her life.

Dr. Deborah White believes that if every Tennessean were to volunteer for one day a month, we could "establish a community built on trust, respect and dignity for all Tennesseans. Reaching out to others," she points out, "requires us to get outside of our boxes, to see the world through the eyes of another, and to listen to voices outside our neighborhoods."

As a professor and administrator at East Tennessee State University, Deborah has implemented service programs in Tennessee higher education for more than fifteen years. Her first project was the creation of Volunteer ETSU, a campus volunteer center operated by and for students. She became a driving force for the East Tennessee Consortium for Service-Learning. For six years, Deborah wrote grants, met with campus leaders, and facilitated meetings and workshops for a consortium that grew to become an eight-college partnership in service-learning. The eight campuses now offer for-credit and extracurricular service opportunities for students. "It is incredible to see how the faculty and students share their experiences and work together to grow their programs," she says. Some schools have partnered with local not-for-profit organizations, some have partnered with local and national parks doing environmental work, and some have partnered with literacy programs. Several of these colleges serve as model programs, training other colleges in their best practices. Deborah believes that when you provide support, people's creativity allows them to work "outside the box." The outcomes of student service have resulted in award-winning theater productions, an improvement in hundreds of children's reading scores, park improvements, and new campus and community service traditions. The national Points of Light Foundation has named each of these programs a "daily point of light."

Deborah believes in the programs she has helped to create. She is proud of her role as the first chair of the board of Greater Johnson City's Promise, which is part of General Colin Powell's national initiative to provide five basic resources for children. Johnson City works to provide adult mentors, a healthy start, marketable skills, safe places to go to after school, and the opportunity to give back in service for every child.

Deborah has definitely mastered thinking outside the box and this link between service and leadership. "I grew up believing I could be president because an uncle teased me into thinking I could be. Every birthday card was addressed to 'The Next President.'" When it is suggested to her that it is not too late to be a candidate, she sighs. Her life is full of teaching, volunteer directives, and commitments to an artist husband, a home, and two growing girls. Some days she'd rather hike up through the mountains overlooking her quiet town, but "it's a double edged sword," she says. "Sitting and thinking is dangerous for people like me. The more time I have to think, the more things I think I need to add to the mosaic of service programs!"

WSMV-Channel 4 Volunteers

Volunteer efforts have always been a vital element of the "Working 4 You" mission. WSMV-Channel 4 is reinforcing this commitment with a Tennessee Volunteer Heroes campaign throughout 2001. In conjunction with the Tennessee Commission on National and Community Service and the Council of Community Services, WSMV celebrates volunteers throughout the state of Tennessee and encourages ongoing volunteer programs in our communities.

In past years, volunteerism has been essential to the success of special projects under the Project Help umbrella. The Project Paycheck effort brought job candidates and employers together, resulting in thousands of newly employed Middle Tennesseans. CPR Saturdays provided life-saving training for over 4,000 community members. And Nashville's Night Out Against Crime encouraged 20,000 people to hit the streets and form partnerships to insure safety in their neighborhoods. In the wake of the 1998 tornado, WSMV supported Releaf Nashville— the local effort to replace 6,500 shade trees on land ravaged by the storm.

An expansion of previous CPR training efforts is currently underway at WSMV,

Tennessee Volunteer Heroes 2001

with a goal of educating 21,000 Middle Tennesseans to administer CPR each year. "4 Your Life: CPR" is an ongoing campaign that calls on volunteers at local malls, hospitals, fire stations, and ambulance stations. The goal is to saves lives in Middle Tennessee through Emergency Medical Service improvements, mass citizen CPR training, and widespread use of Automatic External Defibrillators.

WSMV's corporate owner, Meredith Corporation, further encourages the volunteer spirit. For each hour of volunteer work an employee donates to various nonprofit organizations, Meredith contributes a corresponding dollar amount, giving employees added incentive to volunteer.

In the year 2001, WSMV will support local volunteer efforts through "Tennessee Volunteer Heroes." This exciting campaign celebrates volunteers in Middle Tennessee through a yearlong series of profiles, special programming, and awards luncheons. The campaign will include a Volunteer Calendar that lists local organizations and events in need of volunteers. Additional information on volunteering will be featured on the Channel 4 web site— wsmv.com.

As WSMV strives to serve the citizens of Middle Tennessee, volunteerism remains a primary focus and an integral part of Working 4 You.

If every Tennessean were to volunteer for one day a month, we could...
change the world academically. I started volunteering when my practically deaf niece started kindergarten. It takes all of us working together to make a difference. By volunteering at my grandson's school, I'm allowing the teachers to spend more quality time with our kids. Together we accomplish great things for *our* great things— children, yours and mine. After all, they are our greatest accomplishments. Your children take pride in knowing their parent is in school helping out.
—Mrs. Pat Bone
East Ridge, Hamilton County

If every Tennessean were to volunteer for one day a month, we could...
clean up the environment; raise money for endangered animal protection act; supply happiness to hundreds of kids that are sick; bring each other closer together.

—Sarah Rachel Boulden
Memphis, Shelby County

If every Tennessean were to volunteer for one day a month, we could…
possibly gain a new sense of pride for Tennessee by being involved in improvements, updating and reaching out to new challenges. We could give children the support and encouragement they need to accomplish anything and become productive citizens.

—Betty Boyce
Lebanon
Wilson County

If every Tennessean were to volunteer for one day a month, we could…
visit every home-bound elderly person to provide conversation and assistance. We could make a difference.

—Arlander Boyd
Memphis, Shelby County

If every Tennessean were to volunteer for one day a month, we could…
raise the quality of living for our less privileged citizens without having to have more "programs" by government.

—Deborah Turner Brasfield
Germantown, Shelby County

If every Tennessean were to volunteer for one day a month, we could…
we could accomplish so much. With approximately 5½ million people in the state you would have over 180,000 people working on the same day. Every organization would be overwhelmed with volunteers. Just imagine the new ideas you could get. The state would be a much happier place because everyone would be helping someone. The rewards you get from being a volunteer far outweigh the time spent.

—Jane Brawner
Summertown, Maury County

If every Tennessean were to volunteer for one day a month, we could…
solve many of the human problems that go unaddressed in our communities today. If people were more concerned about the human rights of others, we could reduce violent crime to a negligible level.

—Robin Brewer
Harrison
Hamilton County

If every Tennessean were to volunteer for one day a month, we could…
make a difference in every aspect of life, by being involved with our neglected children, widows that need all kind of help, as well as a kind word or smile, improving our schools, the litter problem, nursing homes, helping the sick in our communities, our parks and waterways.

—Willie Mai Brewington
Whitleyville
Jackson County

If every Tennessean were to volunteer for one day a month, we could... improve the quality of life and sense of worthiness for many people. We would also see improvement in many social problems such as crime, problems in schools, depression and frustration and environmental problems. We are better people when we love and reach out to others, and our lives are enriched and improved.

—Elaine Brown
Nashville, Davidson County

If every Tennessean were to volunteer for one day a month, we could... meet the social needs of every Tennessean, proving that no matter what the situation or need, we are not alone. Tennesseans would learn to be more sensitive and compassionate to their neighbor's trials and tribulations. We would be forced to view our own lives from a different perspective, being more aware of our present blessings.

—Wellmont Hospice Volunteers
Bristol
Sullivan County

If every Tennessean were to volunteer for one day a month, we could... befriend and care for every elderly citizen; begin an effective grassroots effort to clean up our community; provide for the safety and well-being of neighbors; and return a portion of the good we receive to others in our neighborhoods, our county and our state. That in turn would revitalize every citizen's way of life.

—Bill Bruce
Crossville, Cumberland County

If every Tennessean were to volunteer for one day a month, we could... provide a friendlier, safer world for Tennessee children, the future we will grow old with. They in turn would be able, by our example, to keep passing this heritage on.

—Sue Bruce
Chattanooga, Hamilton County

If every Tennessean were to volunteer for one day a month, we could... grow in our understanding of others' needs. The Bible teaches us that it is "more blessed to give than to receive." As mentor, friend, care-giver, tutor, troop leader, we all grow inside to a new awareness of ourselves and others as we help others of all ages and backgrounds transcend limitations.

—Ann Bryan
Nashville
Davidson County

If every Tennessean were to volunteer for one day a month, we could... revolutionize the lives of our two most threatened population segments— the elderly and the very young. With today's frantic pace, many of our elderly and very young are cared for as business commodities. This level of volunteering could provide variety, quality, and renewed spirit in the care of the elderly and very young while bringing comfort to all of us.

—Steve Buckley
Oak Ridge, Anderson County

Tennessee Volunteer Heroes

Norman Acres
From: Helenwood, Scott County
Years of Service: 53
Volunteering Highlights:
Scott County and Tennessee Association of Rescue Squads
Mountain People's Health Council, Past Chairman of the Board
Scott County Cancer Society, Past President
Scott County Adult Literacy Council
American Legion Post # 136
Special Notes: Norman, injured in World War II, has spent his entire adult life giving to others. He helped organize the Scott County Rescue Squad and has held every office in the TN Assoc. of Rescue Squads. Norman taught many of the early First Responder and EMT classes in Scott County. Norman has served as Scott County Chamber Director and has been a troop leader for the Boy Scouts. His children and grandchildren are a tribute to his life, as most of them are active in community service.

Nasar U. Ahmed, PhD
From: Nashville, Davidson County
Years of Service: 14
Volunteering Highlights:
President of Bangladesh Association of Nashville, Tennessee
Founder President of Bangladesh Community of Indiana
Founder leading member of study Circle of Indianapolis
Fundraiser of World Hunger Project
Member of Union of Concerned Scientists (UCS)
Special Notes: He helps build harmony among different racial and ethnic groups being a leading member of committees on Celebration of Cultures, Race Relations Study Circle, and Racial and Ethnic approaches to Community Health on these issues. He volunteers to support: the eliminating hunger and ethnic disparity in health, raising funds, and exchanging information to raise awareness on ethnicity, spirituality, health and well being of Tennesseans as well as world citizens.

Darrell Akins
From: Knoxville, Knox County
Years of Service: 35
Volunteering Highlights:
United Way of Greater Knoxville: Chairman of the Board
Boy Scouts of America, Great Smoky Mtn. Council: President
YMCA Camp Montvale: Board of Directors
Maryville College: Executive Committee, Board of Directors
Florence Crittendon Agency of Knoxville: Life Member
Special Notes: His family and his business keep him so busy, but he is also 100% devoted to giving back to the community and to children. This is evident in his position with the United Way and other organizations.

Melanie Alexander
From: Murfreesboro, Rutherford County
Years of Service: 31
Volunteering Highlights:
United Way of Rutherford County — Board Member and various committees
First Call for Help — Chairman of the Board, Community Liasion
American Heart Association — Heartball Committee
American Cancer Society — Board Member
The Webb School — Secretary Parents Association, Fundraiser Horizons 2000
Special Notes: Melanie has a long history of helping others. She is energetic, caring and reliable. She has reached out to other groups and enthusiastically becomes part of their effort.

If every Tennessean were to volunteer for one day a month, we could… help cure diseases, find homes for the homeless, provide healthcare for the poor, give hope to the hopeless, make children smile, and mentor teenagers, making Tennessee one of the strongest states in our country and truly living up to our name, the "Volunteer State".

—Teresa Bullock
Memphis, Shelby County

Tennessee Volunteer Heroes 2001

Franklin Allen, III
From: Memphis, Shelby County
Years of Service: 2
Volunteering Highlights:
Volunteer Income Tax Assistance Site Coordinator
Special Notes: Pepper Allen is a Volunteer Income Tax Assistance (VITA) Site Coordinator for Catholic High School. He volunteers January through April assisting approximately 500 taxpayers with income tax preparation. Pepper is such a hard worker and very dedicated to the VITA program. He saw a need for our service in the low income community and went on a crusade to recruit over 20 other individuals from local opportunities and local colleges to help in this effort. Pepper is a loving, caring person and exhibits time, patience and expertise in so many ways. He is always willing to help and goes beyond the duties of the VITA volunteers so he can make one more taxpayer satisfied. Pepper brings a kind spirit and very positive attitude to the VITA program and we are very fortunate to have a person of his caliber on our team.

Stan Allen
From: Nashville, Davidson County
Years of Service: 3
Volunteering Highlights:
Woodmont Hills Church of Christ
Nashville Bar Association, Tennessee Bar Association
American Red Cross
Woodmont Christian Church
Building and Entertainment Committee at Arden Place
Special Notes: Stan has overcome some major challenges and changes in his life. He is, however, one of the most delightful people to be around. He loves volunteering. He calls and asks for more to do — and he is always ready with a joke.

If every Tennessean were to volunteer for one day a month, we could...

truly come together as one. Everyone could learn to read, we could feed everybody, we could conquer any disease, comfort the sick and dying, end violence and show unconditional love to all. We could conquer the AIDS epidemic.

—Ken Bundy
Nashville, Davidson County

If every Tennessean were to volunteer for one day a month, we could...

have the best communities, the best amenities and the best quality of life among all the states. I want to live in a place where the people care about, care for and protect their neighbors. Tennessee can be one big neighborhood if we all are pitching in and doing our part.

—Peggy Burton
Tullahoma
Coffee County

American Red Cross
Volunteering Highlights:
All chapters have boards composed of volunteers donating time to lead and serve.
Thousands of persons learned to swim, survive in water, operate safely their small crafts on water.
24 hours a day, services are given to military personnel and their families.
Thousands of volunteers responded to disasters, providing food, clothes, shelter, resources.
Blood donations collected, tested and processed.
Special Notes: In Tennessee we are very fortunate to have the American Red Cross as one of our state's leading volunteer agencies. Most of our chapters in the state were chartered more than 75 years ago. Citizens in our state are much better off because American Red Cross volunteers are there 24 hours day, 7 days a week, 365 days a year. These volunteers are here to help us plan, prepare, and cope with disasters.

Becky Andrew
From: Greeneville, Greene County
Years of Service: 6
Volunteering Highlights:
Asbury UMC
Habitat for Humanity
Gifts for Kids
Math-A-Thon for St. Jude's Hospital
Telemon Migrant Headstart Center
Special Notes: Becky Andrew makes a deep impression on those around her with her volunteer work. Becky connects with people. For example, when a Church Youth Group serves dinner at a homeless shelter, Becky works hard, but when the meal is over, she is the one who consistently sits and talks with the homeless men and women; when we work with children at migrant

Tennessee Volunteer Heroes 2001

> If every Tennessean were to volunteer for one day a month, we could...
> help the less fortunate to such an extent that everyone would receive what they needed from neighbors and friends and the federal government could focus its concerns on other issues. We could once again become a community in the true sense of the word.
>
> —Elizabeth Cable
> Mountain City, Johnson County

Headstart program, Becky is the one who will spend the most time listening and talking with the little children; when we sang Christmas Carols at the nursing home, Becky will be the one who sits and spends time with the grandparent who wants to talk; when we have been on mission trips to South Carolina and Chattanooga, Becky has always been a hard worker, but she is also the one who genuinely gives of herself to the families with whom we work. She listens to others, plays with children, and leaves a lasting impression of love, acceptance and grace with everyone. The way she responds to people, indeed strangers, with kindness and love, have been an example and an inspiration.

The Angel Band
From: Harriman, Roane County
Years of Service: 3
Volunteering Highlights:
Toys for Tots: Roane and Rhea Counties
Operation Reach: Roane County
Hooray for Harriman: benefit concert for new park
Harriman Fire Department: benefit concert for Heat Imaging Device
Royal Care Nursing Home: regular visits singing and having dinner with residents
Special Notes: The caring and love they share with fellow Tennesseans that are less fortunate is amazing, and they ask nothing in return.

Goldie Armstrong
From: Nashville, Davidson County
Years of Service: 7
Volunteering Highlights:
American Red Cross
Special Notes: Goldie has been giving of her time and spirit for many years. She is one of the Red Cross's oldest volunteers and by far the most active. She is conscientious of her duties and always goes above and beyond.

Athens Life Member Club BellSouth Pioneers
From: Athens, McMinn County
Years of Service: 13
Volunteering Highlights:
Made and donated to children in crisis over 1,000 Hug-A-Bears
Signed up Families for food boxes for Friendly Fellows club
Worked at early voting polls for early voting times
BellSouth Pioneer Volunteers
Telephone Pioneers of America
Special Notes: Members of this Club have given unselfishly and freely of their time whenever they are asked, as long as they were physically able.

Dr. N. Max Atnip
From: Cookeville, Putnam County
Years of Service: 29
Volunteering Highlights:
Putnam County's Leadership Putnam
Cookeville Leisure Services Advisory Committee
Cookeville Jaycees Educational Trust Fund: Board Member
Cookeville/Putnam County Chamber of Commerce: Member; former Director
Medvance: Advisory Board of Directors (formerly Cumberland School of Medical Technology)
Special Notes: "I've been fortunate and blessed in so many areas of my life by people who've served as mentors, set good examples for me to follow, and who've left an indelible impression on my life. It would be remiss of me NOT to give back to my fellow

> If every Tennessean were to volunteer for one day a month, we could...
> improve community relations and enhance peer relationships throughout our state. School violence would end and people would join together in harmony.
>
> —Kevin James Cable
> Mountain City
> Johnson County

man and community; not only because it's reciprocal, but because it's the right thing to do! One can set a precedent for others to follow and with enough momentum, fortitude and vision can keep that ball of volunteerism rolling to impact a child, a young adult, a person in midlife, or even a senior citizen. Anyone may be a candidate to be affected by the examples set by a positive role model."

Marene J. Austin
From: Memphis, Shelby County
Years of Service: 4
Volunteering Highlights:
Memphis Housing Authority Housing Development
Jobs Career Center (name changed to Economic Development)
United Way of Mid-South Gifts In Kind International
Memphis Board of Education (Adult Education Division)
Trezvant Vo-Technical Institute
Special Notes: Marene Austin worked her way from welfare to management at Federal Express. In 1996, she started a not-for-profit and has volunteered and graduated over 200 Families First participants through her Choice, Inc. "People Empowering People" program.

Margie Avery
From: Alamo, Crockett County
Years of Service: 18
Volunteering Highlights:
President, Ladies Auxiliary — Crockett County V.F.W.
Volunteer, Cairo Baptist Church Food Bank
Assistant Sunday School Teacher
Northwest Tennessee Economic Development Council (Community Action Agency)
Volunteer, Girl and Boy Scouts

> If every Tennessean were to volunteer
> for one day a month, we could...
> make a major difference in the lives of so many people who live without hope. If Tennesseans could see joy in the face of someone they have helped, it would eventually become their passion to reach out and help those who are in need of their compassion. If only more people could see the good that results from getting involved, our communities would be happier and better places.
>
> —Richard Cadavero
> Collegedale, Hamilton County

> If every Tennessean were to volunteer
> for one day a month, we could...
> identify the most critical needs of society such as housing, child care, education, etc., devise plans to eradicate or alleviate these problems, and volunteers could carry out these plans.
>
> —Harriett Campbell
> Germantown, Shelby County

Special Notes: She has a compassionate, courteous and caring attitude, and is dependable and willing to assist wherever she is needed. Ms. Avery is the mother of two children, has two grandchildren. She is the widow of a World War II veteran who served in the Pacific Islands. She worked sixteen years at a local garment manufacturer and received two special service awards for dedication to duty. She has helped rear her grandchildren and served as a volunteer in their girl and boy scout activities for six years. She has been a community volunteer, transporting neighbors and friends to doctor appointments and hospital visits. She is always willing to help anyone in need, and works several days each week in the office of a local community action agency neighborhood service center. She continues to make a difference in our community.

Amber Bailey
From: La Follette, Campbell County
Years of Service: 1
Volunteering Highlights:
Sunbridge Nursing Home Volunteer
Food Life Services of Campbell County
Campbell County Alliance for Youth
Campbell County Health Fair
TennCare for Children volunteer
Special Notes: Amber is 14 years of age. She has been working diligently with her mentor to give her time and talent in many ways. She finds ways to give back to the community and exhibits a fine volunteer spirit at 14!

Nathan E. Baker
From: Madison, Davidson County
Years of Service: 22
Volunteering Highlights:
American Red Cross: 265 time blood donor; classes in

> If every Tennessean were to volunteer for one day a month, we could... move mountains of pain, trouble and tribulations in people's everyday lives by carrying away one small stone at a time. We could enjoy the cultural diversity of America and learn to accept people for who they are.
>
> —Dionna CarMichael
> Chattanooga
> Hamilton County

Disaster education, HIV/AIDS, Diversity
Nashville Mayor's Advisory Committee for Disability Information
Tennessee Railroad Museum
Mid-TN Council of the Blind
Special Notes: Mr. Baker believes strongly in equality for all. Employers should hire, promote and seek persons with disabilities. It is truly good for their business and good for the state as well as the individual person.

Odell Baker
From: Germantown, Shelby County
Years of Service: 40
Volunteering Highlights:
Germantown Charity Horse Show
Germantown Festival
First Baptist Church, Memphis
Shriners Club, Past President
East Shelby Republican Club, Past President
Special Notes: "I have been honored because of the 25,000 Shelby Countians I have registered to vote and for the newcomer information I have provided for over 35 years. I try to do something every day to help someone."

Samantha Baker
From: Kingsport, Sullivan County
Years of Service: 4
Volunteering Highlights:
Kingsport Animal Shelter
Rotary Club Award
J.C. Penney golden Rule Award, 2000
Michael Mohit Sahni Scholarship (Outstanding Freshman)
Special Notes: Samantha helps lost or abandoned dogs and cats find wonderful, loving homes and live out their final days contently.

Diana M. Baranowski
From: Cookeville, Putnam County
Years of Service: 4
Volunteering Highlights:
Triad Children and Youth Services: President Board of Directors
J.C. Penney Golden Rule Nomination
Special Notes: There are 2 kinds of impact Diana's involvement has: one immediate and the other long term. Diana's involvement with Triad immediately allowed them not to be forced to close the program, having to move already troubled families and youth. The ability of the program to enable families to reunite and continue is untouchable and can be turned into dollars each time we think of prisons, food stamps, welfare, child support, court costs, etc. Diana's leadership and commitment to the relocation of Triad has been phenomenal. She personally gave over 25 hours a week, lowered her semester hours at college, and remained on the board an additional year. Because of her efforts, children will grow and prosper.

Douglas Baron
From: Germantown, Shelby County
Years of Service: 5
Volunteering Highlights:
Germantown High School Key Club: Past President
Germantown High School Fine Arts Department
Germantown 2000 (promoting youth volunteerism)
Who's Who Among American High School Students Award
Germantown Hometown Hero Award
Special Notes: "I have helped in my school and community since the 8th grade. I volunteer for various activities such as: tutoring young underprivileged students; helping out at area hospitals; assisting at LifeBlood of Germantown. I have also participated in

> If every Tennessean were to volunteer for one day a month, we could... greatly improve our social services, health care, education, housing and environment with minimal increase in taxes. Perhaps we all might then recognize the individual benefits volunteers receive in the form of an enhanced sense of belonging, self-esteem and community spirit.
>
> —Chuck Carpenter
> Chattanooga
> Hamilton County

Tennessee Volunteer Heroes 2001

various Germantown Kiwanis Club activities such as Peanut Day, Germantown Festival and Germantown Fourth of July celebration."

Bernard Barton
From: Rickman, Overton County
Years of Service: 30
Volunteering Highlights:
Overton County Lions
Tennessee State Guard
Chaplain for Tennessee Senate and House
Family Officer of the American Legion, Post 4
Hospice Volunteer
Special Notes: "As a resident of Tennessee I have been and continue to be interested in helping Tennessee become a better state by helping those in need by volunteering my services."

Viola G. Batts
From: Memphis, Shelby County
Years of Service: 33
Volunteering Highlights:
The Commercial Appeal's Jefferson Award, 2000
Tennessee Juvenile Court Services Award, Humanitarian of the Year, 1997
JC Penney Golden Rule Award, Senior Division, 1995
McCall's Magazine, Angel of Change Award, 1995
Mayor W.W. Herenton's Make A Difference Award, 1994
Special Notes: Ms. Batts is truly one of the most remarkable people around. She is a true giver and never thinks of herself. For over 33 years, Ms. Batts has donated thousands of hours making food baskets, supervising children on probation, making home investigations in special cases for the Juvenile Court, and many other important job duties. She even got some under-privileged children a paid trip to Disney

> If every Tennessean were to volunteer for one day a month, we could...
> become the paradise state. The main reason would be because people's attitudes would change towards one another. Each person would feel and know the gratification that comes from doing something for someone else without expecting anything in return. Once again, we could win back what America really stands for: "People Helping People".
>
> —Roy L. Chalmers
> Clarksville
> Montgomery County

World this summer — airfare, hotel, admission ticket, and spending money. This lady's energy is boundless.

Mickey (Mary K.) Beazley
From: Brentwood, Williamson County
Volunteering Highlights:
Hospital Hospitality House, Co-Founder
REBIRTH Head Injury Support Group, Co-Founder
St. Thomas Hospital Volunteer
Cheekwood Arts and gardens volunteer
Social Action Committee of Christians and Jews, Charter Member
Special Notes: "I am certainly not heroic, but it is painful to see sadness and suffering. I am strongly convinced that the purpose of life is to extend beyond one's self — and that where there is a need, there cannot be a solution unless we, the human race, create the solution — which definitely *can* be done on all levels, in one way or another, by *all* people.

Diane Beets
From: Knoxville, Knox County
Years of Service: 10
Volunteering Highlights:
Children's Hospital: recruited 40 volunteers to raise over $15,000 for the 1999 phone-a-thon
Habitat for Humanity: Family nurturer for First Tennessee's 3 month building project
Big Brothers and Big Sisters: recruited over 50 volunteers to participate in bowl-a-thon
Special Olympics: volunteers and recruits others
United Way: Allocations Panel
Special Notes: Diane has a concern for her fellow Tennesseans that is difficult to find in most people. Even though she is dealing with severe illness in her family, she found time to volunteer over 300 hours in the first

> If every Tennessean were to volunteer for one day a month, we could...
> not only offer more programs for our youth, but our elderly as well. We need volunteers to help the elderly deal with issues of neglect, poverty, poor nutrition, health care, and more, and volunteers to help our youth deal with issues of teen pregnancy, AIDS Awareness, illegal drugs, crime, violence, and many more.
>
> —Billy L. Cartmell
> Lebanon, Wilson County

> If every Tennessean were to volunteer for one day a month, we could... help accelerate the much-needed progress in achieving the social, economic, cultural, educational and physical well-being of the community we live in and live off of. As a volunteer, the personal gratification and a sense of purpose in life and serving the community is a thing to look forward to each and every day.
>
> —E.S. Chandrasekaran
> Hixson, Hamilton County

3 quarters of 2000. She is a leader and a warrior whom many of her employees, contemporaries, and superiors look up to. She touches everyone she meets with her kind, gentle and generous heart.

Tracey Belcher
From: Memphis, Shelby County
Years of Service: 20
Volunteering Highlights:
Women in Community Service
Women and Children in Crisis
Special Notes: Tracey has her own personal struggle and challenges. She shares her challenges and successes with program participants in Women in Community Service (WICS) Lifeskills for Women at the Shelby County Division of Corrections. When a woman is having trouble, Tracey can always be counted on (even with 4 children of her own) to go running to help and stand by the woman through the crisis and help her get back on the road to success.

Ann Bell
From: Memphis, Shelby County
Years of Service: 8
Volunteering Highlights:
Idewild Presbyterian Church: Librarian; Food Pantry Chairman; serves meals to homeless
University of TN Hematology: teaching assistant; archival files
Special Notes: Dr. Bell has made numerous contributions to the Memphis community, and she has always been a person who believes in helping others. A weekly volunteer, Dr. Bell takes pride in her work with Patient Assistance Programs. These programs are designed to assist patients who have incomes close to the poverty level. If a patient falls within certain financial guidelines, the pharmaceutical companies will provide him/her with needed medication at no cost. This process is very labor intensive, and Dr. Bell assists each week by filling out the necessary paperwork required to enroll patients in these programs. The medical conditions afflicting the patients in these programs range across the scope of medicine, and without this program many of these patients would not receive essential care. Dr. Bell has been essential in the growth of this program, which now sees a turnover of $40,000 per month in medicines.

Ray R. Bell
From: Franklin, Williamson County
Years of Service: 8
Volunteering Highlights:
American Cancer Society: Volunteer Coordinator and driver for Road to Recovery Program
Talking Library: Reader of books on tape for the blind and physically handicapped
1998 Best Program Award winner, Talking Library
Mary Catherine Strobel Award Nominee
Special Notes: Daily work with the American Cancer Society and four days a week with the Talking Library.

Betty Belote
From: Gallatin, Sumner County
Years of Service: 20
Volunteering Highlights:
Sumner Regional Medical Center Volunteer
Hospice Award for Volunteer of the Year, 2000
Board Member, Sumner Foundation
Member of every historic association
Gallatin Day Care Board Member
Special Notes: Betty Belote is one of those rare individuals who shows up when needed, no matter what the event. She has been a dedicated volunteer for

> If every Tennessean were to volunteer for one day a month, we could... improve the quality of life for our young people and senior citizens. Volunteers are fun to be around, kind and loving. If we care, step in, stoop down, and, in love, rebuild a life and restore a soul, who knows, we may entertain angels without knowing it.
>
> —Mrs. Jan Chapman
> Greeneville, Greene County

years. She deserves so much recognition for her selfless devotion to her community and state!

Louise Bentley
From: Jackson, Madison County
Years of Service: 5
Volunteering Highlights:
Jackson-Madison County General Hospital: Patient Relations Volunteer
Guiding Hands for the Blind: Reader
AARP "55 Alive" Mature Drivers Program: West TN Trainer; Class Instructor
Grace Presbyterian Church: Monthly newsletter editor; choir member; GEMS teacher; RIFA Soup Kitchen
Northwest Acres Neighborhood Association: Newsletter editor
Special Notes: Louise has a very caring heart, and that caring is demonstrated through her life of service to not only her community, but to all of West Tennessee. She has significantly, positively affected the lives she has touched! One by one, a long chain of people she has influenced stretches across our region. Her service is not the result of obligations or duties; it is a natural outgrowth of who she is as a person — who she has always been. Louise can't HELP but reach out, because that is what her heart does naturally. She shares. She serves. She replies, "I will!" This is the essence of a life of volunteerism. One human being touching another, for no other reason than to make all our lives better, somehow.

Connie Berry
From: Holladay, Benton County
Years of Service: 1
Volunteering Highlights:
Baptist Memorial Hospice
Special Notes: Connie has gone above and beyond the call of duty as a volunteer for Baptist Memorial Hospice. She stayed all day several times with a Hospice patient, and was the only person who could influence that patient to go to the hospital for respite care. This patient liked Connie so much, he would cry when she would leave. Connie brought food to the home, counseled the caregiver, babysat the family dog, ran errands and is now working in bereavement with the family.

Nisha Bhateja
From: Oak Ridge, Anderson County
Volunteering Highlights:
Oak Ridge Schools Extended Childcare (ECC) Program
President's Student Service Award
Special Notes: "As a volunteer at ECC I was given the responsibility of designing games and activities. This usually includes making up skits, reading to the children, and playing with them outside on the playground. I feel my involvement in the Oak Ridge Schools Extended Childcare Program allowed the children to interact with someone who could relate to them better and gave them the opportunity to have a broader and more diverse range of activities to participate in."

Leo Bilbrey
Special Notes: Special recognition from the Governor and First Lady of Tennessee for excellence in volunteer service.

Happy Birdsong
From: Madison, Davidson County
Years of Service: 62
Volunteering Highlights:
Metro Beautification & Environment Commission: Commissioner 8 years
Girl Scouts of America: 50 years; currently Scout Leader

> If every Tennessean were to volunteer for one day a month, we could...
> create more effective social policy through government, places of worship and civic organizations to help those in need. The greatest gift from volunteering is awareness. We no longer have to depend on filtered images through the media to tell us what's going on with people at risk and why they are in their current social condition. We learn through relationships with people different from us in circumstances but very much alike in hopes, dreams and spirituality.
>
> —Tim A. Chavez
> Brentwood, Williamson County

> If every Tennessean were to volunteer for one day a month, we could...
> ## create such harmony and caring that it would make the rest of our great nation sing, "Follow Tennessee's lead and Make a Difference!"
>
> —Jawanna Chapman
> Russellville
> Hamblen County

Tennessee Volunteer Heroes 2001

> If every Tennessean were to volunteer
> for one day a month, we could...
>
> # we could protect the whole state's environment, voicing our concerns at public meetings and cleaning up the state.
>
> —Mrs. Bertha Chrietzberg
> Murfreesboro, Rutherford County

for TN School for the Blind troop
Boy Scouts of America: 35 years; trained more than 4,000 Boy Scout leaders
Madison Sertoma Club: Chair of "Improve the Community Committee" for 4 years
Madison Chamber of Commerce

Sherry Black
From: Hixson, Hamilton County
Years of Service: 15
Volunteering Highlights:
National Association of Foster Grandparents Program Directors
President of TN Association of Senior Volunteer Directors, Inc.
Past President of Chattanooga Streams of Service
Past President of Directors of Volunteers in Agencies
Member of TN Conference of Social Welfare
Special Notes: Sherry demonstrates outstanding leadership as the Project director of a Tennessee Senior volunteer project.

Becca Bolding
From: Germantown, Shelby County
Volunteering Highlights:
Morgan Woods Theatre: fundraising; work with children
Germantown 2000 Hometown Heroes
Girls Scouts of America: leader over 30 years
Welcome Wagon of Germantown (Now New Neighbors): Past Vice Presdient
Dogwood, IIMS, HHS: fundraising; PTA; ART SMART; choral & thespian support; room mother
Special Notes: "I am honored that someone chose to acknowledge my contributions to our community. There are many who give of themselves every day to make this the special community we live in."

Rae Young Bond
From: Chattanooga, Hamilton County
Years of Service: 5
Volunteering Highlights:
Domestic Violence Coalition, Board member
Community Research Council, Board member
Invest in Children and Parent Place, Steering Committee member
Hamilton County Court Divorce Mediation Pilot Project: convener and organizer
First Things First: Board President and Executive Director
Special Notes: Mrs. Bond is a volunteer Regional Health Council Member who chairs 2 subcommittees and is the lead council member responsible for the monthly health briefings and press conferences. She volunteers approximately 20 hours per month to ensure the success of the health briefings.

Mrs. Pat Bone
From: East Ridge, Hamilton County
Years of Service: 11
Volunteering Highlights:
McBrien PTA, Lifetime membership
1999-2000 Yearbook dedication
Boy Scout partner with grandson
PTA Board Secretary
Special Notes: "Aunt Pat," as she is fondly known, volunteers in our school every day. She does a variety of jobs; making copies, lamination, putting up bulletin boards, making calls to parents regarding PTS, membership, volunteering, etc., assisting classroom teachers, tutoring students, almost any job we give her. She has hugs and smiles for 520 students. She tells people that she has 520 children. You should see their faces!

> If every Tennessean were to volunteer
> for one day a month, we could...
>
> # follow God, follow in Jesus's footsteps and make a real difference. This is what my life has revolved around. This is where my love of volunteerism comes from.
>
> —Doris Chrzanowski
> Burns, Dickson County

Tennessee Volunteer Heroes 2001

Sarah Rachel Boulden
From: Memphis, Shelby County
Years of Service: 3
Volunteering Highlights:
The Memphis Zoo
Le Bonheur Teens
Memphis Youth volunteer of the Year Nominee
Zooboo train
Made negohans w/ Phizer for polar bear medicine
Special Notes: "I started very young and took a significant amount of responsibilities and numerous projects, hundreds of hours."

Betty Boyce
From: Lebanon, Wilson County
Years of Service: 45
Volunteering Highlights:
Lebanon Senior Citizens Center, President, Advisory Board Member
University Medical Center
Special Notes: Betty truly gives of her time and energy to benefit her fellow man. She is dependable, reliable, always available, never seeking to be seen, only to serve with *love*!

Arlander Boyd
From: Memphis, Shelby County
Years of Service: 26
Volunteering Highlights:
Boy Scouts of America
Delta Area Agency on Aging
Senior Citizen's Crime Watch
Block volunteer for Easter Seals, Leukemia Society, American Heart Association
Stillman College, Volunteer College Recruiter
Special Notes: Mr. Boyd provides countless hours of

> If every Tennessean were to volunteer for one day a month, we could...
>
> accomplish many things and become a state of happy and fulfilled people. Volunteering not only accomplishes tasks in need, but it enables people to interact under the most positive circumstances possible.
>
> —John Clark
> Signal Mtn.
> Hamilton County

service to humankind. He feels his extra time should be shared.

Deborah Turner Brasfield
From: Germantown, Shelby County
Years of Service: 12
Volunteering Highlights:
East Memphis Business of Professional Women
Germantown Area Chamber of Commerce
"Memphis Woman" — 50 Women Who Make A Difference
Mertie Buckman Mentor Award — Women's Foundation
Midsouth Women in Business, Iris Award
Special Notes: I have always left room in my life for volunteerism. It is an integral part of my life. I have not limited myself to only political, or religious, but to also the interests of my friends and neighbors.

Jane Brawner
From: Summertown, Maury County
Years of Service: 8
Volunteering Highlights:
American Cancer society, Maury and Lawrence County Units
Camp Horizon, children's camp for cancer patients and their siblings
First United Methodist Church, Mt. Pleasant, TN
Lorena Bourne Women's Circle
Volunteer teacher, Hampshire Ridge United Methodist Church
Special Notes: Jane Brawner's life is one of true dedication to issues she feels strongly about. When teenage daughter Amy was diagnosed with cancer in 1994, Jane and Amy strove together to help others suffering from this disease by supporting the American Cancer society in several volunteer capacities. Despite Amy's death in 1997, Jane's light continues to shine brightly to this day. Remaining active in the Maury

> If every Tennessean were to volunteer for one day a month, we could...
>
> insure that the homeless are fed, clothed and housed; relieve the suffering of the mentally ill and the developmentally disabled; assist the physically ill in hospitals and nursing homes; provide a better educational experience for our children; and reduce the problem of youth with better after-school programs.
>
> —D. Gene Clark
> Nashville, Davidson County

> If every Tennessean were to volunteer for one day a month, we could... have a state that does not rank near the bottom of states in teen drug use, children living in poverty, police protection, high school dropout rate, teens having babies, children without insurance and bilingual education.
>
> —Katherine Clark
> Cookeville
> Putnam County

County unit of the American Cancer Society, she has become a key component of that group. With Jane's chairmanship, the 2000 Relay for Life in Maury County raised $71,000 which was a $20,000 increase from the previous year. Jane is a true hero for using her personal loss to drive her willingness to help others.

William Bray
Special Notes: Special recognition from the Governor and First Lady of Tennessee for excellence in volunteer service.

Robin Brewer
From: Harrison, Hamilton County
Years of Service: 7
Volunteering Highlights:
Nine municipal police jurisdictions, Chattanooga and Hamilton County Sheriff's Department
Four Sessions Court Divisions / Four Circuit Court Divisions
Shelters and Domestic Violence Law Enforcement / Prosecution Task Force / Court Clerks Office
Coalition Against Domestic and Community Violence of Greater Chattanooga, Inc.
District Attorney General's Office
Special Notes: As a founding member of the Coalition Against Domestic & Community Violence, Robin has served as chair of its monitoring, enforcement & advocacy program for 7 years. She has a passion and empathy for victims & children that is outstanding. She has developed rapport with, & respect from law enforcement & the judicial system with judges asking her opinion on cases. Robin goes to court with victims as an advocate regularly; gets referrals from all parts of the justice system; goes with victims to get protective orders; meets with judges to keep them updated about changes in the Coalition; helps train Volunteer Advocates; heads up Law Enforcement Appreciation Day Events annually; serves on the Review Committee for our ADT Alarm Program & our cellular phone program; tirelessly does public speaking & media appearances; and works on Special Events Committee to raise public awareness about domestic violence. Robin has never refused anything asked of her by the Coalition. She is willing to do the most menial tasks & will tackle anything. She can always be counted on to use her own good judgment and initiative to get things done, yet her winning way and sincere commitment gets the best efforts from others she works with.

Willie Mai Brewington
From: Whitleyville, Jackson County
Years of Service: 20
Volunteering Highlights:
(CHEOC) North Spring's Head Start
Jackson County Soil Conservation district, Cahirman for 15 years
Jackson County Health Council
Families First — WHEELS — Always helps hold elections
Gainesboro First United Methodist Church
Special Notes: Willie Mai has a helping hand for everyone, good morals, honesty, and sincerity. She is a Christian, and has 19 years perfect attendance in church! She was the Number 1 Earth Team Volunteer in Tennessee in Conservation Education in 1998.

Gertrude G. Bridgeforth
From: Southaven
Years of Service: 8
Volunteering Highlights:
National Civil Rights Museum: Founding Member; Greeter; Docent; Shop Assistant; Museum Monitor
J.C. Penney Golden Rule Nomination

> If every Tennessean were to volunteer for one day a month, we could... feel the difference. It's a learning experience that you can't get from anything else. I thank God everyday for my health (even though I am disabled) and for allowing me to help others. I met my husband where I worked with Meals on Wheels. We were living at a place for the disabled or those over 65 with no income and I thought I had nothing to give. But, we delivered meals in apartments and it didn't cost any money to help. I've been a battered woman and know how it feels.
>
> —Donna Clouse-West
> Bon Aqua, Hickman County

Tennessee Volunteer Heroes 2001

Special Notes: Gertrude Bridgeforth is a positive, loyal, dependable, articulate volunteer who represents the Museum well both inside the doors and outside the Museum in the broader community. Mrs. Bridgeforth helped shape the volunteer program by offering feedback and direction, and has consistently volunteered her time since 1991.

Elaine Brown
From: Nashville, Davidson County
Years of Service: 15
Volunteering Highlights:
Hands On Nashville
American Red Cross Volunteer, Vanderbilt Site
Founding Member, St. Thomas Advocates, St. Thomas Hospital
Mary Catherine Strobel Award Nominee
United Way Campaign, Vanderbilt site
Special Notes: "I have never thought of myself as a hero — I have not accomplished great things or drastically altered someone's life. But I do hope I have in many small ways been able to share friendship and love with those around me."

Leo F. Brown, Sr.
From: Memphis, Shelby County
Years of Service: 13
Volunteering Highlights:
Auxiliary Probation Service: Senior Deputy Auxiliary Probation Officer
Community Service Award: Shelby State Community College, 1995
Tennessee Higher Education Commission's (THEC) Annual Award for Community Service, 1995
Memphis Black Community: Achievement Award, 1993
Commercial Appeal's Thousand Points of Light, 1989

> If every Tennessean were to volunteer for one day a month, we could...
>
> excite individuals to answer community needs. Through their volunteering, they would learn to creatively solve problems for others in need. They would meet talented and interesting folks. They would enrich their own lives as well.
>
> —Suzanne Mandel Cohn
> Chattanooga, Hamilton County

> If every Tennessean were to volunteer for one day a month, we could...
>
> mentor every child and give each an opportunity to have a positive role model who can mold them into productive, confident and loving human beings.
>
> —Estella Cooper
> Clarkrange, Fentress County

Special Notes: Mr. Brown is Chief of Security for the new Southwest Tennessee College (formerly Shelby State Community College and State Technical Institute). He is on call 24 hours a day, 7 days a week and still finds time to volunteer many hours each month to rehabilitate and re-educate a young person in this community. Mr. Brown says, "if you don't do anything about the problems in your community, then you are a part of the problem." Furthermore, Mr. Brown says of Auxiliary Probation Service (APS), "There's no way I can explain the feeling you have when you know that you were instrumental in helping some young person turn his or her life around."

Bill Bruce
From: Crossville, Cumberland County
Years of Service: 5
Volunteering Highlights:
Maryland Senior Citizens Center; Past President, Currently VP, Building & Committee Chair
Neighborhood Watch Program
Retired Senior Volunteers Program
Fair Park Senior Center
NRA-ILA election Volunteer 2000
Special Notes: Bill is a volunteer alert to the needs of the community, seeing jobs to be done and doing them without being asked. He is a self-starter and consistent finisher.

Sue and "Red" Bruce
From: Chattanooga, Hamilton County
Years of Service: 4
Volunteering Highlights:
J.C. Penney Golden Rule Nomination
Craft Instructor, Lester Coon Apison
Seventh Day Adventist School

> If every Tennessean were to volunteer for one day a month, we could...
>
> # supply transportation and meet the needs of all people with disabilities.
>
> —Greg Cox
> Murfreesboro, Rutherford County

Special Notes: Sue just says "yes" to opportunities.

Ann Bryan
From: Nashville, Davidson County
Years of Service: 42
Volunteering Highlights:
Girls Scouts: Leader
Hospital Volunteer
Salvation Army: Angel Tree Program; Women's Auxiliary; Kare for Kids; Senior Stockings
Cheekwood: Museum Gift Shop Volunteer
War Memorial Children's Concerts Usher
Special Notes: Ann Bryan has great empathy for those in need. Her ability to translate this empathy into action by the generous gift of her time as a volunteer for the Salvation Army qualifies her as a Tennessee Volunteer Hero. Mrs. Bryan has contributed to the welfare of those less fortunate both as a "hands-on" volunteer and by providing volunteer leadership as an officer of the Salvation Army Women's Auxiliary. Working directly with recipients in various Salvation Army programs, she has without hesitation given her time wherever and whenever needed as a daycare volunteer in Kare for Kids daycare for homeless children, as a mall captain for the Angel Tree Program and in the Senior Stockings program, helping plan and oversee the filling of hundreds of Christmas Stockings designed for needs senior citizens. Mrs. Bryan's belief in and enthusiasm for the mission of the Salvation Army is contagious, and she has by her example of hard work and tireless advocacy for that mission become one of our organization's best volunteer recruiters.

Steve Buckley
From: Oak Ridge, Anderson County
Years of Service: 10
Volunteering Highlights:
United Way: Exec Cabinet Member, Knoxville & Anderson County campaigns; Region Coordinator Fed Campaigns
American Cancer Society: Anderson County Bd of Dirs; Relay for Life; 2000 National Excalibur Roundtable
Oak Ridge Public Education Foundation: Director Founding Board
Technology 2020: Chairman elect 2001; Exec Committee Member and Director
Nine Counties, One Vision: Steering Committee Member
Special Notes: The constantly increasing breadth and depth of Steve's volunteer activities have helped thousands of people in East Tennessee to have quality jobs, healthcare, and education. Each year his unique variety of successful activity places demands for service to more organizations and leadership roles within organizations he serves.

Teresa Bullock
From: Memphis, Shelby County
Years of Service: 20
Volunteering Highlights:
National Kidney Foundation, Board President — West TN
Race for the Cure, Komen Foundation
MS Society
Tour for the Cure
Evergreen Historic District Association
Special Notes: Teresa has been serving the community lending her talents and expertise while in college. Teresa never tires giving of herself to others even when faced with such traumatic events as breast cancer and a young son facing renal failure, ultimately receiving a transplant. She is a strong supporter of many causes, not just in words, but in deeds.

> If every Tennessean were to volunteer for one day a month, we could...
> all have a better environment for our children and a safer place for senior citizens to live. We all need to work together for our government, our schools, and our community in order to have better communication with all races to get the job done.
>
> —James T. Crabtree
> Petersburg, Marshall County

Tennessee Volunteer Heroes 2001

Ken Bundy
From: Nashville, Davidson County
Years of Service: 5
Volunteering Highlights:
Nashville CARES Education Department
Nashville CARES Client Services
1999 finalist, Mary Catherine Strobel Award
Clinton/Gore Campaign 1992 & 1996
Gore Campaign 2000
Special Notes: Ken has co-authored training manuals to train speakers to educate youth on HIV risk and prevention, trained others to speak and has done over 75 presentations himself. He works the Heart line at Nashville CARES answering phones and assisting clients. Ken has received letters from young adults thanking him, telling him they have changed their behavior, and that speaking with him probably saved their lives.

Peggy Burton
From: Tullahoma, Coffee County
Years of Service: 30
Volunteering Highlights:
Tullahoma A Capella Singers
South Jackson Goes Country
Tullahoma Celtic Music Festival
South Jackson Street Band
South Jackson Goes Gospel
Special Notes: Peggy has almost single-handedly made Tullahoma a place where good music performed live can be heard. She is very talented and knows how to produce and direct a good show. She is tireless and donates hundreds of hours each year. She is full of optimism and good will. She makes folks around her better. She is a leader, and cares so much for others. Peggy is a voice and piano instructor, has taught music in the Tullahoma schools. For the last 20 years, she has been responsible for originating musical shows and given others a chance to show and develop their musical talent. Most of the shows have been staged to raise funds to save and improve the Historic South Jackson Auditorium and School.

Elizabeth Cable
From: Mountain City, Johnson County
Years of Service: 13
Volunteering Highlights:
Tennessee's VFW-Women's Auxiliary 2000 Volunteer Award
1999 National Prudential Spirit of Community Award for Volunteerism
1998 National Prudential Spirit of Community Award for Volunteerism
…is being featured in McGraw-Hills 4th grade TN History Book, 2001
…was featured in The Tennessee Magazine, Dec., 1999 for volunteer work
Special Notes: Elizabeth has spent hundreds of hours helping the poverty-stricken and handicapped people within her community and throughout the US. She has designed and sewed hundreds of wheelchair caddies and baby blankets.

Kevin James Cable
From: Mountain City, Johnson County
Years of Service: 11
Volunteering Highlights:
Governor Don Sundquist Tennessee Volunteer Commendation Award, 2000
Tennessee's Prudential Spirit of Community Award, 2000
…honored through House Resolution # 134 by State of TN for Volunteerism
Certificate of Congressional recognition from Bill

If every Tennessean were to volunteer for one day a month, we could…
change the *soul* of the state. People caring for people— loneliness dissolves and spirits soar— for both the giver and the receiver. As my life comes to a close, I wish that all who have life ahead of them are able to realize the sense of fulfillment and peace that comes from volunteering.

—Judith Crawford
Nashville
Davidson County

If every Tennessean were to volunteer for one day a month, we could…
satisfy the financial and staffing needs of the volunteer organizations in the community— volunteers would fill the staffing positions that frequently have to be paid positions to obtain workers who accomplish the needed clerical tasks. Money paid for these salaries could be dedicated to serving the needs of the populations targeted by the community organizations.

—Robert Charles Craig, II
Germantown, Shelby County

Tennessee Volunteer Heroes 2001

> **If every Tennessean were to volunteer for one day a month, we could...**
>
> put smiles on many faces, put food on everyone's plate; build homes for all Tennesseans. Volunteering not only helps others, it helps you feel you are a vital member of the community.
>
> —Cathy Crooks
> Murfreesboro, Rutherford County

Jenkins, 2000
Jake Cable Day was Feb 5, 2000 in his community
Special Notes: Kevin has sought to help those within his community who most needed it by giving away baby toboggans, setting up a lending program for physically impaired people, having cots donated for the women's shelter, spear-heading a letter-writing campaign against violence.

Richard Cadavero
From: Collegedale, Hamilton County
Years of Service: 19
Volunteering Highlights:
Children's Home / Chambliss Shelter: food drive and coordinates Christmas Party
Good Samaritan Center — contributes 30-50 boxes of food each year
Chattanooga Soup Kitchen — contributes 30-50 boxes of food each year
Maurice Kirby Child Care Center — feeds a number of families each year
East Fifth Street Child Care Center — feeds a number of families each year
Special Notes: Richard has worked with high school students in community service for the past 19 years. He is the coordinator of Project 17,000 — his students help distribute food baskets to area families (last year 174 families were fed). Coordinator of Christian In Action at Collegedale Academy, fund-raiser which raised tens of thousands of dollars for needy families. Coordinator of Children's Home / Chambliss Shelter Party for past 15 years.

Kenneth Caldwell
From: Jackson, Madison County
Years of Service: 5
Volunteering Highlights:
Office of Minority Health's Teen Violence Alternative Program, Boys & Girls Club
Jackson Halfway House
Founder of Books and Ball Program
Alpha Kappa Alpha's 1998 Outstanding Male Role Model of the Year
Individual Excellence Award, presented by the Mayor for outstanding work with youth
Special Notes: His total commitment to our youth in the area of positive behavior that promotes good health and leadership development.

Camp Creek Care Bears
From: Greeneville, Greene County
Years of Service: 2
Volunteering Highlights:
American Heart Association Walk
Habitat for Humanity
Food Bank
Kinser Park for Keep Greene Green
J.C. Penney Golden Rule Award Nomination
Wonder of Words (WOW)
Special Notes: "Since their inception, the Camp Creek Bears have been very active in their community and school. The impact that this group has made has been tremendous. This is evident by the increase in participating children. When we first began, we were searching for areas in which to become involved. Now, we are receiving requests for our services."

> **If every Tennessean were to volunteer for one day a month, we could...**
>
> have outstanding community pride in each community and self-fulfillment and great feelings of accomplishment by each participating member of our community. Tennessee would be a great place to live and raise families.
>
> —Willard M. Cummings
> Cookeville
> Putnam County

Harriett Campbell
From: Germantown, Shelby County
Years of Service: 20
Volunteering Highlights:
Memphis Symphony League: Chair of Bridge Marathon; Volunteer Receptionist; Young People's Concerts
Memphis Interfaith Organization
Salvation Army: Bell Ringer; Fundraiser; Angel Tree
St. George'e Episcopal Church
Special Notes: A concern to help or improve various facets of the community over a number of years with a consistency of quiet dedication is to some the idea of a Tennessee Volunteer Hero.

Merci Campbell
From: Hendersonville, Sumner County
Years of Service: 10
Volunteering Highlights:
American Red Cross: National Disaster Volunteer; Disaster Program Instructor
Operation Standdown: break and recreation tent
Cub Scouts: neighborhood chair; leader
V.F.W. Auxiliary
Special Notes: Merci has boundless energy and has gone out all over this country to help provide Red Cross relief to Disaster victims.

Dionna CarMichael
From: Chattanooga, Hamilton County
Years of Service: 1
Volunteering Highlights:
DOVIA
Signal Centers/ Families First
Catholic Charities
Venus Lacy Foundation
Community Based Training

> If every Tennessean were to volunteer for one day a month, we could...
> scale back on the services now provided by our state government, saving taxpayer dollars. Local volunteers know their community's unique needs and can direct volunteer programs to meet those needs.
>
> —Mary M. Cunningham
> Kingsport
> Sullivan County

> If every Tennessean were to volunteer for one day a month, we could...
> build healthier communities, enhance the lives of seniors, children, the disenfranchised and disadvantaged, and connect with that special part of ourselves and one another which is what life ought to be about.
>
> —Matthew Cushing
> Nashville
> Davidson County

Special Notes: Dianna is a true modern day hero who assists women on a welfare-to-work program. She shows these ladies that someone cares and that they can achieve as long as they believe. She is an outstanding volunteer! Her faith in God and belief in a better way of service qualify her as a Volunteer Hero. She has boundless determination, dedication and compassion for others.

Chuck Carpenter
From: Chattanooga, Hamilton County
Years of Service: 3
Volunteering Highlights:
Bridge Refugee & Sponsorship Services: Board VP; Chair Finance Committee; Advisory Committee
St. Thaddeus Episcopal Church: Chairman of Finance and Planned Giving
Service Corps of Retired executives: Vice Chair and Business Counselor
Hamilton County Juvenile Court: Foster Care Review Board Member
DuBose Conference Center: Treasurer of Board of Directors
Special Notes: Chuck has made a significant impact on the revitalization of Bridge Refugee Services, on the morale at Bridge and in the lives of five refugee families. He has committed more than 1,000 hours since June, 1997.

Church Health Center Volunteer Nurses Team
From: Memphis, Shelby County
Volunteering Highlights:
Church Health Center, Inc.
Special Notes: The volunteer nursing program has had a significant impact on the Center. Without the help

Tennessee Volunteer Heroes 2001

> If every Tennessean were to volunteer for one day a month, we could...
>
> # build enough houses to eliminate poverty housing within 5 years.
>
> —Phil Dalton
> Talbott, Hamblen County

of nurses, the evening clinic would not be possible. The Center has grown from caring for 12 patients on the first day to providing a medical home for over 22,000 of the working poor. Thanks to the commitment and genuine devotion of dedicated men and women, who understand that caring for patients in a loving environment is truly caring for and loving our neighbors.

Billy L. Cartmell
From: Lebanon, Wilson County
Years of Service: 22
Volunteering Highlights:
National Youth Sports Coaches Association
A.R.T. (All Races Together) Lebanon High School
Mary Catherine Strobel Award Nominee
Lebanon Special School District Schools Uniform Committee
Mayor's Community Spirit Award
Special Notes: Twenty-two years as a youth coach and counselor, Director of Head Homes Community Park Summer Program, 1998-94. Presently serves as the Recreation Director at the Market Street Community Center, for the Wilson County Civic League.

CASA of Northeast Tennessee
Volunteering Highlights:
J.C. Penney Golden Rule Award Nomination
Special Notes: CASA of Northeast Tennessee has been serving, for the past 14 years, the unseen children who are victims of abuse or neglect, and, through no fault of their own, come into the court system. Although those who work in juvenile court try, our overburdened court system does not have much time to search out or assess the needs of each child. This is where CASAs volunteers offer a child a powerful voice in court. Although we can see the immediate result of our volunteer work in the faces of children who have been removed from harm's way, the healing of a family takes time and patience. This is not something that can be accomplished overnight, in a week or even a month. Our volunteers work with families for the best interest of the child, working to improve the environment in the child's home to assure the child can return to a safe place, and will also have the opportunity to grow and develop to his or her best potential. The true impact of this volunteer work will be seen when these children become parents themselves. Most volunteers lift the spirits of those they help, but a CASA does even more: they plant hope where there was none. The work of a CASA volunteer is not glamorous, and it is not easy. The very people we are trying to help sometimes resent us and may even vent their anger over the court system towards the CASA volunteer. With all of this, the CASA worker does not give up, we know the importance of the work we do.

Roy L. Chalmers
From: Clarksville, Montgomery County
Years of Service: 4
Volunteering Highlights:
Clarksville-Montgomery County Community Action Agency
Clarksville-Montgomery County United Way
Ajax Turner Senior Citizen Center
8 Elementary Schools
Special Notes: Outstanding leadership as the Project Director of a Tennessee Senior volunteer project.

> If every Tennessean were to volunteer for one day a month, we could...
> raise enough money to find a cure for cancer, build houses for the poor and homeless, give troubled teens good role models and much needed guidance, staff the care facilities for the elderly and make the volunteers from Tennessee the happiest, most fulfilled people in the USA!
>
> —Genivee Daniels
> Germantown
> Shelby County

E.S. Chandrasekaran
From: Hixson, Hamilton County
Years of Service: 7
Volunteering Highlights:
JC Penney Golden Rule Award for Outstanding
  Volunteerism in the Greater Chattanooga Area
Chattanooga Girls' Choir
Chattanooga School for the Arts and Sciences (CSAS)
Hamilton County School system Magnet School:
  School Advisory Board
Allied Arts of greater Chattanooga
Special Notes: His devotion and leadership to the Chattanooga Girls' Choir to assist in the cultural development of young ladies in grades 4-12.

Georgeanne Chapman
From: Nashville, Davidson County
Years of Service: 38
Volunteering Highlights:
Martha O'Brien Center
Book 'Em
Reading is Fundamental
Parthenon Patrons
Friends of Warner Park
Special Notes: Georgeanne has worked to open up the world of reading for children in the James A. Cayce Homes. As a young girl of 14 in the early 1960's, Georgeanne started coming over to the Martha O'Brien Center to read to children in the Cayce Community. She would take a book cart around the neighborhood and sit outside and read to the children. Then the children would check out a book to take home with them — and return it to Georgeanne the next week. Georgeanne has given of her talents and time in many different ways throughout the past 38 years. She served on Public Relations committee for the center in the early 80's.

> If every Tennessean were to volunteer
> for one day a month, we could...
>
> ## not only assist others, but teach positive role models that embody strong moral values and personal integrity in helping build a strong America where we help others in need.
>
> —J. Millen Darnell
> Germantown, Shelby County

> If every Tennessean were to volunteer
> for one day a month, we could...
>
> ## show consistency in our efforts to solve any problems that our youth are facing.
>
> —Charles Davis
> Nashville, Davidson County

She helped an important special event called the "Miss Martha's Ice Cream Crankin'" get its start in the late 80's, served Meals on Wheels to house-bound community members for a time, and continuously championed for the support of Martha O'Brien Center in her church and the greater Nashville community. This desire to kindle the passion for books and reading in children has stayed alive in her through the years. Five years ago she helped initiate a project with her fellow church members to have members come to the center on a regular basis and read to the children. Georgeanne's impact on children has been monumental.

Mrs. Jan Chapman
From: Greeneville, Greene County
Years of Service: 20
Volunteering Highlights:
First Baptist Church: past Dir of Clothes Closet;
  Fellowship Event Director; Vacation Bible School
Laughlin Memorial Hospital: Board of Directors;
  Volunteer since 1980
Fundraising Committee for Tusculum College, Heart
  Association and Cancer Society
Past Memb: Humane Society, Library, YMCA, Arts Guild,
  Little Theater; Youth Builders; Tutorial Reading Pgm
Member: Living Christmas Tree Chorus; Sanctuary
  Choir; Moose Club; Medical Auxiliary
Special Notes: "As a wife, mother and grandmother, I am proud to honor God and my country by doing Volunteer work in the great State of Tennessee. As a volunteer and a member of the healthcare family, I feel I have helped in some small way with the quality of medical service to our community. I also feel that the greatest measure of success is not based on what we have accumulated, but on how much we have helped others. Thank you for choosing to honor Volunteers in Tennessee."

Tennessee Volunteer Heroes 2001

> If every Tennessean were to volunteer for one day a month, we could...
>
> ## make life with all its richness accessible to everyone. Reaching out to others, helping them to help themselves assures that we all benefit.
>
> —Donna Davis
> Memphis
> Shelby County

Jawanna Chapman
From: Russellville, Hamblen County
Volunteering Highlights:
Tennessee's Community Assistance Corporation, Executive Director
Lakeway Center for the Handicapped, Board Member
Tennessee Housing and Redevolpment Association, Affiliate Member
Tennessee Federation of Republican Women; Region 4A, Vice President
Ridin High Therapudic Program, Parent Volunteer
Special Notes: Outstanding leadership as a supervisor of Volunteers in Service to America (VISTA)

Chattanooga/Hamilton City Medical Alliance
From: Chattanooga, Hamilton County
Years of Service: 6
Volunteering Highlights:
Family and Children's Services of Chattanooga, Inc.
J.C. Penney Golden Rule Award Nomination
Special Notes: The Chattanooga/Hamilton City Medical Alliance "adopted" the Family Violence Services Shelter (FVSS) in 1997. The first event was hosting a shower for shelter residents. The items given not only provided for the immediate needs of the residents, but supplied much-needed items for months to come. This was followed by "Save the Shelter Day," which provided donations of clothing, household items, toiletries, and furniture gathered by members of the Medical Alliance to be given to clients as they moved out of the Shelter to begin life on their own. In addition to the donations and hard work of the Medical Alliance, they donated $4,000 from the proceeds of their fashion show as an earmarked contribution to the FVSS. The Medical Alliance also furnished a playground for the children who live in the shelter. The following year, the Medical Alliance donated $10,000 to the Shelter, and several members of the Alliance became regular visitors to the Shelter. With each visit, they brought new bed linens, pillows for couches, curtains, televisions, and microwave ovens. In addition, the Medical Alliance members bring their own families to the Shelter for an annual Christmas Party, complete with Santa. While providing the basic needs of the Shelter, the Medical Alliance has helped the Shelter staff realize that we are not alone in the struggle to help victims of violence. Emotionally, we were all helped by the presence of Alliance members who came bearing gifts. We have been blessed by more than gifts; we have made friends for life. It is a grand feeling to know that we have someone to call if we need help — any kind of help.

Tim A. Chavez
From: Brentwood, Williamson County
Years of Service: 33
Volunteering Highlights:
Metro Nashville Schools; initiated campaign for used personal computers, results 130 PCs & 500 CD-Roms
Apollo Middle School; established language computer lab partnering with GE employees
Edgehill United Methodist Church; Neighborhood Sunday morning breakfast program
Project S.A.V.E. (Students and Teachers Against Violent Environments) — John Henry Hale Homes children
Glenview Elementary School; facilitated donation of used musical instruments
Special Notes: "Besides my volunteering, I use my position as a newspaper columnist to match resources with needs. I have an invaluable forum. With it, I believe comes the moral responsibility to use it for the good of the community. So I go out and see

> If every Tennessean were to volunteer for one day a month, we could...
>
> ## lighten the burden on the faithful and accomplish so much more that is needed to be done to make the state a happier place for all.
>
> —Leroy Davis
> Crossville, Cumberland County

the community problem, the volunteer effort that has started because of it, and what readers can do to get involved. I determine the volunteer effort's credibility and record of activity and accomplishment. I believe this kind of reporting and writing helps readers make a more informed decision on whether a specific volunteer effort meets their interests and personal schedules."

Mrs. Bertha Chrietzberg
From: Murfreesboro, Rutherford County
Years of Service: 30
Volunteering Highlights:
Black Fox Wetlands, Founding Member
Friends of the Greenway, Original Board Member
Tennessee Trails
Tennessee Native Plant Society
Friends of Fall Creek Falls
Special Notes: Mrs. Chrietzberg works tirelessly for saving the natural beauty of Tennessee. She was a founding member of Tennessee Trails, wildflower Society, Garden Club, Friends of the Greenway (Murfreesboro Greenway System), Plant Rescue and Edible Plants Member

Doris Chrzanowski
From: Burns, Dickson County
Years of Service: 20
Volunteering Highlights:
The Renaissance Center
Bon Aqua United Methodist Church
Centerville Nursing Home
FCE (Family, Community and Education)
Special Notes: Doris's commitment to church and to civic and educational organizations is her greatest joy.

If every Tennessean were to volunteer for one day a month, we could...

make a big difference in crime, the homeless, and homebound people.

—Alene Deal
Nashville, Davidson County

D. Gene Clark
From: Nashville, Davidson County
Years of Service: 40
Volunteering Highlights:
American Red Cross, Disaster Services Volunteer
Vanderbilt University Medical Center, Lay member of committee for Protection of Human Subjects
Hillsboro Presbyterian Church: Room in the Inn Volunteer
Special Notes: Mr. Clark has devoted may hours of volunteer time. Service includes non-profit organizations, churches, civic groups, community groups and credit unions. Gene is the expert in damage assessment for the Red Cross. His work after the 1998 tornado was instrumental in providing quick relief to the disaster victims.

John Clark
From: Signal Mtn., Hamilton County
Years of Service: 6
Volunteering Highlights:
Signal Mtn. Recreation, Inc.: President
Signal Mtn. Soccer League: President 1996-97
Signal Mtn. Fire & Ice Girls Select Soccer Team: Coach — State Champs 1997
American Association of Textile Colorist and Chemists
Signal Crest United Methodist Church
Special Notes: Mr. Clark's untiring efforts in bringing the Signal Mtn. Soccer Complex to completion were outstanding. His organizational skills in fund raising, work details, getting the irrigation system installed, sod installation and nurturing the grass are outstanding.

If every Tennessean were to volunteer for one day a month, we could...

provide all the volunteer positions needed and would not put a strain on just a few people.

—Sandy Davis
Crossville
Cumberland County

Tennessee Volunteer Heroes 2001

> *If every Tennessean were to volunteer for one day a month, we could...* make our community and state a much better place. It makes me happy to do for others. When people thank me, I say, "If it makes you feel good, just think how happy it makes me!"
>
> —Mary Virginia Dean
> Springfield, Robertson County

Katherine Clark
From: Cookeville, Putnam County
Years of Service: 16
Volunteering Highlights:
Putnam County Farm Bureau women, chairman last 5 years
Family and Community Education Club
Putnam County Senior Citizens, Board of Directors, Secretary
Jefferson Ave. Church of Christ
Putnam County Fair, Chairman of Quilt division
Special Notes: "I have volunteered many hours trying to make my home county a better place to live. I learned from working with the Putnam County Farm Bureau Farm Tour that many students knew nothing about where their food comes from; now they have a better idea."

Dorothy Cleaves
From: Memphis, Shelby County
Years of Service: 5
Volunteering Highlights:
Memphis Urban League: Chair, Board of Directors
Memphis Distinguished Sales and Marketing Award, 1991 and 1992
J.C. Penney Golden Rule Award Nomination
Special Notes: through Dorothy's efforts, she has enabled the League to help hundreds of low-income people in Memphis and Shelby County become employed and independent through the Workforce Development and Training, Medical Office Technology Training, Skills Bank and Education Initiative Programs.

Donna Clouse-West
From: Bon Aqua, Hickman County
Years of Service: 27
Volunteering Highlights:
Meals on Wheels
Battered Women's Shelters
Adopt a Grandparent
Senior Citizens Center
Human Society
Special Notes: "When my mom was a nurse, I would go to work with her at a nursing home and read or write letters, visit patients, and help employees do what was necessary. At 18, I became a candy stripper at another nursing home, doing both jobs. I have also volunteered at daycare one summer after school, adopted a nursing home patient as my grandmother who had no family."

Suzanne Mandel Cohn
From: Chattanooga, Hamilton County
Years of Service: 58
Volunteering Highlights:
JC Penney Golden Rule Award Winner, 1994
Hospice Volunteer Award, 1993
Founder, Past President, Chattanooga Area Food Bank
Mizpah Congregation
InterFaith Hospitality Network
Special Notes: Sue is always looking for ways to brighten the lives of others and invites as many people as possible to join in her mission. Sue found her niche in 1993 when she started the K.O.O.L (Knitters Out Of Love) project at Hospice of Chattanooga. As a volunteer, she recruited more than 100 volunteers to knit or crochet afghans to donate to the agency's terminally ill patients. Many of the knitters are homebound themselves and can't get out to do volunteer work at an agency. This project gives those knitters an opportunity to volunteer. Sue

> *If every Tennessean were to volunteer for one day a month, we could...* make the city a better place for all residents, but every person can and should contribute by helping others daily, in some way, never expecting someone else will help. Do your duty, be active, help keep the community clean.
>
> —Bruce W. DeForest
> Germantown, Shelby County

makes her rounds to homes and churches to collect the finished product. The K.O.O.L volunteer catalogs each item with a listing of who made it, a description and the number donated to that point. She then packages the afghans in large clear plastic bags and encloses a hospice card. Once bundled, Sue delivers the bags to hospice where social workers and nurses pick them up to deliver to patients.

Estella Cooper
From: Clarkrange, Fentress County
Years of Service: 40
Volunteering Highlights:
Save our Cumberland Mountains
Girl Scouts of America
Save the Children Organization
AmeriCorps Vista
Head Start Center (LBJ&C)
Special Notes: What qualifies her as a Volunteer Hero? Her undying spirit and energy, exemplified by her constant efforts to provide help and opportunities for people throughout.

Greg Cox
From: Murfreesboro, Rutherford County
Volunteering Highlights:
Nashville CARES
Vanderbilt HIV Clinical Trials
United Cerebral Palsy
Woodmont Hills Church of Christ
Room In the Inn
Special Notes: Greg puts in as much time volunteering as he does working at his job. He is an interfaith care team leader at Nashville CARES. He has provided transportation, errands and emotional support to clients at Nashville CARES. He coordinates the needs of the client with other team members. Greg has volunteered in vaccine clinical trials at Vanderbilt, not knowing how it would affect his health.

James T. Crabtree
From: Petersburg, Marshall County
Years of Service: 10
Volunteering Highlights:
Lions Club
Fellowship Baptist Church
Senior Citizens, Meals on Wheels
Food Harvest
1996 Olympic Torch Relay
Special Notes: James has true compassion for human life, physically and spiritually for his family, community and church. He asks nothing in return and wants to do more. He goes out of his way to help anyone, and at the same time spreads the word of God to give them hope each and every day.

Dr. Judith Craig
From: Germantown, Shelby County
Volunteering Highlights:
S.M.A.R.T. (St. Mary's, Manassas, Alabama
 Redevelopment Team)
Germantown 2000 Hometown Heroes
Special Notes: Dr. Craig is the only volunteer phoned in the event of problems with our computer program.

Robert Charles Craig, II
From: Germantown, Shelby County
Years of Service: 20
Volunteering Highlights:
SMART, Vice President of Finance, Endowment Chair
Methodist Neighborhood Center
Harwood Day School, Mentoring computer skills

If every Tennessean were to volunteer
for one day a month, we could...

make a difference for those without guidance and for those without food and clothing. Even one person can make a difference in their community.

—Carolyn D. Demonbreun
Nashville
Davidson County

If every Tennessean were to volunteer
for one day a month, we could...

make a difference in the lives of every citizen in Tennessee. We could mentor, feed, clothe, educate, **encourage and help turn people's** lives around to a degree that is unheard of now.

—Virginia (Ginny) DeHart
Memphis, Shelby County

Tennessee Volunteer Heroes 2001

> If every Tennessean were to volunteer for one day a month, we could... brighten lives and give hope where light and hope are needed. We could help a developmentally disabled individual gain new skills, or give a helping hand to a family hurting because of a terminal illness.
>
> —Bharti Desai
> Chattanooga
> Hamilton County

Emmanuel United Methodist Church, volunteer for Neighborhood Home Construction
Civitan International and Memphis Civitan Club
Special Notes: Over the past 20 years Bob has faithfully served the cause of mentally and developmentally challenged children through his service to Civitan International, through the Civitan Candy Box project which places peppermints in restaurants across the country. Every penny of these funds goes to the local organizations for challenged children and to the Civitan International research Center at the University of Alabama at Birmingham to find a cure for prenatal diseases especially Downs Syndrome. During these 20 years, Bob has raised over $200,000 through the Candy Box project, plus the Civitan International Breakthrough Golf tournament and a 5K Run sponsored by the Memphis Civitan Park. He also serves the needs of disadvantaged children in the inner city neighborhood of Winchester Park in Memphis through SMART organization for which he has been responsible for obtaining a community home and office space.

Judith Crawford
From: Nashville, Davidson County
Years of Service: 30
Volunteering Highlights:
Jr. League of Nashville: Sustainer Volunteer of the Year, 1994
Family Resource Center Vanderbilt Childrens Hospital
Gilda's Club of Nashville
Race for the Cure, Honary Survivor 1998
Mary Catherine Strobel Nominee, 1998
Special Notes: "I developed breast cancer in 1978, with many reoccurrences and still manage to give many healthy moments to volunteerism — fulfilling life. I have no regrets now that cancer has the upper hand."

Cathy Crooks
From: Murfreesboro, Rutherford County
Years of Service: 2
Volunteering Highlights:
Therapy Dogs International
Delta Society, National Pet-Assisted Therapy Organization
Volunteer Paws: Founding member, Rutherford County
Special Notes: Cathy and her dog provide animal-assisted therapy in local nursing homes and assisted living facilities. Cathy also assists with the certification process for certifying new pets and their owners to provide animal-assisted therapy.

Willard M. Cummings
From: Cookeville, Putnam County
Years of Service: 15
Volunteering Highlights:
Cookeville Evening Lions Club: Director; 3rd, 2nd, 1st VP; President; Zone Chairman; Region Chairman, District Governor; Melvin Jones Fellow; Lion of the Year, District Lion of the Decade; State and District Lion of Distinction, International Leadership Award; 3 International President Certificates
J.C. Penney Golden Rule Award Nomination
Tennessee Lions Eye Center for Children: Operation KidSight; photoscreening; fundraising
Special Notes: His dedication to community service qualifies him as a volunteer hero. He volunteers hundreds of hours each year to help save the sight of Tennessee's children.

> If every Tennessean were to volunteer for one day a month, we could... improve the quality of life for *all* Tennesseans and make a better Tennessee. Volunteering obviously benefits the *receiver* of the action— too often, we overlook the benefit received by the *giver*. Volunteering requires us to be our best selves, often requiring us to develop skills we don't use in our daily professional and personal lives. We then become better "selves" in our daily routine. Volunteering, then, is a *win-win* endeavor.
>
> —Diana Diaz
> Gallatin
> Sumner County

Mary M. Cunningham
From: Kingsport, Sullivan County
Years of Service: 40
Volunteering Highlights:
Meals on Wheels of Kingsport
Eastman Hiking/Canoeing Club, affiliate of
  Appalachian Trail Conference
Sequoyah Council, Boy Scouts, 10 years active merit
  badge counselor & hikemaster
Bays Mountain Park, former volunteer naturalist, now
  Park Commissioner
Frontier Health, former Board Member & President;
  Board Member of affiliated programs
Special Notes: "With over 25 years with Meals on Wheels, I have witnessed tremendous growth in the program. I have assumed responsibilities commensurate with this growth. This has kept the organization all volunteer and allows most of the funds to be spent directly on the recipients. Although I perform many administrative tasks, I still cook once a month and very frequently deliver meals to our 220 clients."

Matthew Cushing
From: Nashville, Davidson County
Volunteering Highlights:
N.A.S.W.
Crisis Intervention Center
Glenview Neighborhood Association
Mental Health Association
Successful Clinical Social Worker for Nashville CARES
Special Notes: Matthew is a very dedicated volunteer. He has a lot of background in mental health issues. His experiences have taken him to where he is today. He is a very warm, kind and compassionate man. He is a wonderful volunteer and has given his heart to so many people and continues to do so everyday.

If every Tennessean were to volunteer for one day a month, we could...

ease the pain and confusion of those in need and try to give them the strength and courage to attain their goals and feel worthwhile.

—Helen W. DiRenzo
Memphis, Shelby County

 If every Tennessean were to volunteer for one day a month, we could...

reach out to the homebound, go and visit and talk with them, let them know they are not alone and forgotten. With a smile and a few kind words, we could bring some sunshine into their lonely hours. God gives us that gift, and we should use it every day in our lives.

—Anne Doherty
Clarksville, Montgomery County

Horace Lee Cyree
From: Arrington, Rutherford County
Years of Service: 33
Volunteering Highlights:
Veterans of Foreign Wars, officer, Post 8422
American Legion
Masonic Order
Al Menah Shine Temple
Almaville Volunteer Fire Department
Special Notes: Lee Cyree is dedicated to helping Veterans. He volunteers his time at the York Veterans Administration Hospital in such activities as organizing bingo, collecting donated clothing, organizing a carnival and horse show every year, and transporting Veterans to hospitals. He serves as Chairman of the VFW Memorial Day Service at Stones River National Battlefield. He also serves as co-coordinator of Veterans Affairs for Rutherford County — an unpaid position.

Phil Dalton
From: Talbott, Hamblen County
Years of Service: 3
Volunteering Highlights:
AmeriCorps VISTA / Hamblen County Habitat for
  Humanity
Hamblen County Sheriff's Department, Retired
Post Office, Retired
Army: Retired
Special Notes: His unique dedicated spirit and contagious enthusiasm inspire everyone he comes in contact with to want to better themselves and help others.

Tennessee Volunteer Heroes 2001

> If every Tennessean were to volunteer for one day a month, we could...
>
> ## provide a safer, cleaner environment for our children, where neighborhoods and communities work together to form a united people.
>
> —Frances Donaldson
> Celina
> Clay County

Douglas R. Daniel
From: Memphis, Shelby County
Years of Service: 6
Volunteering Highlights:
Habitat for Humanity of Greater Memphis, Inc.
Family Services Committee Chairperson
St. Jude Children's Hospital: Board of Directors
J.C. Penney Golden Rule Award Nomination
Crisis Center
Special Notes: Due in large part to Doug's leadership, 185 low-income families have been successfully trained, nurtured, and qualified for the responsibilities of home ownership. As a result of this high number of homes build for low-income families, Habitat for Humanity of Greater Memphis, Inc. is currently the number one affiliate in the Mid-America Region and ranks 15th in the nation.

Genivee Daniels
From: Germantown, Shelby County
Years of Service: 15
Volunteering Highlights:
Memphis Affiliate of the Susan G. Komen Breast Cancer Foundation: past Treasurer; fundraiser
Abused Women Services: chaired Celebrity Cook off
New Neighbors of Germantown: President; Vice President; Historian: Publicity Chairman
Germantown Youth Commission: Advisor
Leaadership Germantown Alumni Association: Vice President
Special Notes: Genivee deserves the title of "Volunteer Hero" because of her efforts to give to her community — hours of volunteer work with abused women and children, her support of Race for the Cure to raise money for breast cancer education and research, her dedication to New Neighbors of Germantown and their endeavors to give monies to local charities and her volunteer work at her church.

J. Millen Darnell
From: Germantown, Shelby County
Years of Service: 51
Volunteering Highlights:
Overseas missionary to the Indians of the high Andes Mountains
44 years as a registered Boy Scout
City of Germantown: Chaplain; compiled 3 histories of the city
Kiwanis Club: President
Memphis Ministries Association: President
Special Notes: "7,000 boys and girls were in the scouting program at Farmington Presbyterian Church when I was the minister of that church."

Charles Davis
From: Nashville, Davidson County
Years of Service: 18
Volunteering Highlights:
National Basketball Association (NBA)
Charles Davis Foundation, Founder
1996 Outstanding Young American — U.S. Junior Chamber of Commerce
Vanderbilt University
Special Notes: Charles Davis shares his athletic talents, his attainments and wisdom with inner city kids teaching them as a mentor to believe in themselves and life's opportunities through his foundation.

> If every Tennessean were to volunteer for one day a month, we could...
>
> ## go from being the 41st in the country in math and English, to being the first or second.
>
> —M. Chris Douglass
> Murfreesboro, Rutherford County

Dana C. Davis
From: Kingsport, Sullivan County
Years of Service: 9
Volunteering Highlights:
Kingsport Youth Tobacco Prevention Team
Character Counts
TN State Health Department
Dana and Company
MOOSE — Youth Awareness
Special Notes: Dana is a Prudential Spirit of Community Award winner, Campaign for Tobacco Free Kids Advocate of the Year, and was inducted to the Pizza Hut National Geographic Kids Hall of Fame.

Donna Davis
From: Memphis, Shelby County
Years of Service: 2
Volunteering Highlights:
Metropolitan Inter-Faith Association (MIFA)
March of Dimes
Mayor's Advisory Council for Citizens with Disabilities
Center for Independent Living
Kings Daughters
Special Notes: Donna has been a "front line" volunteer for Metropolitan Inter-Faith Association (MIFA) Emergency Services Division for over two years. She works two mornings a week helping families in crisis. The work takes dedication and exceptional people skills. When clients arrive at Emergency Services, they are in distress, scared, confused and often angry. Donna takes it all in stride, offering a smile and words of encouragement.

> If every Tennessean were to volunteer for one day a month, we could...
>
> accomplish our goals in many places: hospitals; Red Cross; churches; scouts; helping the underprivileged; the sick; senior citizens; the handicapped; children. There is always room for one more helper.
>
> —John Lawrence Dreher, Jr.
> Nashville
> Davidson County

Leroy Davis
From: Crossville, Cumberland County
Years of Service: 2
Volunteering Highlights:
Fair Park Senior Center
Maryland Senior Center
Hilltoppers Senior Center
Cumberland County Palyhouse
Pamona Methodist Church
Special Notes: Leroy is always making people laugh, is always ready to help someone, and is very compassionate and understanding.

Mary Anna Davis
From: Memphis, Shelby County
Years of Service: 3
Volunteering Highlights:
Oak Forest Elementary: President PTO
J.C. Penney Golden Rule Award Nomination
Special Notes: Mary Anna puts the needs of the school first by providing her time to help ensure that our school receives many things that we cannot provide. She solicits donations of products/services to be sold at the school's annual auction. Businesses receive free advertising, families receive quality merchandise, and students receive educational supplies for their classrooms.

Sandy Davis
From: Crossville, Cumberland County
Years of Service: 2
Volunteering Highlights:
Fair Park Senior Center
Maryland Senior Center
Hilltoppers Senior Center
Cumberland County Playhouse
Country Place Nursing Home

> If every Tennessean were to volunteer for one day a month, we could...
>
> make Tennessee even better! (Which would be tough to do— we are already the best state in the nation!)
>
> —Adam Dread
> Nashville, Davidson County

Tennessee Volunteer Heroes 2001

> If every Tennessean were to volunteer for one day a month, we could...
>
> *Touch* the lives of every Tennessean! *Change* the lives of many Tennesseans! Those who give through volunteering will expand their appreciation of the human condition and the value of advantages such as health, education and human worth. Those who receive through volunteerism will experience the gifts of love and time from others given from the heart, with no expectation for a personal return. *All* Tennesseans would grow in stature.
>
> —Elaine Duncan
> Chattanooga
> Hamilton County

Special Notes: Sandy has a good disposition, loves to help people and always has a big smile.

Alene Deal
From: Nashville, Davidson County
Years of Service: 30
Volunteering Highlights:
Easter Seals
Lung Association
March of Dimes
Senior Citizens, Inc: Volunteer of the Week; Certificate of Appreciation
Muscular Dystrophy

Mary Virginia Dean
From: Springfield, Robertson County
Years of Service: 14
Volunteering Highlights:
Springfield NHC: visit residents, deliver mail, read
Robertson County Senior Citizens: Influenza shots yearly, Blood Pressure weekly
American A.H.A, Memorial Chairman
Sunday School Teacher for 45 years
Deliver tapes of sermons weekly to shut-ins
Special Notes: "As a retired R.N., I have been pleased to give injections of ordered medication to many people."

Bruce W. DeForest
From: Germantown, Shelby County
Years of Service: 19
Volunteering Highlights:
Germantown Public Library
Friend of the Library
Germantown Park Subdivision
Germantown 2000 Hometown Heroes
Special Notes: Mr. DeForest deserves recognition as a Volunteer Hero because of his outstanding creative activities in his subdivision.

Virginia (Ginny) DeHart
From: Memphis, Shelby County
Years of Service: 1
Volunteering Highlights:
Metropolitan Inter-Faith Association
Brinkley Hieghts Alliance
Grahamwood Elementary School
Special Notes: "I am not a 'hero'. I feel very blessed to have the health and the financial resources so that I can give my time to worthy causes. I have been so blessed that I just want to share."

Carolyn D. Demonbreun
From: Nashville, Davidson County
Years of Service: 43
Volunteering Highlights:
Nashville Baptist Association
Shelby Ave. Baptist Church
Easy Nashville Cooperative Ministry
Second Harvest Food Bank
Women's Prison
Special Notes: "I really have no qualifications. I just love and like to help others that are in need."

Bharti Desai
From: Chattanooga, Hamilton County
Volunteering Highlights:
Hospice of Chattanooga
Orange Grove Center, Inc.
Special Notes: Orange Grove is a community-based facility serving individuals with developmental disabilities. Ms. Desai, Orange Grove's only international volunteer, is a soft

> If every Tennessean were to volunteer for one day a month, we could...
>
> have a rippling effect of kindness starting with ourselves and then reaching out to others. This would make for a much better Tennessee.
>
> —Abby Dunn
> Goodlettsville
> Sumner County

spoken, easy-going lady. She easily establishes a rapport with whoever she comes in contact with, and is always a willing helper in any way asked. Duties assigned include one-on-one assistance with lunch and implementation of stated objectives that are especially designed to meet that person's goals and visions. Extremely dependable, Ms. Desai often shows initiative by assisting other staff, often bringing "goodies" for all to enjoy. Her classroom supervisor often says of her "What does she *not* do?" A most valuable asset, Ms. Desai is counted on each Tuesday to help those she serves on physical therapy equipment, lunch, computers or whatever she sees needs to be done. It is a treat to have someone who is pleasant and willing to volunteer her time. Ms. Desai is more than a volunteer, she is a friend and co-worker.

Diana Diaz
From: Gallatin, Sumner County
Years of Service: 14
Volunteering Highlights:
Friends of Hendersonville Hospital, President
First United Methodist Church, Hendersonville
Room in the Inn
American Cancer Society
Special Notes: Diana's volunteer heroism is best portrayed through her dedication to cancer patients and their families. She has been a strong advocate for patient service programs all across the state. She has facilitated "I Can Cope" sessions in her county, an 8-week educational program for cancer patients and their families. Her background as an oncology nurse enables her to communicate effectively with cancer patients, helping them to understand more about their disease and how they can best get through treatment. She has also served as a statewide trainer for the program, enabling hundreds of other volunteers

> *If every Tennessean were to volunteer for one day a month, we could...*
> change the communities, city, state, country and world. We could end hunger and homelessness, we could empower the homeless and motivate the disenfranchised. We could build a better world for not only Tennesseans, but for Americans.
>
> —Bethany Durham
> Memphis, Shelby County

> *If every Tennessean were to volunteer for one day a month, we could...*
> change attitudes, which would result in litter-free communities and roadsides. Community events and activities would have plenty of help to plan and carry out their projects. Our young people would grow up with a volunteer work ethic that would help them consider the needs of others while becoming productive members of the community.
>
> —Mike Edmonds
> Johnson City
> Washington County

to take this program back to their communities. Diane always goes the "extra mile" to help a cancer patient with whatever his or her needs are. Two years ago, she won the St. George Award from the American Cancer Society, the highest honor the Society gives a volunteer.

Cindy P. Dickens
From: Cookeville, Putnam County
Years of Service: 3
Volunteering Highlights:
Putnam County 4-H
J.C. Penney Golden Rule Award Nomination
Special Notes: Mrs. Cindy Dickens has performed several volunteer services for Putnam County's 4-H program. She works on a daily basis with the 100 students in her 5th grade classes encouraging them to be involved with 4-H. She volunteers in her classroom each month allowing the 4-H agents to come in and present their programs. Outside the classroom, Mrs. Dickens volunteers her personal time to work with the county 4-H agents and the county elementary students by judging the County Clover Bowl Contest.

Edith Dietzen
From: Chattanooga, Hamilton County
Years of Service: 15
Volunteering Highlights:
Ladies of Charity Store Volunteer/Coordinator/Board Member
Our Lady of Perpetual Help School — Monday Office Volunteer
Our Lady of Perpetual help Church — Office
Special Notes: For 10 years, Edith has coordinated the volunteer schedule for the Ladies of Charity Resale Store. While serving her own volunteer hours, at age 80, she frequently fills in at the last moment.

Tennessee Volunteer Heroes 2001

> If every Tennessean were to volunteer for one day a month, we could... help elderly citizens with their needs, such as home repair, yard work and shopping. Also, we could assist slow-learning children in their school systems, improving their skills in basic classes of math, reading, English and writing.
>
> —Lamar Edwards
> Knoxville, Knox County

Helen W. DiRenzo
From: Memphis, Shelby County
Years of Service: 9
Volunteering Highlights:
YWCA Abused Women's Services
J.C. Penney Golden Rule Award Nomination
Special Notes: "I really care about the women and children passing through the shelter. They are in pain and the children have seen so much pain and violence. I like to feel my hugs help these women and children."

Disaster Action Team First Responders
From: McDonald, Tennessee
Years of Service: 1
Volunteering Highlights:
American Red Cross
J.C. Penney Golden Rule Recognition
Special Notes: These committed volunteers come from all walks of life. Each sets aside one week of his or her life monthly with a commitment to remain available for American Red Cross Disaster Relief. Disaster victims do not have to wait or wonder where to turn.

Anne Doherty
From: Clarksville, Montgomery County
Years of Service: 10
Volunteering Highlights:
Loaves and Fishes Soup Kitchen
Immaculate Conception Church
Visits the sick in Nursing Homes
Dr. Ed Atkinson Volunteer of the Year 2000
Distributes bulk food to other agencies feeding the needy/homeless
Special Notes: Ms. Doherty's mission is to do whatever she can to feed the hungry. As a teenager in World War II Austria, she came to know what real hunger is. Because of her compassion, she volunteers 6 days a week at our local soup kitchen.

Frances Donaldson
From: Celina, Clay County
Years of Service: 20
Volunteering Highlights:
Clay County Partnership Board Member
Clay County Museum Board Member
4-H Club
American Cancer Society
Volunteers for church functions
Special Notes: She has volunteered many years to help civic organizations and the community. She has a special interest in preserving history in our county, and has volunteered many hours trying to achieve that goal.

R.R. Donnelley
From: Gallatin, Sumner County
Years of Service: 25
Special Notes: For 25 years, R.R. Donnelley has worked with the City of Gallatin, the State of Tennessee, historic, civic and social groups to form a better city, community, state and nation.

M. Chris Douglass
From: Murfreesboro, Rutherford County
Years of Service: 2
Volunteering Highlights:
AmeriCorps — Emerald Youth Foundation: Mentor and Teacher
New Hope Missionary Baptist Church
West View Elementary School
Special Notes: Chris Douglass, an urban "kid" in Knoxville, decided to give back to his community through

> If every Tennessean were to volunteer for one day a month, we could... help reach the hearts of those who are lost, help heal the wounds of the infirm, help feed those who are hungry, touch the lives of those who are alone, brighten the world of those who are hurting and help preserve the physical world for all of us.
>
> —Emily B. Elliott
> Bartlett, Shelby County

AmeriCorps membership at Emerald Youth Foundation after being involved there as a participant for several years. He served as an excellent male, African American role model to dozens of inner city children, and has now returned to college.

Patrick J. Doyle, Ed.D.
From: Murfreesboro, Rutherford County
Volunteering Highlights:
Special Notes: Dr. Patrick Doyle, a professor of biology at Middle Tennessee State University, is the force behind recycling on campus. Since 1972, he has shaped the recycling habits of faculty and staff. Dr. Doyle now presides over a modest fleet of trucks and a cadre of diligent workers and receives release time to administer the campus-wide recycling program. His work benefits the environment and the lives of MTSU students.

Adam Dread
From: Nashville, Davidson County
Years of Service: 24
Volunteering Highlights:
The Cystic Fibrosis Foundation, Board
The Community Resource Center, Oyster Easter
Belcourt YES!
March of Dimes
The Surfrider Foundation
Special Notes: "There's nothing more powerful than a bad boy doing good works."

John Lawrence Dreher, Jr.
From: Nashville, Davidson County
Years of Service: 60
Volunteering Highlights:
Boy Scouts of America: Silver Beaver Award; 60 years at the troop, council and national levels

> If every Tennessean were to volunteer for one day a month, we could...
>
> ## make Tennessee not only the best state in the South, but the best state in the country.
>
> —Elwood Ervin
> Celina, Clay County

> If every Tennessean were to volunteer for one day a month, we could...
>
> ## make a lot of unhappy, disabled, lonely people happy.
>
> —Bill Estep
> Elizabethton
> Carter County

Knot Hole Baseball Coach: 22 years, lead teams to 3 city championships
Toys for Tots (TFT): 36 years; organized Nashville's TFT campaign and TFT store; collected toys
Telephone Pioneers of America: 40 years local and state level, main emphasis working with the blind
American Red Cross: 19 years; blood drives
Special Notes: John Dreher has volunteered his time with many different organizations over the past 60+ years. He gives of his time and talents unselfishly as a caring volunteer. He has touched the lives of many, young and old and has left a positive mark on each. He possesses the true spirit of a volunteer.

Judith Dronebarger
From: Cookeville, Putnam County
Years of Service: 4
Volunteering Highlights:
Putnam County Habitat for Humanity: Chairman of Family Nurturing and Education committee
J.C. Penney Golden Rule Award Nomination
Special Notes: Judy has been involved with Habitat since 1996, in all phases of Habitat from the family selection committee to the construction and land development. Judy's volunteer efforts have had a tremendous effect on the community. She has not only volunteered her time and talents, but has spent her own money for food and supplies.

Elaine Duncan
From: Chattanooga, Hamilton County
Years of Service: 17
Volunteering Highlights:
Family & Children's Services of Chatt.: Board Pres; Aux Group Pres; Fundraising/Personnel Community Chair
Brownie / Girl Scout Leader

Tennessee Volunteer Heroes 2001

> If every Tennessean were to volunteer for one day a month, we could...
>
> meet the needs of many more people, and our communities would be better and happier places to live. Those who volunteer would feel better, too!
>
> —Carol Etherington
> Nashville
> Davidson County

United Way Board
Allied Arts Board
Church Committees
Special Notes: When their own family was growing, Elaine and her husband, Stuart, were a "resource family" for Family and Children's Services of Chattanooga, providing a wholesome environment, love and support for abused, neglected and runaway teen girls. Elaine's work with FCS led to involvement in leadership and fundraising roles, as well. Elaine has inspired her children to carry the volunteer flag, too. Daughter Malone sponsors an annual Easter drive to provide toys for children of families in need.

Abby Dunn
From: Goodlettsville, Sumner County
Years of Service: 5
Volunteering Highlights:
American Red Cross: National Disaster Volunteer
Hospital and Hospice Patient Representative
Nursing Home Volunteer
Daughter of the American Revolution
Junior Service League
Special Notes: Abby's outgoing personality is irreplaceable on the disaster operations she has participated in both locally and nationally.

Bethany Durham
From: Memphis, Shelby County
Years of Service: 4
Volunteering Highlights:
Teens for Peace
Beta Club, National and State
Vice President of DECA
Key Club
Special Notes: Bethany has qualified herself by giving countless hours of service to the Exchange Club Family Center, consistently for four years.

Assistant D.A. Lee Dryer
From: Franklin, Williamson County
Special Notes from a Grateful Citizen: Sometimes in our lives, things happen that make you really take notice. On October 23, 1995, my daughter Stacey Dale Grissom was murdered. What I took for granted was gone. I met Assistant District Attorney Lee Dyer. This man has been a great friend. He takes time out of his busy life, donating his time to go with me to area churches, to help me tell my story and hope if only one child or person hears my story we have done something. He talks with children and adults, telling them about things people don't know until they face it. He sheds tears as his words come from the heart. He doesn't let his title stand in his way. I thank God for him — he is for the people. You can tell that he feels your pain and hurt. You never get the feeling that it is his job. Lee Dyer is a true Tennessee Hero.

Jennifer Easley
From: Cookeville, Putnam County
Years of Service: 10
Volunteering Highlights:
Girl Scouts of America
Camp Horizon: Jr. Counselor
Leadership Putnam Youth Academy Class of 1999
I Care Award: nominee
J.C. Penney Golden Rule Award Nomination
The 2000 Prudential Spirit of Community Award: nominee
Special Notes: "I feel that my helping in Girl Scouts has helped build up the confidence of some of the little girls who may be overweight or not as accepted as others

> If every Tennessean were to volunteer for one day a month, we could...
>
> meet the emergency needs of every one of our five million citizens.
>
> —F. Miles Ezell, Jr.
> Nashville, Davidson County

in school. I can also tell that I mean something to kids I work with at church and through Girl Scouts when I get hugs when I see them out in the community. When I work with people through my volunteer work, they tell me I am doing a great job and that they really appreciate what I am doing. They also tell me that they would love me to come back and help whenever I have time.

Vicky Easley
From: Cookeville, Putnam County
Years of Service: 12
Volunteering Highlights:
Girl Scout Leader and Volunteer of the Year
Cub Scout Saint George Award
Girl Scout Saint Ann Award
BPW's Volunteer of the Year
J.C. Penney Golden Rule Award Nomination
Boy Scout Long rifle Award
Special Notes: Vickie has been a role model for many girls and boys that she has worked with through the years. She has helped them grow strong and confident of themselves. She has been an inspiration to many adults that have worked with her. The community agencies know if they need some helping hands they can call Vickie and her girls or boys will be there to help. There was little for girl scouts to do in this area. Vickie came up with some events for her girls to participate in. When she saw how well her girls liked them, she hosted events inviting all of the girls in the region to come and participate. Vicky does he best to keep the cost of these events down so every girl who wants to participate can.

East TN Consortium for Service Learning
From: Johnson City and Various Counties
Years of Service: 6
Volunteering Highlights:

> If every Tennessean were to volunteer for one day a month, we could...
>
> make this state a lot better place. There wouldn't be people doing without meals, rides to doctors, companionship, etc. We need to put our heart into our neighbors.
>
> —Mildred Farmer
> Madison
> Davidson County

> If every Tennessean were to volunteer for one day a month, we could...
>
> alleviate many of the homelessness and hunger problems, help direct misguided youth from dysfunctional homes, reverse the trend of gang activities, show drug addicts that their situation is not hopeless, and show love and kindness to those incarcerated.
>
> —Velvetta Fields
> Memphis
> Shelby County

Learn and Serve America
America Reads
America's Promise
Service to State and National Parks
Campus Compact
Special Notes: The Consortium has connected over 6,000 students, faculty and staff in meaningful service to their respective communities and to East Tennessee.

Mike Edmonds
From: Johnson City, Washington County
Years of Service: 12
Volunteering Highlights:
Johnson City/Washington County/Jonesborough Chamber of Commerce
Johnson City Parks and Recreation
Warrior's Path State Park
Keep America Beautiful: 1992 National 1st Place; 1997 National 2nd Place
1995, K-12 Environmental Awareness Award from T.D.E.C.
Special Notes: He has inspired his 5th grade students to be involved in numerous community events and programs. His science club can be counted on each year to help organize and carry out several projects. Project examples include: planting over 2500 trees in Warrior's Path State Park; organizing children's games for Earth Day events; roadside litter pickup; bagging mulch from Chipping of the Green; storm drain stenciling; stream monitoring; collected over 26,000 student signatures on Earth Day 2000 pledge and gave them to the Tennessee Senate.

Lamar Edwards
From: Knoxville, Knox County
Years of Service: 28
Volunteering Highlights:
Past Chapter President, Telephone Pioneers of America

Tennessee Volunteer Heroes 2001

> **If every Tennessean were to volunteer for one day a month, we could...**
> build better communities. Volunteering helps one build a sense of pride through observing work accomplished. One also gains a better knowledge of community concerns and activities. Volunteering helps build better communities when we all work together to accomplish goals and fulfill the needs of others.
>
> —Margaret Ellen Finley
> Johnson City, Washington County

National Kidney Foundation, Board Member
Homeowners Association, President
BellSouth Pioneer Volunteers
Special Notes: Lamar works tirelessly in his efforts to help raise awareness of the National Kidney Foundation. Lamar has also been a mainstay in a tutoring project with the Knoxville Life Member club of the BellSouth Pioneer Volunteers. He is dependable and gives 110% to whatever he is involved in.

Lum Edwards
From: Nashville, Davidson County
Years of Service: 7
Volunteering Highlights:
American Red Cross
BellSouth Pioneer Volunteers, Nashville Life Member Club
Special Notes: Lum has been driving for the Red Cross for some time. He sets aside every Wednesday and will go wherever he is needed.

Emily B. Elliott
From: Bartlett, Shelby County
Years of Service: 10
Volunteering Highlights:
Appalachian Service Project (serves East Tennessee, Kentucky, Virginia and West Virginia)
March of Dimes: Fundraising Communications Chair
American Cancer Society: Relay for Life
United Methodist Church: St Johns Soup Kitchen vol; Youth Choir Tour Counselor: Wesley Madison Tower Vol
TN Dept. of Environment & Conservation Stream 2000
Special Notes: In addition to volunteering for the many humanitarian projects and charities listed above, Emily also serves as Bartlett Alderman, and serves voluntarily on the Planning Commission, Arts Council, and Family Assistance Commission. She also works full time as a nurse.

Gene Elliott
From: Soddy Daisy, Hamilton County
Years of Service: 10
Volunteering Highlights:
Chattanooga Area Food Bank
Lion's Club: President; Lion of the Year; Lion of the Decade
J.C. Penney Golden Rule Award Nomination
Special Notes: Gene has been community-minded most of his life, first in his many years as a chemistry and math teacher, then as a feed store owner. Any individual in the Chattanooga area needing food assistance can obtain a voucher from one of our partner agencies. They then bring the voucher to the Chattanooga Area Food Bank to be filled by a volunteer like Gene. On an average day, Gene will fill 80 or more vouchers. He will look into the eyes of desperate parents, hungry children, and needful elderly. Asking for help is never easy — pride is very difficult to swallow, but Gene makes it a little easier. He never judges or inquires. He simply gives them food, a smile, and hopefully a little dignity. Gene is loyal, compassionate, caring, faithful and dependable.

Emerald Youth Foundation AmeriCorps
From: Knoxville, Knox County
Years of Service: 3
Volunteering Highlights:
700+ children pre-school through 12th grade
After-school programs
Sport programs
Tutoring
Emerald Community Youth Center
Special Notes: This AmeriCorps program is committed to serving young people of the inner-city, urban Knoxville, equipping them to be leaders in their neighborhoods.

> **If every Tennessean were to volunteer for one day a month, we could...**
> make the community better and there would not be as many crimes and violence. It would teach Tennesseans to show respect for properties that have been loaned to everyone. It would make them feel like better people, and realize that money is not everything. By volunteering, you enrich yourself more than you ever could with money. If you give to the community what the community has given to you, the community will help you in trying times.
>
> —Kristin Fisk
> Cookeville
> Putnam County

Tennessee Volunteer Heroes 2001

Elwood Ervin
From: Celina, Clay County
Years of Service: 20
Volunteering Highlights:
Clay County Partnership
Celina Lion's Club
Celina Fire Department
Celebrity Waiter for American Center Society
United Way
Special Notes: He has been very active for several years in the community. He continues to promote our county and works to recruit new industry to our area as a member of the Economic Development Board.

Bill Estep
From: Elizabethton, Carter County
Years of Service: 25
Volunteering Highlights:
Shriner Crippled Children's Hospital, transports children
Shriners, Fundraising via sale of Shriner newspapers
Shriner Children's Christmas Parties, collects bicycles
Disabled American Veterans, provides transportation to and from appointments
Disabled American Veterans, sponsors Christmas Parties for hospitalized Veterans
Special Notes: Bill loves our country, loves people, cares about children.

Carol Etherington
From: Nashville, Davidson County
Years of Service: 20
Volunteering Highlights:
American Red Cross in many capacities
YWCA
Tennessee Council of Community Services

If every Tennessean were to volunteer
for one day a month, we could...

realize how alike we really are. Just by helping others, we would greatly improve our sense of community and put an end to divisiveness and distrust.

—Robert Flynn
Humboldt
Gibson/Madison County

If every Tennessean were to volunteer
for one day a month, we could...

see that no elderly persons goes hungry for food and company; that no child is without nurture; that no handicapped person would face a barrier without help; that every individual, regardless of gender, race or religion would receive the help he or she needs to fulfill his or her potential.

—Harriet H. Foley
Nashville
Davidson County

Mental Health — International Red Cross Delegate to Cambodia, etc.
International Florence Nightingale Award, 1997
Special Notes: Carol is a Volunteer Hero, having spent a lifetime as both volunteer and paid as an RN serving in the USA and in war-torn countries from Cambodia to Sierra Leone, as well as in the Nashville and Tennessee area. She is a registered nurse and teaches at the Vanderbilt School of Nursing.

F. Miles Ezell, Jr.
From: Nashville, Davidson County
Years of Service: 50
Volunteering Highlights:
American Red Cross, Nashville Area Chapter
David Lipscomb University: Board Chair 1991-97; Board Member 1996-2000
A.G.A.P.E.: Board Chair 24 years; Board Member 6 times
Philanthropist of the Year, 1997
Youth Encouragement Services — Past President
Special Notes: Miles gives an endless amount of time, blood, and financial resources to the Red Cross and the entire Nashville Community. He has been an outstanding volunteer leader for 50 years and inspires others to give of themselves.

Mildred Farmer
From: Madison, Davidson County
Years of Service: 14
Volunteering Highlights:
Metro Social Services Nutrition Group
Cumberland View Towers clubs
Special Notes: Mildred is always available to serve meals and volunteers her time to the nutrition program. She takes people out to eat "just to get away."

Tennessee Volunteer Heroes 2001

> If every Tennessean were to volunteer for one day a month, we could...
>
> address the needs in all communities throughout Tennessee and beyond. This would start a flame that could light the way to a better world for all.
>
> —Lori Gonsch Foster
> Germantown, Shelby County

Hazel Fields
From: Nashville, Davidson County
Years of Service: 11
Volunteering Highlights:
American Red Cross
Reach to Recovery
Senior Citizens
Schader Lane church of Christ and mission work in Africa
Community Groups
Special Notes: Hazel has demonstrated work as a volunteer for 11 years and very successful doing both leadership and direct service to people. She has been Chair of Awards and Recognition and is a member of the Chapter board. She is very active in special projects.

Velvetta Fields
From: Memphis, Shelby County
Years of Service: 2
Volunteering Highlights:
Women in Community Service, Inc. (WICS): Mentor
12-step sponsor
Prison Ministry
Street Ministry
Overcomer's Unit: State President
Special Notes: Velvetta takes her vacation time from work to come speak and teach female inmates at the Shelby County Division of Corrections. She uses her spare time to act as a mentor to a number of women when they are released into the community. She is indefatigable in her efforts. She inspires by word, by action and by example.

Margaret Ellen Finley
From: Johnson City, Washington County
Years of Service: 20
Volunteering Highlights:
American Red Cross of Johnson City/Washington County
Civitas of Johnson City
Co-founder of Community Crisis Advisory Team
Tennessee Conference on Social Welfare
HIV/Aids education Instructor
Special Notes: Ellen does everything she can to help make Tennessee the best state in the union. Her compassion, dedication and willingness to help are an inspiration to everyone who knows her.

Anne Fisher
From: Memphis, Shelby County
Years of Service: 4
Volunteering Highlights:
New Hope Christian Academy
J.C. Penney Golden Rule Award Nomination
Special Notes: Mrs. Fisher has volunteered to teach Art Education to inner-city children once per week for the past three years. Mrs. Fisher's work educating children is never done. Her unconditional hard work at New Hope, coupled with providing our students with such a rich experience ultimately enhances their ability to express themselves artistically. It is simply amazing to see our students develop an appreciation of the arts. Small motor skills, the ability to work with a variety of art supplies, and understanding color, line, design and pattern shape are among the many program benefits. Most importantly, our students know that Mrs. Fisher genuinely loves them.

> If every Tennessean were to volunteer for one day a month, we could...
>
> have better schools, clean up the environment and lower taxes.
>
> —Hugh O. Fox
> Athens, McMinn County

Tennessee Volunteer Heroes 2001

Barbara A. Fisher
From: Germantown, Shelby County
Years of Service: 6
Volunteering Highlights:
Shelby County Republican Women's Club: Exec. Board; Corresponding Secretary; Treasurer; Finance Chair
Germantown Senior Advisory Commission:
Germantown Garden Club: Treasurer; Corresponding Secretary; Recording Secretary
Poplar Estates Garden Club: Recording Secretary
Special Notes: One of the six finalists for the Jo Reed Volunteerism Award given annually at the City of Germantown.

Kristin Fisk
From: Cookeville, Putnam County
Years of Service: 8
J.C. Penney Golden Rule Award Nomination
Volunteering Highlights:
Girl Scouts of America, Gold Award Recipient
Muscular Dystrophy Association, Camp counselor
Camp Horizon, Special Needs Junior Counselor
Who's Who Among American High School Students
JC Penney Golden Rule Award Winner
Special Notes: "I have been volunteering since I first started Girl Scouting at the age of about five. When you are little you do lots of volunteer work because that is what little kids do. When I was about eight, I started volunteering on my own. I would go with older Girl Scout Troops to nursing homes and sing and help them with bingo. I went to Walnut Village, homes for the elderly and rake yards, pick up trash and whatever was needed. In seventh grade, I became a Junior Volunteer at Cookeville Regional Medical Center. I work at an MDA Camp for one week and at Camp Horizon for two weeks every summer. I feel the community gives so much to you it is only right you give something back. Volunteering makes you a better person. If you start at an early age, you will appreciate the values of life more when you become an adult. This can be a step in the right direction to end some of the violence."

Maggie Joy Flynn
From: Humboldt, Madison County
Years of Service: 42
Volunteering Highlights:
American Cancer Society
United Way
American Heart Association
Jackson Symphony Orchestra
Kiwanis Center for Child Development
Special Notes: Maggie is constantly volunteering for something. She often goes from one meeting to the next for numerous organizations she supports.

Robert Flynn
From: Humboldt, Gibson/Madison County
Years of Service: 22
Volunteering Highlights:
United Way of West TN: Board Member and officer
American Red Cross: Lifeline Blood Services; 14 gallon blood donor
Kiwanis Club of Jackson
Girl Scout Council, San Fernando Valley: former Board Member
United Way of Los Angeles: Mendenhal Award Winner, 1995
Special Notes: Bob Flynn is a dedicated leader among volunteers who serve our community. He thinks beyond what we are doing to what we are capable of doing to make life better for people in need.

If every Tennessean were to volunteer for one day a month, we could...

bridge the gap between all racial and financial barriers, making Tennessee the model state of the south.

—Martha "Eve" Freeman
Hendersonville, Sumner County

If every Tennessean were to volunteer for one day a month, we could...

make a difference in our state. Our state would be more beautiful. Citizens facing a challenging time in their lives would have support. Children could be nurtured and developed, and each volunteer would learn the true meaning of helping someone else.

—Kealie E. Frazier
Medina

> If every Tennessean were to volunteer for one day a month, we could... open a lot of eyes and minds to the real needs volunteer organizations fill in the lives of our citizens. We could also give our volunteers a great sense of personal fulfillment in knowing they *do* make a difference in our communities.
>
> —Melba Fristick
> Germantown, Shelby County

Harriet H. Foley
From: Nashville, Davidson County
Years of Service: 40
Volunteering Highlights:
St. Luke's Community Center — Founder Child Development Center, Past Pres. Advisory Board
This-N-That Thrift Shop — Founder and Board President
YWCA — Board President; Domestic Violence Shelter founder; Chair of 100 year celebration
United Way of Middle TN — Vice chair of Board; Many committee chairs
Senior Citizens Inc., Board President; Endowment Board Founder; Capitol Campaign Steering Committee
Special Notes: Harriet Foley is the quintessential volunteer. Not only has she been a stalwart proponent of the mission of Senior Citizens, Inc., she has also played an important part in the creation and the continued success of many organizations in Nashville. Harriett Foley best represents the fine spirit of a Tennessee Volunteer.

Ford Credit/PRIMUS Financial Services
From: Franklin, Williamson County
Years of Service: 10
Volunteering Highlights:
Juvenile Diabetes Foundation: 1230 walkers in year 2000 walk!
Junior Achievement: Classroom teachers: Bowl-a-thon teams
Our Kids, Inc.
Second Harvest Food Bank
American Red Cross, Williamson County Chapter
Special Notes: The company encourages volunteerism by providing up to 16 hours paid time away from duties for employee groups to volunteer in the community and by promoting company-sponsored volunteer events annually.

Lori Gonsch Foster
From: Germantown, Shelby County
Years of Service: 20
Volunteering Highlights:
Germantown Animal Control Commission
Germantown Animal Shelter: Volunteer; Pet Adoption; Euthanasia Rescue
Memphis Museums: Pink Palace Crafts Fair; Lichterman Nature Center
Holy Spirit Catholic Church: Haiti medical mission assistance; St. Peter's Picnic
English Meadows Neighborhood Association Welcome Committee: Newsletter Distribution Chair
Special Notes: I am an example of the joy one can get from volunteering and I hope it will encourage others to get involved with the community by volunteering their time and efforts.

Hugh O. Fox
From: Athens, McMinn County
Years of Service: 50
Volunteering Highlights:
McMinn County Rescue Squad
McMinn County Rural Fire, Chief four years
Senior Citizen Board Member, Fundraising Committee
Friendly Fellow Christmas boxes for over 900 families
Neighborhood watch
Special Notes: Mr. Fox has spent fifty years volunteering his time helping those who need help.

Natalie R. Frager
Special Notes: Special recognition from the Governor and First Lady of Tennessee for excellence in volunteer service.

> If every Tennessean were to volunteer for one day a month, we could... overcome disease, poverty, and provide great child care. Older people would be served. Civilization would move rapidly forward.
>
> —Violet Fuson
> Smithville, Dekalb County

Tennessee Volunteer Heroes 2001

Franklin Memorial Chapel
From: Franklin, Williamson County
Years of Service: 28
Volunteering Highlights:
Franklin Memorial Chapel
Mt. Hope Cemetery
Franklin Monument Company
Church of Christ
Gospel Singing
Special Notes: "Franklin Memorial Chapel was my true Tennessee Hero. On October 23, 1995, my daughter Stacey Dale Grissom was murdered. How many of us think we are going to outlive our children? Not me. But, believe you me, it can happen. I didn't have any burial or life insurance, and didn't know what I was going to do. The staff at Franklin Memorial Chapel donated their time to help me out in my hour of need. All I had to pay for was the casket, at cost. I am so proud to call Tennessee my home. We are the most loving and caring state I know. Thank you Franklin Memorial Chapel — you are true Tennessee Heroes."

Kealie E. Frazier
From: Medina
Years of Service: 8
Volunteering Highlights:
"Smoke Arthritis" Barbeque: 1st Coordinator
"Up Til Dawn"
Martha O'Brien Center: Youth; Meals on Wheels; Clerical work
Boys and Girls Clubs of Murfreesboro
Mountain TOP: High School Mission Trip and Alternative Spring Break
Special Notes: Kealie was the Director of "Up Til Dawn" a campus-wide fundraising event benefiting St. Jude Children's Research Hospital in Memphis. MTSU is

> If every Tennessean were to volunteer for one day a month, we could...
>
> eliminate poverty, homelessness, and hunger. Child neglect, abuse and abandonment would lie in decline as well as crime. We would be a more loving and caring state.
>
> —Bill Gaetano
> Dickson, Dickson County

> If every Tennessean were to volunteer for one day a month, we could...
>
> learn greater respect and honor for one another. People can often develop feelings of self-worth when they are served and when they serve others.
>
> —Patrizia Garilli
> Memphis
> Shelby County

known as being a "suitcase college" with apathetic students. Yet, Kealie's extraordinary commitment to this project garnering over $21,000, making it the largest student fundraiser in MTSU history. In addition, Kealie was able to involve over 50 students in the planning and execution of the event. In all, over 500 students participated in "Up Til Dawn" making it an event MTSU was very proud of.

Martha "Eve" Freeman
From: Hendersonville, Sumner County
Years of Service: 10
Volunteering Highlights:
Friends of the Great Smoky Mountains
The Nashville Zoo
Sumner County Museum
Native American Indian Association of Tennessee
Volunteer State College Foundation
Special Notes: Eve voluntarily creates, produces and hosts a cable television program (*Eve Freeman Interviews the People* for Tennessee, which has aired nightly for the past 10 years. Eve invites experts to speak on topics such as: American Red Cross; Community Child Care; Senior Citizens; education; medical news; literacy; animals; arts; Tennessee State Parks.

Melba Fristick
From: Germantown, Shelby County
Volunteering Highlights:
Germantown Festival: coordinator
Our Lady of Perpetual Help Church: Parish Council; Family Life Committee
City of Germantown: past chair Library; Park and Recreation Commission
University of Memphis: Highland 100; Phi Mu

Tennessee Volunteer Heroes 2001

> If every Tennessean were to volunteer for one day a month, we could...
>
> ## understand our community and its citizens so much better. All people are interesting.
>
> —Winnie R. Gaskell
> Murfreesboro
> Rutherford County

Ray Frizzell
From: Nashville, Davidson County
Years of Service: 25
Volunteering Highlights:
BellSouth Pioneer Volunteers
Boy Scouts of America: Executive Board Member;
  Selection Committee for Silver Beaver Awards Group
Freed Hardeman University, Advisory Board Member
Crieve Hall Baptist Church; Elder
Directs English classes to Spanish population of Crieve
  Hall Church of Christ
Special Notes: Ray established and raises funds annually to serve an inner-city Boy Scout Troup as Scout Master for 25 years. During this time, he has recruited a diverse group of adult "role model" individuals to provide leadership and "real life" examples for the scouts. During his tenure as scout master, they have been recognized as a "Quality Troop" for 23 of his 25 years. This troop has served over 500 scouts, with 21 becoming Eagle Scouts. He has helped young men to master outdoor camping and high adventure skills, gain self confidence, and to prepare for life as leaders.

Myra Fuller
From: Chattanooga, Hamilton County
Years of Service: 10
Volunteering Highlights:
Children's Home/Chambliss Shelter — Partner in
  Education: mentoring, surplus materials, fund-raising
Ronald McDonald House: Founding Board Member,
  active Board Member
Possible Dream Foundation
American Lung Association — 1998 Woman of
  Distinction Award
Combined Federal Campaign — Day of Caring
Special Notes: Myra has a great compassion for helping people in need, especially abused, neglected and dependant children. She has a talent for motivating others to give of themselves in service projects or in providing financial assistance. There is an obvious sense of fulfillment she receives from reaching out to others in need.

Violet Fuson
From: Smithville, Dekalb County
Years of Service: 20
Volunteering Highlights:
Project Help
Jacobs Pillar United Methodist Church: Piano Player;
  District Treasurer United Methodist Women
Dekalb Retired Teachers
AARP, President
Meals on Wheels
Special Notes: Violet has a history of volunteering with many organizations.

Bill Gaetano
From: Dickson, Dickson County
Years of Service: 14
Volunteering Highlights:
CareNet Preganancy Services of Middle Tennessee
Dickson County Help Center
Meals on Wheels
CASA
Oakmont Accelerated Reading
Special Notes: He has a heart for seeing and a genuine concern for those in need. His life is volunteering. He volunteers at more places by far than those listed above.

> If every Tennessean were to volunteer for one day a month, we could...
>
> ## see a difference in our attitude and awareness of needs in Tennessee. We would realize the wonderful efforts being implemented to make life easier for those not as fortunate. Volunteering is a win-win situation for the Volunteers and the Organizations.
>
> —Sally Geny
> Nashville, Davidson County

George Gardner
From: Murfreesboro, Rutherford County
Volunteering Highlights:
MTSU Foundation
Middle Tennessee Symphony Guild
Murfreesboro Airport Authority
Children's Discovery House, Past President
Murfreesboro Arts Center
Special Notes: Mr. Gardner single-handedly raised the funds to build a new Discovery Center in Murfreesboro, and provided hours of hands on assistance ranging from board meetings to manning booths at the street fair.

Patrizia Garilli
From: Memphis, Shelby County
Years of Service: 4
Volunteering Highlights:
Metropolitan Inter-Faith Association (MIFA)
Memphis — Shelby County Public Library
Poetry Society of Tennessee
Volunteer Center of Memphis: Adult Volunteer of 1998
JC Penney Golden Rule Awards finalist
Special Notes: "I do not feel like a hero, but I do care about the importance of demonstrating kindness and friendliness toward all people and the willingness to serve them to the best of our capabilities."

Winnie R. Gaskell
From: Murfreesboro, Rutherford County
Years of Service: 7
Volunteering Highlights:
Hospice of Murfreesboro
Meals on Wheels
Cannonsburgh Pioneer Village in Murfreesboro
Special Notes: "I'm not a hero, just enjoy working with Hospice and the feeling I may have done things to help someone."

> If every Tennessean were to volunteer for one day a month, we could...
> eliminate attitudes that create barriers that keep us at odds with one another. We could eliminate fear and hatred, and replace them with understanding and compassion. And who knows what that could lead to?
>
> —Peter T. Giannini
> Germantown
> Shelby County

 If every Tennessean were to volunteer for one day a month, we could...
significantly alleviate the very real needs of those who are in pain, those who need special assistance to learn to crawl, walk, feed and care for themselves or talk, and those who need support in times more difficult that most of us can imagine. We could foster a community of acceptance— a place where all citizens, even those with special needs or extraordinary afflictions, would be respected and accepted without question.

—Paul Gilbert
Nashville
Davidson County

Sue Geist
From: Hermitage, Davidson County
Years of Service: 1
Volunteering Highlights:
American Red Cross
Special Notes: Sue has had to overcome many challenges and obstacles, but she has a spirit and willingness about her that is inspirational. She volunteers frequently and loves it.

Sally Geny
From: Nashville, Davidson County
Years of Service: 3
Volunteering Highlights:
Nashville's Table
Second Harvest Food Bank
Youth Encouragement Services
Special Notes: "I volunteer one day a week for various organizations. I feel it is one of the most rewarding things I have ever experienced. They seem grateful for the help, and I am so happy to be associated with these extraordinary and dedicated people."

Peter T. Giannini
From: Germantown, Shelby County
Years of Service: 20
Volunteering Highlights:
Memphis in May, Transportation Steering Committee
Habitat for Humanity
Saint Peter's Home for Girls
J.C. Penney Golden Rule Award Nomination
Memphis Zoo; Center for Southern Folklore
Special Notes: Peter is always willing to help others, no matter how time consuming or difficult the task. He involved his entire family in volunteering as well. He is a natural leader who encourages others.

> If every Tennessean were to volunteer for one day a month, we could... touch the life of another person in a positive way. We could turn a frown into a smile and soothe a broken heart if only for a little while. We could help a lonely teenager to understand how we all make mistakes, but we learn from them and go on. We could save the state thousands of dollars while making our communities and cities cleaner and safer places to live.
>
> —Lilly R. Gilkey
> Memphis, Shelby County

Paul Gilbert
From: Nashville, Davidson County
Volunteering Highlights:
High Hopes, Inc.
Special Notes: "I simply learned of the needs of High Hopes (and of the kids that it serves) and was immediately determined to do everything in my power to satisfy those needs. My only desire in doing so was to improve the lives of the kids that depend on the services and support provided by High Hopes. High Hopes, Inc. is a non-profit preschool for children with special needs. I set 2 goals when I first discovered High Hopes. 1) to increase its visibility in the community so that families in need would know where to go at the time they most need the support. 2) To increase the financial resources of High Hopes so that the kids could receive the best services possible, and that no child would be turned away due to financial need. Although we have to work at these main goals, I feel great about the progress we have made over the last three years."

Lilly R. Gilkey
From: Memphis, Shelby County
Years of Service: 21
Volunteering Highlights:
Juvenile Court Auxilliary Officer, Chief, Board Member
United Way Fund Allocation Committee Member
Tennessee Association of Public Purchasing West Tn Rep
National Institute of Government Purchasing
J.C. Penney Golden Rule Award Nomination
Sunday School Teacher, ages 9-12
Special Notes: A couple of the many awards he has received: JC Penney Golden Rule Award, 2000; the Brother Jesse H. Bishop Humanitarian Award, 1998

Mary Lou Goins
From: Woodbury, Cannon County
Years of Service: 29
Volunteering Highlights:
4-H Club: Vol Leader, Cannon Cty, District & State levels; Alumni Recordbook Chair; judging team coach
First Baptist Church, Woodbury: Sunday School teacher; Asst. Librarian; Clerk; Media Director
Cannon County Child Protection Council/Health Council: CPC Chair; TN Highway Safety Chair
Town of Woodbury: 1st Female elected Alderperson & Vice-Mayor; Woodbury Parks & Recreation Board
Cannon County Dixie Youth: lifetime member; coach; scorekeeper; secretary
Special Notes: Mary Lou has been an active volunteer in her community working to help youth attain the highest possible goals and objectives that they can attain. She also has worked to improve education, environment, community pride and resources in her community.

Golden Notes / Lewis Center Chorus
From: Memphis, Shelby County
Years of Service: 26
Volunteering Highlights:
Mid-South Fair Sr. American Talent Contest — 2nd place in 1987
Mphs/Shelby County Council on Aging Sr. Group of the Year Finalist
City of Memphis Division of Park Services
Alzheimer's Day Services, Inc.
J.C. Penney Golden Rule Award Nomination
Special Notes: The chorus (a group of 25 individuals ages 55 plus) volunteer at least 2 hours a week practicing and performing a repertoire of religious hymns, patriotic songs, and old favorites for nursing homes, senior centers, retirement centers, churches, etc.

> If every Tennessean were to volunteer for one day a month, we could... give a gift to ourselves through others. Volunteering allows us to discover who we are by being able to see who others are, not because we have to, but because we choose to. It helps us to see the circle that joins us together and the truths within that circle.
>
> —Annie M. Goodhue
> Nashville, Davidson County

Annie M. Goodhue
From: Nashville, Davidson County
Volunteering Highlights:
YMCA: Shelter for Domestic Violence, children's program
Try Angle House
Better Decisions Program: TN Prison for Women
Woodland Hills Youth Development Center
Friends of Woodland Hills: Board; Co-Chair Community Support Committee Programs
Special Notes: While many volunteers initially want to work with our children's program, this volunteer job traditionally has a high turnover rate. It can be very frustrating and heart-wrenching job. However, consistency is so important to children, and by Annie coming each and every week for 10 years — huge obstacles are overcome. Trust being at the top of the list! Children who are living in chaos — never knowing what to expect at home — are filled with fear, tension, anger, confusion, guilt, anxiety, isolation, and often hopelessness. When a child is injured, the physical scars can be readily seen, but it's the emotional scars that are the most devastating. Annie has learned so many skills and tools that allow her to effectively communicate with children. She understands when the "act out" and is there to listen and support them in their own ways. Often it is the children who ask their mothers to return to the group so they can spend more time with Annie. Violence is a learned behavior. Annie is doing everything in her power to break the cycle of violence in these families.

Adrianna Gordon
From: Nashville, Davidson County
Years of Service: 2
Volunteering Highlights:
Vanderbilt Medical Center
Women's Birthing Center

> *If every Tennessean were to volunteer for one day a month, we could...*
>
> ## truly make a difference in the lives of those less fortunate, particularly the children, who are most vulnerable.
>
> —Adrianna Gordon
> Nashville, Davidson County

> *If every Tennessean were to volunteer for one day a month, we could...*
>
> ## see a vast difference in the comfort and happiness level of every citizen within the state borders.
>
> —Vicki Gordon
> Lebanon
> Wilson County

Waverly-Belmont Clinic
United Neighborhood Health Services
AmeriCorps
Special Notes: Her initiative, determination, positive attitude and team spirit qualify her as a Volunteer Hero!

Sheryl Gorden
From: Memphis, Shelby County
Years of Service: 5
Volunteering Highlights:
Temple Israel
Partner In Education (PIE): Board Member; President; Vice President
Parent Hospitality Committee: Chairman
Spring Fling and Silent Auction: Chairman
Coffeeville Public Library
J.C. Penney Golden Rule Award Nomination
Special Notes: Mrs. Gordon is one of those dear, special people you encounter in your life and realize that by encountering her, you have touched God. Her love of the school is beyond words and she has placed that love into volunteer action. This parent and entrepreneur has proven to be a rare jewel to White Station High School. She has touched the lives of our students, faculty and staff.

Vicki Gordon
From: Lebanon, Wilson County
Years of Service: 25
Volunteering Highlights:
Immanuel Baptist Church, Sunday School Teacher
Lebanon Community Spirit 2000 Award
Past PTA and Sports Booster Club Member
Special Notes: Vicki spearheaded the inception and has tirelessly served as chairman of the Wilson County Relay for Life event, which over the past few years has raised over $300,000 for research, education and patient

Tennessee Volunteer Heroes 2001

> If every Tennessean were to volunteer for one day a month, we could...
>
> provide food and housing for every needy citizen in the state. Tennessee would become a model for every other state.
>
> —Andrew Gray
> Nashville, Davidson County

service programs of the American Cancer Society. In addition to the Relay, Vicki serves as lead volunteer in Wilson County by instilling educational programs and patient services within the community. Vicki's willingness to drive a patient to his/her treatment, lead an educational program or provide the local cancer center with materials is a rare commodity in the volunteer world. She recruits other volunteers so the number of patients helped continues to grow.

Andrew Gray
From: Nashville, Davidson County
Years of Service: 3
Volunteering Highlights:
St. Vincent DePaul Childcare
Our Kids
Habitat for Humanity
MBA Soup Kitchen
Mission Work in Bolivia
Special Notes: For the past 3 years, he has served as volunteer with the organizations above 2-10 hours weekly.

Roland Gray, M.D.
From: Nashville, Davidson County
Volunteering Highlights:
Renewal House — Medical Director
Alcohol and Drug Council — Family Program Supervision
Tennessee Medical Foundation
Davidson County Drug Court
Discovery Place — Medical Director
Special Notes: As Medical Director of Renewal House, Dr. Gray has assisted clients and their children with their physical, mental and spiritual needs. He has also helped train the staff in addiction issues.

Shirley Greenfield
From: Nashville, Davidson County
Years of Service: 45
Volunteering Highlights:
St. Thomas Hospital: Stephem Minister, Pastoral Care; Quarterly Newsletter; Cancer Day Volunteer
The Temple: Sr. Temple Chair
Asociation for Retarded Citizens; Dickson County Chair
Council of Jewish Women
Sponsor of imigrant family
Special Notes: Shirley is talented in many areas: writing, sewing, listening to name a few. She shares all of her talents to help people in need.

Bob Gregory
From: Brentwood, Williamson County
Volunteering Highlights:
American Red Cross: coordinating PRIMUS blood drives since 1992; Board of directors; chair annual golf tournament; chair volunteer donor recognition event; Chair Development Committee
Chair United Way/Proffitt's ticket sales
Special Notes: Bob is a dedicated Red Cross volunteer having served on the Board of Directors of the Williamson County Chapter and organizing the chapter's largest blood drive (quarterly).

David W. Gregory, M.D.
From: Nashville, Davidson County
Years of Service: 11
Volunteering Highlights:
Siloam Family Health Center: Founder; Chair Board of Directors 89-99; Vol Medical Director, Physician
Hillsboro Presbyterian Church, Elder on session
Special Notes: Siloam Family Health Center is a faith-based primary care clinic that serves refugees and

> If every Tennessean were to volunteer for one day a month, we could...
>
> improve the lives of every less-fortunate citizen in Tennessee. The rewards of volunteer work far outweigh the effort. In time, the volunteer comes to truly understand "The Greatest of These is Charity".
>
> —Roland Gray
> Nashville
> Davidson County

neighborhood residents who lack access to mainstream healthcare system. Siloam also is a site for training students and young physicians in primary care of refugees.

Tommy D. Grider
From: Cookeville, Putnam County
Years of Service: 4
Volunteering Highlights:
Trustee — Tennessee Baptist Children's Home
Putnam County Humane Society
Honored with students by Tennessee and US Humane Societies
Honored with students by Tennessee House and Senate
JC Penney Golden Rule Award Nominee
Special Notes: During the last 4 years, Tommy has led students in the Raider TV program at Avery Trace Middle School to produce live telethons to benefit the local Humane Society and Ronald McDonald House.

Rev. Bill Griffith
From: Cleveland, Bradley County
Years of Service: 20
Volunteering Highlights:
Volunteer Chaplain: Cleveland Fire Dept; Police Dept; Rescue Squad; E.M.A.; Sheriff's Dept
Men of Ministry: Director (feeds 450+ families per month)
Crisis Response Ministry: Director (responds to scene of major crisis providing assistance & relief)
Big Brother & Big Sister: worked to pass joint resolution in Congress honoring & supporting program
Emergency Svcs Memorial Wall: coordinator of bulding effort in 99, remembering fallen emergcy svc wkrs
Special Notes: Rev. Bill Griffith is a volunteer and a hero in the truest sense of the word. All of his time and efforts are spent helping others. He reaches out to the sick, homeless, hungry and the heavy-laden. He always does so with a smile, and with intense encouragement.

David Griffith
From: Tullahoma, Coffee County
Years of Service: 19
Volunteering Highlights:
Tullahoma Senior Citizens — Construction of new building
Shriners — Keep Coffee County Beautiful, President, Past ambassador for Tullahoma and Normandy areas
Beautification Committee, City of Tullahoma
Kiwanis — Literacy Council, volunteer of the Year Award
Director, Tullahoma Utility Board
Special Notes: Received *Volunteer of the Year* award from City of Tullahoma Kiwanis.

Debra Grimes
From: Nashville, Davidson County
Years of Service: 9
Volunteering Highlights:
CASA of Davidson County, Board President
Hands On Nashville, Board Member, volunteer
Oasis Center, Inc., Artists for Oasis
United Way of Nashville/Davidson county, VRT
Downtown Rotary

Cathy Griswold
From: Hermitage, Davidson County
Years of Service: 13
Volunteering Highlights:
Boy Scouts of America
Mary Catherine Strobel Volunteer of the Year for Meigs Magnet School
Den Leader Award, Cub Scouter Award, Long rifle Award — Boy Scouts of America
Fund Raising Chair Dodson Elem, & Tulip Grove Elem.;

If every Tennessean were to volunteer for one day a month, we could…

validate in our own hearts the truth of the Biblical precept that it is far better to give than to receive.

—David W. Gregory
Nashville
Davidson County

If every Tennessean were to volunteer for one day a month, we could…

be a catalyst to repair the world, eliminate illiteracy, assist new mothers with child care, form visiting groups for isolated and elderly, be mentors and buddies for troubled youth, work for understanding between new Americans and community, deliver books to the homebound, and beautify our state.

—Shirley Greenfield
Nashville, Davidson County

Tennessee Volunteer Heroes 2001

> *If every Tennessean were to volunteer for one day a month, we could...*
>
> extinguish many of the problems faced by individuals and groups. If Tennesseans would give just one day a month, the need for government intervention in our lives would be lessened and Tennessee would be better for it.
>
> —Tommy D. Grider
> Cookeville, Putnam County

Vol Coord. Meigs Magnet; Band Booster Chair
Youth Sailing Program, Harbor Island Yacht Club
Special Notes: "'Hero' is such a big word, but I do like to mentor the youth I am blessed to serve. It is a joy to watch them bloom into young adults who have self-confidence and purpose in their lives. I believe we are called to help one another when and where we can."

Jennie C. Groce
From: Byrdstown, Pickett County
Years of Service: 50
Volunteering Highlights:
Lions Club
D.A.R.: Murfreesboro; Cookeville as Chaplain
Veterans Administration Hospital, Murfreesboro
Volunteer mission with her church in Venezuela
Volunteers at three hospitals
Special Notes: Jeanne cares for others and wants to serve or love everyone, even the unlovely. She enjoys getting out and being with others. She says she is really the one that is helped.

Mollie E. Gross
From: Johnson City, Washington County
Years of Service: 2
Volunteering Highlights:
Pine Oaks Assisted Living Center
University High School: President 9th Grade Class; President Math Club: Honor student
Suzuki Studies Program, East TN State University
J.C. Penney Golden Rule Award Nomination
First United Methodist Church: UMYF
Johnson City Ballet, Senior Company
Special Notes: Molly is thirteen and has been volunteering at the Pine Oaks Assisted Living Center for two years. Molly assists the staff in motivating residents to get involved in activities. She has a winning attitude and a captivating personality. She helps in a CAN capacity when the need arises — like helping serve drinks and salad during meals in the dining room, helping the confused residents locate their rooms, and assisting them in locating the next activity scheduled. Molly comes to the Center three days a week and stays an average of 3-5 hours at a time. Molly has assisted in a variety of activities at our facility. She has performed flute concerts on special holidays, she danced and taught the Hula at our annual Luau, assisted residents for a variety of craft activities, helps schedules volunteers, helped decorate for parties; assisted in decorating bulletin boards, gotten free tickets to the Johnson City Ballet Company's "The Nutcracker". Molly never has a bad day. She has a neverending smile and a heart of gold to go with it. It is difficult to find an individual as young as Molly who is willing to give as much of herself. She is every parent's dream and the ideal role model for young people everywhere.

Mert Guin
From: Memphis, Shelby County
Years of Service: 17
Volunteering Highlights:
Union Planters Bank: IMPACT Volunteers (Individuals Making Progress and Changing Tomorrow)
J.C. Penney Golden Rule Award Nomination
WKNO, Channel 10: Advisory Board
MIFA Starry Nights: Kiosk Manager
Special Notes: Mert has been a very active member of IMPACT, since 1983. She has devoted most of her volunteer time in 1999 to WKNO Channel 10 and MIFA Starry Nights. Thousands of people in our community enjoy the services and programs provided by these agencies. Mert has a heart for serving others and truly enjoys helping the community.

> *If every Tennessean were to volunteer for one day a month, we could...*
>
> make an overwhelming difference in our communities. "To whom much is given, much is required." For those of us who have been given a great deal, we can make a tremendous difference in the lives of people around us, if we'll give back our time, our resources and our gifts.
>
> —Rev. Bill Griffith
> Cleveland
> Bradley County

Tennessee Volunteer Heroes 2001

Ola Mae Hagewood
From: Cumberland Furnace, Dickson County
Years of Service: 10
Volunteering Highlights:
Mary Catherine Strobel Award Nominee
Senior Citizens
Nursing Homes
Special Notes: Ms. Hagewood is dedicated to what she does and loves helping others. She is 81 years old but you could never tell it. She loves people and being around others. She is dedicated to what she does and loves helping people.

Ruth Thomas Hale
From: Charleston, Bradley County
Years of Service: 50
Volunteering Highlights:
Tennessee 4-H Foundation: Fund Development; Quilt Making; Alumni, Inc.
First Baptist Church
Cleveland Hospital
Museum at Five Points
Special Notes: She is a dynamic, caring individual who leaves everything and everyone she touches greatly improved and enriched. She is a leader, a servant, a mentor, a teacher, a neighbor — a wonderful friend to many.

Annie Laurie Hall
From: Germantown, Shelby County
Years of Service: 36
Volunteering Highlights:
Germantown City Beautification: Chairman
Germantown Horse Show
Germantown Arts Alliance
Suburban and Poplar Estates Garden Clubs

If every Tennessean were to volunteer for one day a month, we could...

do almost anything. I think of mentoring children with single parents, helping the homebound have better lives, lifting up the disadvantaged, being sure that our senior citizens continue to be valued and have a good quality of life. We could help all poor, crippled and disabled adults, lost children, and those who have been led astray.

—David Griffith
Tullahoma, Coffee County

 If every Tennessean were to volunteer for one day a month, we could...

ease the woes of the world.

—Debra Grimes
Nashville
Davidson County

Germantown Methodist Church: Various boards
Special Notes: "I try to volunteer every place that I am needed."

Chuck Hall
From: Hixson, Hamilton County
Years of Service: 21
Volunteering Highlights:
Chattanooga Hamilton County Rescue: Chairman of the Board
Dallas Bay Fire Dept: Chairman of the Board
First Things First: Public Policy Member for Fathering Dads of Tennessee
Friends of the Festival: Past Board Member
Special Notes: He provides positive, compassionate and professional energy to insure that the citizens of Hamilton County will benefit.

Anita Hamblen
From: Nashville, Davidson County
Years of Service: 45
Volunteering Highlights:
St. Henry's Women's Council: past Commity Service Chair
American Red Cross
American Heart Association
Special Notes: Anita's warmth and sense of humor positively affect the patients, staff, visitors and her fellow volunteers.

Tammy Haney
From: Pulaski, Giles County
Volunteering Highlights:
Girl Scouts
Garden Club
Co-publisher of Family Cookbook
First Baptist Church

Tennessee Volunteer Heroes 2001

> If every Tennessean were to volunteer
> for one day a month, we could…
> eliminate illiteracy, hunger in our community, and make the world a much brighter place. Our youth would have the mentors they so desperately need, and the volunteers themselves would find that their lives are enriched and fulfilled in ways that they never expected. We would all be better people if we learned to take the time to help others.
>
> —Cathy Griswold
> Hermitage
> Davidson County

School Volunteer
Special Notes: Tammy is always available to help with any volunteer project that will benefit someone who needs help. She is the most unselfish person we know. She gives 110% in everything she does.

Frances Hanger
From: Winchester, Franklin County
Years of Service: 15
Volunteering Highlights:
Franklin County Literacy Council
Emergency Services for Foster Children
BellSouth Pioneer Volunteers; Partner of the Year Award, chairs various committees and projects
Goshen Cumberland Presbyterian Church Women's Group
Middle Tennessee Camp Bluebird, Adult Cancer Camp
Special Notes: Frances unselfishly gives her time and talents to various organizations throughout her community, including her church. Both young and old respect her and value her friendship. No matter the need, Frances is the first one on site and usually the last one to leave. She gives straight from the heart, and it is felt by all who are privileged to know her.

W. David Hanisco
From: Memphis, Shelby County
Years of Service: 13
Volunteering Highlights:
Lions: Pres District 12L Lions Foundation; Regional Chair District 12: Region 1; Lions Sight Van
United States Coast Guard Auxiliary: Vice Captain Division 8 Eastern; Division Public Affairs Office
Student Volunteers for Optometric Services to Humanity: South and Central American Villages
Memphis In May: Chairman Party Operations; Speakers Committee; Ambassador
Hands On Memphis
Special Notes: David never says "No" when asked to serve, or when he sees a need to serve, especially when it will help the well being of the underprivileged, his country, his city his neighborhood or his church. He unselfishly volunteers many hours, days and funds in these endeavors.

Donna Hardin
From: Bartlett, Shelby County
Years of Service: 15
Volunteering Highlights:
Special Kids and Families, Inc.
Operation Feed
Ellendale School
March of Dimes
American Red Cross
Special Notes: She is a hero for her dedication and selflessness assisting with practically every special event sponsored by Special Kids and Families since its inception.

Lynn Harding
From: Chattanooga, Hamilton County
Years of Service: 11
Volunteering Highlights:
Chattanooga CARES: past President Board of Directors
Y-ME of Chattanooga: Peer Counselor; VP Board of Directors; Chair Education & Outreach Committee
Don Harwell Award from CARES for outstanding service: 1996
CARES Volunteer of the Year: 1998
Junior League Community Service Award: 1998
Special Notes: Lynn Harding is a Tennessee Hero because she continues to make a difference in the lives of people who are burdened with AIDS and breast cancer, two diseases that are killing Tennesseans.

> If every Tennessean were to volunteer
> for one day a month, we could…
> make a difference for our communities and state, improving life for our fellow man in schools, hospitals and nursing homes, living our Christian calling and/or faith. We could help buy needed equipment for hospitals. Our VA Hospital and nursing homes have a special need for visitors as some residents never have a visitor, they are from all over the U.S. and some are far from home.
>
> —Jennie C. Groce
> Byrdstown, Pickett County

Tennessee Volunteer Heroes 2001

Ronald Lee Harmon
From: Nashville, Davidson County
Years of Service: 6
Volunteering Highlights:
Salvation Army, Angel Tree Program
Disaster Relief, 1998 Tornado
Salvation Army, Canteen — fed needy children in the park
Salvation Army; Adopt-A-Family at Christmas
Special Notes: "I do not consider myself to be a hero, only a servant. The ongoing needs of others drives me to volunteer and be of service to the Salvation Army."

Betty Harper
From: Dickson, Dickson County
Years of Service: 3
Volunteering Highlights:
Humane Society of Dickson County
Americn Heart Association
Education Edge
Meals on Wheels
Community Foundation for Dickson County
Special Notes: Betty is a hero because of her dedication to any project she takes on. Betty's compassion and tenacity are unequaled!

John Harris
From: Knoxville, Knox County
Years of Service: 2
Volunteering Highlights:
RSVP Board Member
AmeriCorps Leader Program: Alumni
CAC AmeriCorps Program: Alumni
Lambda Chi Alpha Fraternity
Team VOLS
Special Notes: John is a hero because of his outstanding leadership and service in the CAC AmeriCorps Programs.

If every Tennessean were to volunteer for one day a month, we could…

make our state a model for other areas of the country to admire and imitate. It would improve the lives of many of our fellow Tennesseans!

—Mollie E. Gross
Johnson City
Washington County

If every Tennessean were to volunteer for one day a month, we could…

make a difference in the lives of so many people. It makes you feel good to help someone.

—Ola Mae Hagewood
Cumberland Furnace
Dickson County

He served two full time terms — 1 year with the Urban Agriculture Team and 1 year as an AmeriCorps Leader.

Jan Harvey
From: Germantown, Shelby County
Years of Service: 20
Volunteering Highlights:
Memphis Race for the Cure: started and chaired group registration: co-chaired Race Pledge Program
Reach to Recovery: Chairman "Cash for Cancer"; outreach to newly diagnosed women
Women Helping Other Women (WHOW): mails monthly reminders for support meeting; substitute facilitatior
Memphis Cancer Center Foundation: Co-chair 2000 National Cance Survivor Day Celebration
Baptist East Hospital: volunteer in newborn nursery
Special Notes: "I was chosen for this honor because I have a husband and children who have always supported my volunteer efforts (and usually get drafted into helping), and because I'm fortunate to have the time and the good health to reach out to others."

J. Matthew Hassan
From: Nashville, Davidson County
Years of Service: 2
Volunteering Highlights:
Reconciliation
Special Notes: Hassan is a 3rd year medical student at Vanderbilt University with a schedule that keeps him on campus from 7:30am to 6p, on most weekdays, and studying frequently until midnight. But, he has made time to volunteer with the children of prisoners every Tuesday night. Matthew is dependable and kind, two things the Reconciliation kids really need.

Tennessee Volunteer Heroes 2001

> If every Tennessean were to volunteer for one day a month, we could… probably eliminate juvenile delinquency and help the volunteer have more self esteem. In St. Mark, 10:45 it says we are "not to be ministered unto, but to minister." Serving others has a way of satisfying the soul. It does make a difference.
>
> —Ruth Thomas Hale
> Charleston, Bradley County

David Hassler
From: Byrdstown, Pickett County
Years of Service: 60
Volunteering Highlights:
Hull-York Lakeland Resources Conservation and Development Council, Past President
Pickett County Library, Chairman of the Board of Trustees
Pickett Chamber of Commerce Executive Committee
Abandoned Coal Mine Reclamation Committee, Past Chair
"Certificate of Merit" significant contributions to preservation of historical heritage
Special Notes: Mr. Hassler has demonstrated outstanding community service to allow all residents of Pickett County a better place to live.

Lawrence W. Haws
From: Gray, Washington County
Years of Service: 20
Volunteering Highlights:
American Red Cross of Johnson City/Washington County
Boy Scouts of America
Washington County Emergency Management Agency
Mason
Community Police program
Special Notes: Lawrence volunteers at least 20 hours a week, making our community safer and stronger.

Judith Grigsby Hayes
From: Thompson Station, Williamson County
Volunteering Highlights:
Williamson County Commissioner, Third District
Williamson County/Franklin Chamber of Commerce, Board Member
Williamson County Chair of Tourism
Williamson County Heritage Foundation
Williamson County Historical Society

Marge Heeder
From: Franklin, Williamson County
Years of Service: 40
Volunteering Highlights:
St. Thomas Hospital
Glendale United Methodist Church
Special Notes: Marge has volunteered nearly 20,000 hours over 27 years at St. Thomas Hospital. There are not enough words to express the positive impact she has made helping people in need. She is AWESOME!

Ray Heeder
From: Franklin, Williamson County
Years of Service: 30
Volunteering Highlights:
St. Thomas Hospital
Glendale United Methodist Church
Special Notes: Ray is gentle and kind, two trains greatly needed as a volunteer in a hospital setting. He has given more than 14,000 hours to serve people in need.

Anne Helgeland
From: Nashville, Davidson County
Years of Service: 45
Volunteering Highlights:
TN Commission for National and Community Service: Chair 1994-96
Hands on Nashville: project coordinator for "Hands On Nashville" Day
Volunteer Administrators Network: former president; volunteer service project chair
Elder Care Board: helped set up elder Care Hotline 800 # for nationwide service to caregivers
Special Notes: Anne is a Volunteer Hero because of her outstanding performance and leadership as an RSVP Project Director for Senior Volunteers and leadership as

> If every Tennessean were to volunteer for one day a month, we could…
>
> have a wonderful and beautiful state.
>
> —Annie Laurie Hall
> Germantown, Shelby County

Tennessee Volunteer Heroes 2001

Chair of TN Commission for National and Community Service.

Peggy Hemperly
From: Memphis, Shelby
Volunteering Highlights:
Shelby County Republican Women's Club — 30 years
Shelby County Republican Party — 30 years
Delta Area Agency — 10 years taking care of needy individuals
American Red Cross — 45 years, chairman of all services
School for the Blind — 10 years, taught braille at Jewish community center
Special Notes: Peggy loves helping others. She wants to help people have a better life — to be happier. She is 93 years young and still volunteers all the time!

Fred & Mai Dee Hendricks
From: Bell Buckle, Bedford County
Years of Service: 12
Volunteering Highlights:
Bedford Countians United for a Better Tomorrow (BUFAT)
Food Source, Shelbyville
Gilliland Historical Resource Center
Senior Citizens Center, Shelbyville
Save Our Cumberland Mountains
Special Notes: Fred and Mai Dee are Volunteer Heroes because of their complete unselfishness as a team.

Lorraine Hendricks
From: Sevierville, Sevier County
Years of Service: 17
Volunteering Highlights:
Boys and Girls Club of the Smoky Mountains
Fort Sanders Sevier Medical Center

If every Tennessean were to volunteer for one day a month, we could...

change the world! The friendships, the sharing and the caring as a result of my volunteering have changed my life.

—Anita Hamblen
Nashville, Davidson County

If every Tennessean were to volunteer for one day a month, we could...

improve our communities, our state, and our nation. Our lives should be centered around our church, our families and our communities.

—Tammy Haney
Pulaski
Giles County

Kids Voting of East TN
Health Improvement Council of Sevier County
United Way of Sevier County
Special Notes: Lorraine is currently actively volunteering in 12 not-for-profit organizations. She is on the Board of Directors in 8 of these organizations.

Jerry Herman
From: Madison, Davidson County
Years of Service: 25
Volunteering Highlights:
Tennessee Commission on National and Community Service, Commissioner
Juvenile Court: Foster Care Review Board, Sevier and Davidson Counties
TN & Area 10 Special Olympics, Coach and Coordinator
Sevierville Housing Authority, Commissioner
Community Health Council, Sevier County

Dixie Lee Hill
From: Hornsby, Tennessee
Years of Service: 4
Volunteering Highlights:
Western Mental Health Institute
American Cancer Society Relay For Life
American Red Cross Blood Drive
Western Mental Health Institute "Best All Around" Volunteer, 1999
J.C. Penney Golden Rule Recognition
Special Notes: Dixie definitely has made a great difference with her willingness to help and her ability to accomplish any task she tries. The staff assistance Dixie has given directly affects patient care, helping in the treatment process, thus helping to improve the quality of life and dignity of those she serves. She has provided that contact that is vital to mental patients'

Tennessee Volunteer Heroes 2001

> **If every Tennessean were to volunteer for one day a month, we could...**
>
> give a positive reinforcement to the homeless, the elderly, and youth. We could develop building blocks of hope for others who are needing encouragement, food, shelter or a friend.
>
> —Frances Hanger
> Winchester, Franklin County

care and treatment through her encouragement and participation in the patient parties she helped to plan and/or initiate. During the 4 years that Dixie has volunteered, her services have touched many of our 220+ psychiatric patients and nearly all of our 550 staff members. Staff in many of the areas learned who she is this past year because of her visibility and involvement. Dixie is a positive influence to others in her community and at her high school in Selmer as she continues to be an advocate for Western, the mentally ill, and volunteering.

Marian J. Himmelreich
From: Germantown, Shelby County
Years of Service: 28
Volunteering Highlights:
Germantown Symphony Orchestra: performer and fundraiser
Memphis Zoo: docent and animal presenter
YWCA: Swim teacher and board member
American Red Cross
American Heart Association
Special Notes: Marian has been first violinist in the Germantown Orchestra for 25 years. She is also busy as den mother, Montessori art teacher, water safety and CPR instructor, docent for the Memphis Zoo. Marian swam across the Mississippi River for a YMCA fundraiser.

Charlie Hines
From: Memphis, Shelby County
Years of Service: 25
Volunteering Highlights:
Memphis Literacy Council
Metro Memphis Club N.ANBPW
Memphis City Schools, Whitney elementary
Memphis Area Day Care Centers
Special Notes: Charlie provides at his own expense his time, ideas, concerns and strengths to the groups or organizations with which he is involved.

Joni Hite
From: Greeneville, Greene County
Years of Service: 1
Volunteering Highlights:
4-H
Church Bible Bowl, nursery worker
Library worker at Chuckey Elementary
Round Robin member and peer tutor
Special Notes: Joni volunteered 244 hours at Woodhaven Child Care Center during the summer. She helped the staff care for and teach children between the ages of six months and five years. She voluntarily prepared and carried out lesson plans for the one year old children's class. During the school year, Joni volunteers as a peer tutor at Chuckey Elementary School where she is a student. Joni is 13 years old!

Debbie Hitt
From: White House, Sumner County
Years of Service: 8
Volunteering Highlights:
Girl Scouts of America
White House Santa's Breakfast
Temple Baptist Church: Sunday School; Hostess Committee
Special Notes: Debbie is a Volunteer Hero because of her commitment to care of young children with disabilities and their families.

> **If every Tennessean were to volunteer for one day a month, we could...**
>
> inform the public in safety practices to save lives, and prevent serious injury and property loss. We could serve our community and make life more pleasant for everyone, thereby repaying our world for our fortunes of life, and saving millions of dollars for our country, state, local government and community.
>
> —W. David Hanisco
> Memphis, Shelby County

Tennessee Volunteer Heroes 2001

Richard T. Hoffman, Jr.
From: Memphis, Shelby County
Years of Service: 5
Volunteering Highlights:
Memphis In May: Chairman 2000
Wonders International Cultural Series: Docent and Speakers Bureau
Memphis Brooks Museum of Art: Special Events Volunteer
Memphis Overton Park Zoo: Zoo Rendezvous Volunteer
WKNO Public Radio: Membership Pledge Volunteer
Special Notes: He assumed chairmanship of the 2000 Memphis In May World Championship Barbecue Contest, appointed a new steering committee, and organized a successful contest.

Cherrie Holden
From: Germantown, Shelby County
Years of Service: 11
Volunteering Highlights:
Tennessee Court of the Judiciary Judge
Tennessee State Board of Education: District 7 Representative
National Association of Recording Arts & Sciences, Memphis Chapter: Board Member & Secretary/Treasurer
O'Landa Draper Ministries, Inc.: Founding Board Member
Shelby County Republican Party: campaign volunteer; Candidate Recruitment Committee; Website Editor
Special Notes: "Germantown has long encouraged volunteerism among its citizens. I am one of many that willingly give their time to the betterment of their community."

Liz Holden
From: Rockwood, Roane County
Years of Service: 25
Volunteering Highlights:

> If every Tennessean were to volunteer for one day a month, we could...
>
> # improve life for a lot of well-deserving people.
>
> —Donna Hardin
> Bartlett
> Shelby County

> If every Tennessean were to volunteer for one day a month, we could...
>
> make it possible for people to realize that AIDS threatens not just a few but all of us, or we could make it possible for women to understand how important it is to take responsibility for our health and protect ourselves against the ravages of breast cancer.
>
> —Lynn Harding
> Chattanooga, Hamilton County

Save Our Cumberland Mountains
Trustee at Volunteer Fire Department
Trustee at Westal Baptist Church
BellSouth Pioneer Volunteers, President Roane-Cumberland Life Member Club
Life Member of the Year, BellSouth Pioneer Volunteers
Special Notes: Liz is a true leader and organizer. She is sincere, an inspiration and a wonderful example of what volunteering is all about.

Virginia Holland
From: Waverly, Humphreys County
Years of Service: 17
Volunteering Highlights:
Chamber of Commerce Outstanding Volunteer Award
Waverly Health Care Honor Award and Sunshine Award
American Heart Outstanding Award
St. Jude Honors Award and Plaque
Humphreys County Museum Volunteer Award
Special Notes: "I am proud to be a volunteer and help as many people as I have. I enjoy every day of it. The people help me as much as I help them."

Katie Hollis
From: Nashville, Davidson County
Years of Service: 47
Volunteering Highlights:
American Red Cross
Veterans Administration Medical Center
Southern Hills Medical Center
Elementary Schools
Special Notes: Katie is a Volunteer Hero because of her long and faithful service as a volunteer throughout her life in several different localities and as a blood donor, Blood Center Volunteer and hospital volunteer. She is always available for new and special assignments.

> If every Tennessean were to volunteer for one day a month, we could... teach a child to feed himself or herself by learning a trade. We could give confidence back to battered women. We could share God's love.
>
> —Ronald Lee Harmon
> Nashville
> Davidson County

Lucy Hollis
From: Tullahoma, Coffee County
Years of Service: 33
Volunteering Highlights:
Tullahoma Regional Fine Arts Center
Tennessee Arts Commission
Tennessee Federation of Women's Clubs
Tullahoma Chamber of Commerce
Tennessee Art Education Association
Special Notes: Lucy came here in the late 1960's as a young art teacher. Tullahoma would have no Fine Arts Center without Lucy. She has put Tullahoma on the map for the arts with all she has done to teach, bring art shows and art trains here and being a state and national leader for the arts.

Connie Hollman
From: Lawrenceburg, Lawrence County
Years of Service: 9
Volunteering Highlights:
Blue Grass Regional Library, Board Member
Lawrence County Library Association, Treasurer
Lawrence County Retired Teachers, Treasurer
Tennessee Ornithological Society, Field Counter
Meals-On-Wheels Volunteer
Special Notes: Whether counting birds at daybreak or delivering meals in the pouring rain, Connie Hollman gives tirelessly of her time and energy. She truly exemplifies the Tennessee Volunteer spirit.

Halden A. Hooper, M.D.
From: Gallatin, Sumner County
Years of Service: 40
Volunteering Highlights:
American Red Cross: Blood Regional Board; various leadership roles
Gallatin Health Association
Volunteer State Community College
Sumner County Medical Society
Sumner Foundation: Vice-President
Special Notes: Dr. Hooper deserves to be called a "Volunteer Hero" because of a lifetime of serving others. He has pioneered in many health service areas. No task is too menial. Even his many awards are dwarfed by his modesty.

Wanda Hooper
From: Nashville, Davidson County
Years of Service: 30
Volunteering Highlights:
St. Thomas Hospital Advocates
American Heart Association
United Way of Middle Tennessee
Children's Hospital at Vanderbilt University Hospital
Tennessee Nurses Association
Special Notes: Wanda personifies volunteerism. She organizes events and communities with ease and grace. Tennessee is fortunate to have her making a difference in our great state.

Jeffrey T. Horner
From: Greeneville, Greene County
Years of Service: 3
Volunteering Highlights:
Adult Basic Education
UETHDA
J.C. Penney Golden Rule Award Nomination
National Park Service
Tusculum College
Walters State Community College
Special Notes: Jeff's influence does not stop in the classroom — he is very active in the community. Early in

> If every Tennessean were to volunteer for one day a month, we could... be better role models for our children. If we as parents, teachers and community leaders could set strong examples of responsibility and duty to our younger generations, we could systematically address social and cultural problems.
>
> —Betty Harper
> Dickson, Dickson County

Tennessee Volunteer Heroes 2001

the semester, students are encouraged to participate in various service learning activities. Mr. Horner is great at generating support for a worthy cause. These activities are presented not merely as ways to add to a resume, but as fun activities that enrich lives in two directions. His college students benefit in that they learn from the activities, build frinedships, and have a good time together. The school children whom they serve are exposed to learning in ways that they probably have not been before, and more likely would not have been if not for the individual behind these projects: Jeff.

Chaplain Joe. W. Horton, Sr.
From: Bolivar, Hardeman County
Years of Service: 10
Volunteering Highlights:
The Hardeman County Ministers Fellowship Association: Treasurer
West TN Central District Association (Pastor/Layman Conference): Officer
Hardeman County Chaplains' Association: President
Hardeman County Corrections Corporation of America: Spiritual Coordinator
Hardeman County Literacy Council: Future Directions Membership Chairman
Special Notes: "I was led to 'Retire' to a full-time Ministry capacity, to devote all my time to preaching the 'Good News of Salvation' and working in many capacities for the betterment of mankind. My personal dream is to go wherever the Lord leads me!"

Housing Services Corps
From: Robbins, Scott and Morgan Counties
Years of Service: 5
Volunteering Highlights:
Habitat for Humanity: houses for 107 families; 153 families attended homeowner course
75 miles of trail maintenance
Rehabilitated a local women's shelter
600 students completed a budgeting class
Strorage building for a local food pantry
Special Notes: "I am committed to providing the highest quality of life for families in Scott and Morgan Counties."

H.G. "Sonny" Hunter, Jr.
From: Kingston, Roane County
Years of Service: 10
Volunteering Highlights:
East Tennessee Regional Leadership Association, Class of 2000
Roane County American Heart Association, Board
American Cancer Society
United Way
March of Dimes
Special Notes: Sonny serves many community-oriented groups, clubs and individuals. Sonny qualifies because he contributes to our community!

Catherine A. Hurdle
From: Memphis, Shelby County
Years of Service: 5
Volunteering Highlights:
BellSouth Pioneer Volunteers: Volunteer of the Year
Race for the Cure
Habitat for Humanity
Salvation Army Angel Tree
Junior Achievement
Special Notes: Catherine is one of the most dedicated volunteers ever! Simply ask her to help and she's there. She's a wonderfully kind and compassionate person.

> *If every Tennessean were to volunteer for one day a month, we could...*
> teach younger citizens the values of volunteerism in changing the quality of life for every citizen in towns, counties, states and countries. We could improve the morality of those younger people who have had no moral guidance from irresponsible parents or peers. We could change the living conditions of the less fortunate. We could improve the environmental quality of our country. We could attain a degree of life that man has only dreamed of.
>
> —David Hassler
> Byrdstown
> Pickett County

> *If every Tennessean were to volunteer for one day a month, we could...*
> build better communities, strengthen the skills of our schoolchildren, clean our environment, and, most importantly, help our neighbors... through service in our churches, community centers and local government organizations.
>
> —John Harris
> Knoxville, Knox County

Tennessee Volunteer Heroes 2001

> If every Tennessean were to volunteer for one day a month, we could...
>
> be very proud that we are holding true to our heritage of being the "Volunteer" state. There would be less hunger, fewer homeless people, a cleaner state and environment, and a greater feeling of love and self-worth with much less loneliness. Tennessee is great and with all of us trying together, it could only be better.
>
> —Judith Grigsby Hayes
> Thompson Station, Williamson County

Teresa Ivey
From: Maryville
Years of Service: 2
Volunteering Highlights:
Maryville Housing Authority
Habitat for Humanity
J.C. Penney Golden Rule Recognition
Special Notes: Teresa has performed outstanding volunteer service for the residents at Maryville Housing Authority. She is well respected by staff and residents in her community. Many residents confide in her with their problems and challenges and look to her for encouragement.

Mayor Cherry Jackson
From: Thompson Station, Williamson County
Volunteering Highlights:
Thompson Station Community Association
Thompson Station Arts and Crafts Festival: Chair
Reconstruction of Thompson Station's Depot
Thompson Station Volunteer Library
Thompson Station Senior Citizens
Special Notes: Acting as the Mayor of Thompson Station is a non-paying job. Cherry loves her community and loves to help other people. She is interested in making Thompson Station a better place for all residents.

Shirley Jackson
From: Bartlett, Shelby County
Years of Service: 5
Volunteering Highlights:
J.C. Penney Golden Rule Award Nomination
Truancy Prevention Service of Juvenile Court
Special Notes: Shirley Jackson serves as a commissioned volunteer Truant Officer for the Juvenile Court of Memphis and Shelby County. Truant officers visit the homes of truant children who have been referred to the Court by the schools for chronic unexcused absences. This year, Shirley supervised the efforts of truant officers who have touched the lives of over 750 students. Because truancy is regarded as the gateway offense to criminal behavior, the successful impact of Ms. Jackson and her team of truant officers is measured by the high percentage of children who have returned to regular school attendance. Because of the guidance and intervention by the truant officers, these children have been successfully turned away from a life of crime.

Martha Jamison
From: Memphis, Shelby County
Years of Service: 25
Volunteering Highlights:
AmeriCorps, Memphis
Head Start, Chulahoma, MS
CPO Office, Fort Riley, Kansas
Memphis City Schools
CYF Director, Shady Grove CME Shurch
Special Notes: Martha is a Volunteer Hero because of her willingness to cooperate, her ability to lead and follow and her positive attitude. She is honest and dependable, trustworthy, considerate and intelligent.

Jack Jennings
From: Tullahoma, Coffee County
Years of Service: 20
Volunteering Highlights:
Coffee County Leadership in Progress
Tennessee's Backroads Heritage, Inc.
Tullahoma Celtic Music Fest
Historic Preservation Society of Tullahoma, Inc.
Tullahoma Design Shop, writing long term strategic plan
Special Notes: Jack has donated skills, knowledge, experience and hundreds of hours in the last 10 years

> If every Tennessean were to volunteer for one day a month, we could...
>
> build a model of neighbor helping neighbor that would cause the world to beat a path to our door.
>
> —Anne Helgeland
> Nashville
> Davidson County

Tennessee Volunteer Heroes 2001

to more than a dozen groups in Coffee County to help others succeed, make a difference, and enhance the quality of life in the county. Jack is determined to leave Coffee County better than it was when he moved back.

Becca Jensen
From: Nashville, Davidson County
Years of Service: 3
Volunteering Highlights:
Oasis Center, Peer Education Program and Youth Member of Oasis Board of Directors
Nashville Youth Pulse: Volunteer; Project Coordinator; TN Planning Team Pulse Day, 1998, 1999, 2000
Mayor's Youth Council
Special Notes: Becca has spent a great deal of her high school years volunteering in many different cpacities. She has raised the bar for youth participation in community development.

John Sevier Middle School
From: Kingsport, Sullivan County
Years of Service: 7
Volunteering Highlights:
Boys & Girls Club
J.C. Penney Golden Rule Award Nomination
Salvation Army
Safe House
Small Miracles Therapeutic
Hunger First
Special Notes: The students and staff of John Sevier Middle School have consistently demonstrated a strong commitment to community service and service learning projects. Their philosophy is based upon the assumption that students must learn how to be "givers" as well as receivers. One of the goals of the John Sevier Middle School is to become a "community" of learners and to accept the challenges and responsibilities associated with developing maturity and the realization that each individual can change the world one deed at a time. Middle School students are at a very impressionable stage in their lives. It is our belief that the actions of these students and staff members are exemplary and could serve as an excellent model for other schools, organizations and communities.

> If every Tennessean were to volunteer for one day a month, we could…
>
> # eliminate hunger in Tennessee.
>
> —Fred & Mai Dee Hendricks
> Bell Buckle, Bedford County

Carol Johnson
From: Germantown, Shelby County
Years of Service: 30
Volunteering Highlights:
St. George's Episcopal Church
Farmington Elementary School
Farmington PTA
Kappa Delta Pi, International Honor Society in Education
Master's Degree in Special Education
Special Notes: "I believe that God has given each of us gifts and talents to use in service to others in order to make this world a better place. I try to apply this belief to my life and do the best that I can with what I have been given."

Judy Johnson
From: Smyrna, Rutherford County
Years of Service: 15
Volunteering Highlights:
Crisis Intervention Center, Volunteer
Hospice of Murfreesboro: Co-Facilitator of grief support group; weekly patient care
Sewanee Learning Disability Center: past teacher art classes, fundraising, youth activities
Baptist Hospital: developed a children's program

> If every Tennessean were to volunteer for one day a month, we could…
>
> # make such a difference in this world and we could help make people so much happier. It makes a person a better person by volunteering.
>
> —Peggy Hemperly
> Memphis
> Shelby County

> If every Tennessean were to volunteer for one day a month, we could... begin to build the bridge between the Tennessee in our eyes, and the Tennessee in our hearts. Volunteers are critical in helping us turn attention from our problems to the solutions.
>
> —Jerry Herman
> Madison, Davidson County

United Way: served on the Promoting Health and Healing Council
Special Notes: Judy's selfless dedication positive attitude and commitment are just three of her special, heroic qualities. She has done an enormous amount of work to help better our surrounding communities. She is everything anyone would ever want to have in a volunteer. She has touched a countless number of lives and keeps on doing so every day.

Michele Johnson
From: Nashville, Davidson County
Years of Service: 21
Volunteering Highlights:
Tennessee Justice Center, co-founder and staff attorney
Renewal House
Tennessee Voices for Children: Board Member; Policy Committee Chair
High Hopes Therapeutic School: Past Board Member
Family Voices of Tennessee: Past Advisory Board Member

Brenda Joines
From: Maryville, Blount County
Years of Service: 11
Volunteering Highlights:
BellSouth Pioneer Volunteers, President Smoky Mtn. Council
Junior Achievement, East Tennessee
American Diabetes of East Tennessee
Coach, Challengers — (Little League Baseball Team for handicapped children)
Pioneer of the Year, BellSouth Pioneer Volunteers
Special Notes: Brenda lives the values of volunteerism. She is dedicated and enthusiastic with all in which she is involved, and especially enjoys working with senior citizens.

Ivan R. Jones
From: Cookeville, Putnam County
Years of Service: 2
Volunteering Highlights:
Lazarus House Hospice: 1999 Volunteer of the Year
Celebration of Life Reception
J.C. Penney Golden Rule Award Nomination
Photographer for Annual 5K Run
Boot at County Fair
Special Notes: Lazarus House Hospice cares for patients who have six months or less to live. Volunteers are trained to provide direct support to these patients and their families. Ivan came to Lazarus House asking to serve. After his training, he made his time available to provide the support needed by his patients. Ivan is a volunteer who works with the caregiver more than the patient. His task is never-ending because he continues to support the caregivers after the initial circumstances that brought them together. His special kind of caring is the continuing and tireless effort that sustains meaningful life at the time when people need it most.

Jonathan M. Jones
Special Notes: Special recognition from the Governor and First Lady of Tennessee for excellence in volunteer service.

Virginia Jones
From: Nashville, Davidson County
Volunteering Highlights:
St. Thomas Hospital
Special Notes: Virginia works a difficult volunteer shift at St. Thomas Gift Shop. Her commitment is fantastic.

> If every Tennessean were to volunteer for one day a month, we could... build a better society. As expressed by the poet Edwin Markham: "Why build these cities glorious if man unbuilded goes? In vain we build the world, unless the builder also grows."
>
> —Marian J. Himmelreich
> Germantown, Shelby County

Wanda Jones
From: Germantown, Shelby County
Years of Service: 9
Volunteering Highlights:
The Village Toymaker
Germantown Presbyterian Church
Methodist Hospital, Germantown
Special Notes: "It is the volunteer's pleasure to be helpful."

Molly Kaplan
From: St. Louis
Years of Service: 7
Volunteering Highlights:
Special Olympics
Harpeth Hall School
Community Service Senior Award
Cum Laude Award
Presidents Student Service Award
Special Notes: Molly is a leader of volunteerism at school, in her synagogue and in the community. She is a very compassionate young woman, quick to identify community needs and implement an appropriate solution. She quietly plans volunteer projects and programs, and enthusiastically recruits her peers to join in her volunteer efforts.

Lorraine Kaufman
From: Memphis, Shelby County
Years of Service: 8
Volunteering Highlights:
President of the Board, Senior Leaders, Inc.
Advisory Council for the Delta Area Agency on Aging
5 year advocate for the funding of community-based services to help seniors remain at home
Founders of the Senior Link Hotline

If every Tennessean were to volunteer for one day a month, we could...

provide more services and care to the needy people and/or organizations of our state. We could also provide extra help in the classrooms of poor school systems.

—Charlie Hines
Memphis, Shelby County

 If every Tennessean were to volunteer for one day a month, we could...

improve the lives and touch the hearts of people. We could make our state a better place to live for present and future generations.

—Joni Hite
Greeneville, Greene County

Board Member of neighborhood organization
Special Notes: Lorraine has been a lifelong volunteer utilizing her 70+ years of experience to set in motion an organization that makes it possible for seniors to live their lives to the fullest.

Don E. Keeble
From: Vonore, Monroe County
Years of Service: 26
Volunteering Highlights:
American Red Cross, Monroe County, Chairperson
Boys and Girls Clubs
State 4-H council
United Way, Monroe County, Board of Directors
Fort Loudon Historic Association
Special Notes: Mr. Keeble exemplifies giving back to the community from which he's received so much. He is a native of Tennessee. He not only leads but works in the nuts and bolts of each task.

Helen Kelley
From: Chattanooga, Hamilton County
Years of Service: 41
Volunteering Highlights:
READ of Chattanooga
Senior Neighbors; RSVP and RAPP programs
Foster Grandparent Program assisting special needs children
Intergenerational Book Club
Special Notes: Ms. Helen Kelley, at age 80, has graciously given her time, talents and heart to young and old in our community most of her adult life and is still going strong!

Tennessee Volunteer Heroes 2001

> If every Tennessean were to volunteer for one day a month, we could...
>
> ## make a difference, maybe not every time, but like ripples on a pond that keep spreading.
>
> —Debbie Hitt
> White House
> Sumner County

June Kendall
From: Bartlett, Shelby County
Years of Service: 20
Volunteering Highlights:
J.C. Penney Golden Rule Award Nomination
Lifeblood, MSRBC
Special Notes: Ms. Kendall's service has affected hundreds of people in our community. Her own blood donations alone have helped as many as 210 people. Because of her, 88 more people donated blood than have done so before, which affects 264 lives. The other volunteer activities she gives to Lifeblood are not so easily quantified, but she is definitely responsible for several hundred more lives being saved.

Paul Kennedy
From: Nashville, Davidson County
Years of Service: 6
Volunteering Highlights:
Crieve Hall Church of Christ
Nashville School of Preaching and Biblical and Studies
Restoration Radio Network
American Red Cross
Special Notes: Paul has overcome many challenges and obstacles and yet he is eager to do all he can. He rarely says no and can always be counted on to do what he has committed to.

Randall Killman
From: Celina, Clay County
Years of Service: 5
Volunteering Highlights:
Clay County Industrial Board Director
Clay County Partnership, Board Member
Celina Lion's Club, President
Leadership of Upper Cumberland

Rock Springs Church of Christ
Special Notes: He volunteers his time on a daily basis helping to recruit new industry to our area. Helping to promote our county and providing a better place for our children to grow up is a major goal of his.

Rita Kittrell
From: Charlotte, Dickson County
Years of Service: 13
Volunteering Highlights:
The Renaissance Center — Ambassador of Year
Musician for St. Christopher's Church for 13 years
Crisis Pregnancy Center
March of Dimes
American Heart Association
Special Notes: Rita's commitment to church, community, and quality of life in Tennessee qualifies her as a Volunteer Hero.

Eva L. Knabb
From: Chattanooga, Hamilton County
Years of Service: 5
Volunteering Highlights:
American Red Cross Coordinator of Health Services, national level
Served in Jackson, TN tornado; Putnam County; Hamilton County; Puerto Rico; Oklahoma
Raises a granddaughter alone
Teaches Community Disaster Education in elementary schools
Does casework follow-up for health needs of disaster clients
Special Notes: As a registered nurse, Eva volunteers in the American Red Cross Disaster Health Services locally, statewide, and nationally. She serves on our Disaster Action Team remaining on call for local disasters one week per month. She is an extremely caring individual who never hesitates to extend herself in the service to others.

> If every Tennessean were to volunteer for one day a month, we could...
>
> ## raise enough money and/or construct a sufficient number of single family houses to provide safe, new, owner-occupied homes for a significant number of hard working, low income families across the State.
>
> —Richard T. Hoffman, Jr.
> Memphis
> Shelby County

Tennessee Volunteer Heroes 2001

Joe Knight
From: Arlington, Shelby County
Years of Service: 1
Volunteering Highlights:
J.C. Penney Golden Rule Award Nomination
Metropolitan Inter-Faith Association (MIFA)
Special Notes: Mr. Knight worked almost every day for at least 3 hours. On days he wasn't scheduled to work, he would call in to make sure shifts were covered and offer his time and service. Sometimes he would grace us with his presence without calling only to find himself useful in some form or fashion. He has a positive effect on clients and on other volunteers because of his smile and cheerful spirit.

Kent E. Koederitz
From: Johnson City, Washington County
Years of Service: 11
Volunteering Highlights:
Johnson City Hazardous Materials Response Team, Chief
Instructor for Hazardous Materials, Fire and Rescue Response
Local Emergency Planning Committee, Washington County, Chairman
J.C. Penney Golden Rule Award Nomination
Johnson City School system
Boy Scouts of America; Adult Assistant
Special Notes: "I don't consider myself a Tennessee Volunteer Hero. I am honored to be considered for inclusion with this group. I perform the duties as Hazardous Materials Response Team Chief. I use my skills in fire rescue to fulfill a need of the region."

> If every Tennessean were to volunteer for one day a month, we could...
> renew the spirit of the giving of one's self to others that belonged to our forefathers— the same pioneering spirit that led to our state being known as "The Volunteer State." Our families, our communities, our cities, our counties and our state would be strengthened far beyond any state in the nation due to a renewed sense of neighborly love.
>
> —Cherrie Holden
> Germantown
> Shelby County

> If every Tennessean were to volunteer for one day a month, we could...
> **wipe out illiteracy, thereby guaranteeing the basic needs for each citizen— food, clothing and shelter.**
>
> —Liz Holden
> Rockwood
> Roane County

Larry Kuka
From: Harrison, Hamilton County
Years of Service: 28
Volunteering Highlights:
Church of Jesus Christ of Later Day Saints: Branch President; Teacher
Boy Scouts of America: Scoutmaster; Explorer Post Advisor
Big Brothers and Big Sisters of Chattanooga: Activity Chair
Hamilton County Sheriff Department: Reserve Officer Patrol and Special Events
Republican Party
Special Notes: "I have tried to serve others in my business and personal life and will continue to do so."

Nickie Louise Lancaster
From: Hermitage, Davidson County
Years of Service: 30
Volunteering Highlights:
American Red Cross
Easter Seals of Tennessee
Polio Heroes and International Polio Network
Catholic Church — St. Mary's of Seven Sorrows
School Nursing and Boy Scouts
Special Notes: Nickie is a Volunteer Hero because of her lifetime of volunteering in the fields of youth development, safety services, and health education programs with local and national recognition. She has done all this in spite of being a polio survivor.

Mary B. Lanier
Special Notes: Special recognition from the Governor and First Lady of Tennessee for excellence in volunteer service.

> If every Tennessean were to volunteer for one day a month, we could...
>
> we could take care of most problems, and each volunteer would have a good feeling. We would all be better off.
>
> —Katie Hollis
> Nashville, Davidson County

Reneé LaRose
From: College Grove, Williamson County
Years of Service: 8
Volunteering Highlights:
1995 MFA — in painting at Vermont College, Vermont
Salvation Army Stepping Stones Park co-creator, designer, project coordinator and volunteer
Visual Arts Alliance of Nashville, Board Member
Taught painting, drawing and art appreciation at MTSU and Watkins Art Institute
Artist in collection of Metro Nash Airpt, Bridgestone, Trans-Financial Corp, Warner Reprise Records
Special Notes: Renee's generosity and vision in helping to provide a place of spiritual sanctuary and beauty for those whose lives are torn by domestic violence and poverty qualifies her as a true Tennessee Volunteer Hero. Working with fellow Nashville artist Sherry Hunter, she conceived the idea of Stepping Stones Park at the Salvation Army Area Command Transitional Housing facility. Through the gift of her considerable creative talent and the generous donation of her time, she helped create this small park completely surrounded by a wall inlaid with ceramic tile designs — designs placed there lovingly by thousands of volunteers from Nashville and across the country. The park serves as a place of beauty and peace where those in the Salvation Army Transitional Housing Program can come together in fellowship or a place where they can retreat alone to pray, dream or plan. It is an oasis of peace and beauty in an inner city neighborhood. Renee has given thousands of hours of time over the last eight years to plan, raise funds for the project, and work along side, instruct and guide the volunteers who have helped create the park's beautiful mosaic wall. Her insight into the spiritual and emotional needs of those caught in this cycle and her desire to meet that need in a unique and personal way has had an unexpected and very profound result. In a setting where basic human needs such as food, clothing and shelter are often so urgent and obvious, the visual impact of the beautiful mosaic wall and Renee's personal testimony to each group of volunteers who have worked on the project have awakened thousands of volunteers over the past eight years to hidden spiritual and emotional needs of those living in poverty. The participation of these volunteers has helped to expand the awareness of the plight of the homeless and those caught in domestic violence and the ways the community can help change their lives. The gift of her creative talent to offer consolation and beauty to those in crisis in a unique and concrete way qualifies her as a true Volunteer Hero.

John Lavecchia
From: Memphis, Shelby County
Years of Service: 2
Volunteering Highlights:
URICO
Outstanding Young Man of America, 1970
Memphis Jaycees Outstanding Young Educator, 1970
J.C. Penney Golden Rule Award Nomination
Christian Brothers High School Hall of Fame Inductee, 1984
Who's Who in Tennessee Distinguished Service Award, 1991
Special Notes: John assists the maintenance and social services staff of Estival Communities, a transitional housing program for homeless families. John understands it is not enough to provide shelter. When the staff might not have time to provide small touches like pictures or placemats, John takes the time to make the apartment feel like home. It is impossible to describe the incredible impact this gesture has for a family who has not had a home of their own for some time.

> If every Tennessean were to volunteer for one day a month, we could...
>
> become the most beautiful place in the world. We know this is God's country, and volunteers are needed to care for what our ancestors built, and to preserve the past and nurture the future for our children.
>
> —Lucy Hollis
> Tullahoma
> Coffee County

Tennessee Volunteer Heroes 2001

Barbara Lawson
From: Greeneville, Greene County
Years of Service: 30
Volunteering Highlights:
Greene County Partnership's Youth Community Action Team
J.C. Penney Golden Rule Award Nomination
Youth Council and Youth Leadership Program
Youth Leadership Program
Special Notes: Barbara and her son Lennie agreed to chair the Youth CAT. More than 25 volunteers signed up to work with Barbara. This exciting group has truly made a difference regarding youth in our community. Barbara also took on the responsibility of the Youth Council, comprised of students from area high schools who participate in community service projects. A few projects introduced by Barbara included assisting with Thanksgiving dinners throughout the community, ringing bells for Salvation Army, helping residents at Morningside decorate for Christmas, and serving hot chocolate at "Christmas in the Park." Barbara continues to work with the Youth CAT monthly, work with the Youth Council on numerous service projects and meet with them once a month on Saturdays, as well as direct the Youth Leadership Program. Her love and concern for the youth in our community is never ending.

Leadership Putnam BBQ Team
From: Cookeville, Putnam County
Years of Service: 5
Volunteering Highlights:
Little League: pit crew prepared 1,000 hamburgers for sale at a fundraiser
Monterey High School, Project Graduation: pit crew prepared barbecue chicken and pork for J.C. Penney Golden Rule Award Nomination fundraiser
Habitat for Humanity: pit crew prepared many gallons of gumbo for "Gumbo Cookin on the Square"
YMCA soccer teams: pit crew prepared Boston Butts at 3 different times
Citizens Police Academy: pit crew prepared ribs for each graduating class
Special Notes: For many years, the Leadership Putnam Alumni Association has participated in the Cookeville Cook-off. The reputation of the "Pit Crew" as excellent BBQ cooks and community volunteers has led to invitations from many other organizations to raise money by preparing BBQ for sale at their fundraising events.

Pat Lebkuecher
From: Hendersonville, Sumner County
Volunteering Highlights:
American Red Cross: Disaster Action Team Captain; National Disaster Volunteer
Rotary: Medical Mission to Guatemala; Word Community Service Chair
Sumner Literacy Council
American Cancer Society: Relay for Life
Special Notes: Mrs. Lebkuecher is busy everyday working to make the disaster program work here in Nashville. She is on committees to help recruit and teach Red Cross volunteers. She works and is available for us to call day or night to help disaster victims.

Rip Lebkuecher
From: Hendersonville, Sumner County
Years of Service: 10
Volunteering Highlights:
American Red Cross Disaster Action Team Captain
American Red Cross National Response Disaster Volunteers
Volunteer State Community Foundation
American Cancer Society: Relay for Life
Literacy Council of Sumner County, Hendersonville

> If every Tennessean were to volunteer for one day a month, we could... change the face of Tennessee by: cleaning up trash on our highways; offering love and caring to our youngest, oldest and disabled citizens; building affordable homes for the poor; teaching the adult illiterate to read; extending a helping hand to the addicted; educating youth on dangers of drugs, alcohol, and unprotected sex; seeking a gentler treatment of our environment; and a multitude of similar projects.
>
> —Halden A. Hooper
> Gallatin
> Sumner County

> If every Tennessean were to volunteer for one day a month, we could... relieve not only the pain and suffering of many Tennesseans, but also the loneliness that many of our aged and physically challenged citizens feel. Equally important, we could set an example of assistance that future citizens of Tennessee could emulate and thus guarantee the continuation of caring and service above self.
>
> —Connie Hollman
> Lawrenceburg, Lawrence County

Tennessee Volunteer Heroes 2001

> If every Tennessean were to volunteer for one day a month, we could... better resolve a lot of issues that plague our communities and help make Tennessee a happier and better place to live. We could also make a lot of friends and form lasting relationships that would serve to perpetuate hope and the volunteer spirit.
>
> —Wanda Hooper
> Nashville, Davidson County

Special Notes: Rip Lebkuecher works to build the Disaster Action Teams in Nashville. He studies, teaches and mentors other volunteers to reach their potential, which is building a cycle of success at the American Red Cross in Nashville.

Paul LeBlanc
From: Cordova, Shelby County
Years of Service: 10
Volunteering Highlights:
Kate Bond Elementary School Volunteer
Memphis Belle Association
J.C. Penney Golden Rule Award Winner
March of Dimes
Naval Support Facility- Millington, Retired Affairs Office
Special Notes: This father of 10 and grandfather volunteers 2 days each week in the Kate Bond library. Faithfully, every Monday and Friday, he assists our librarian in checking books in and out to the students. He has become quite adept at library skills such as shelving books, cleaning them, and processing newly received books. He learned to operate 2 different computer systems as well as the Dewey Classification System for library books. He's served as a test proctor during achievement test week, works directly with students, provides a smile and pleasant conversation to those that need a friend, and gives a stern look when it is needed. He's pleasant and social with the staff, and has a marvelous sense of humor that just brightens everyone's day. We appreciate all Mr. LeBlanc does for our students and our staff, when he could be home enjoying his retirement. We are grateful for the hours of dedication he has provided to our school and would be thoroughly lost if he ever missed a day. But more importantly, we would miss him, Mr. LeBlanc the person, not just what he contributes to our school. He is a part of our Kate Bond family.

Leslie N. Lee
From: Memphis, Shelby County
Years of Service: 15
Volunteering Highlights:
Memphis City Schools, Adopt-A-School Program
Baptist Memorial Health Care Foundation
Junior Achievement
Exchange Club Family Center
Memphis Chamber of Commerce 2005 Business/Education Partnership

Martha Leiper
From: Signal Mountain, Hamilton County
Years of Service: 4
Volunteering Highlights:
Room in the Inn: Pres. & VP; member Exec., Mgt & Resource Committees; Chair, Building Committee
St. Jude Home & School Association, Treasurer
Society of Financial Analysts, Past President
Special Notes: Martha is an effective and organized leader. She is an active volunteer for the board, but also prepares a meal for the shelter once a month. Martha volunteers her time and contributes her life skills at our numerous fundraisers.

Frank and Ruby Leslie
From: Nashville, Davidson County
Years of Service: 9 and 20
Volunteering Highlights:
American Red Cross
Vultee Church of Christ
General Hospital
Donelson/Summit Hospital
Central State
Special Notes: Without a thought for unfavorable weather or road conditions, last minute requests or late

> If every Tennessean were to volunteer for one day a month, we could... gain God's grace, favor and blessing in ways far beyond all we can think or imagine. We don't face the challenges of life alone; God is the Mighty Fortress and he will never abandon us. He uses times of extreme difficulty to teach us how to be persistent in our faith and love for him. Seek his guidance above that of the world! Yes, we could touch every problem or need that raises its ugly head in instant victory and success!
>
> —Chaplain Joe. W. Horton, Sr.
> Bolivar
> Hardeman County

night hours, the Leslies deliver crucial blood products to area hospitals. They have logged 230,000 miles and 17,000 hours of volunteer service!

Peg LeVan
From: Knoxville, Knox County
Years of Service: 42
Volunteering Highlights:
Established and supervises health clinics in 33 schools
Structured/supervises volunteer program to aid veterans in VA Outpatient Clinics
Structured/supervises volunteer program of recreation in nursing homes
Trained volunteers for community Operation Health check
Served on state Council, Regional Council, National Red Cross Panels and Committees
Special Notes: Through the American Red Cross, Peg has met a number of community needs in establishing volunteer programs be assessing needs, designing programs, staffing volunteers and providing a volunteer support system.

Allison Lewis
From: Germantown, Shelby County
Volunteering Highlights:
March of Dimes
Bethany Home Project 98 and 99
Germantown High School Key Club
Germantown High School Beta Club
National Honor Society

Lucille Shattuck Lewis
From: Hixson, Hamilton County
Years of Service: 45
Volunteering Highlights:
Association of Childhood Education International

> If every Tennessean were to volunteer for one day a month, we could...
>
> be recognized once again as the true Volunteer state, serving our communities with everyone's participation and accomplishing the good deeds and services needed in an aggressive and timely manner, for the benefit of all.
>
> —Catherine A. Hurdle
> Memphis, Shelby County

Early Childhood Advisory Committee for TN Department of Education
Creative Discovery Museum Board
Who's Who in American Education Administration
The Chattanooga Association for the Education of Young Children presents the "Lu Lewis" Award annually
Special Notes: Lu's heart is with children. She is viewed by her peers and by the Chattanooga community as the "expert" in early childhood education. She has chaired children's events, preschool advisory boards, and local community banquets, in addition to serving as consultant to the education system, Parents as First Teachers development committee, Chattanooga Venture early childhood task force, Junior League, and local Girl Scouts. Lu is an avid storyteller. Believing that reading to your children is one of the most important "gifts" you can give your children, she currently leads the Books for Babes effort for United Way of Greater Chattanooga/Invest in Children.

Mildred Littrell
From: Jackson, Madison County
Years of Service: 9
Volunteering Highlights:
Western Mental Health Institute
Altrusa Club
Timber Springs Adolescent Program
J.C. Penney Golden Rule Award Nomination
1999 Eagle Award for Outstanding Volunteerism
Special Notes: Mrs. Littrell began volunteering at the Western Mental Health Institute in 1991, with a group from the Altrusa Club. She became the leader of this group in 1996 and began as a special volunteer on the children's unit soon afterward. She is touching the lives of many women and children. She is donating a service that is needed and definitely one that contributes to

> If every Tennessean were to volunteer for one day a month, we could...
>
> boost community pride. This creates fresh ideas, energy and enthusiasm. "We make a living by what we get, we make a life by what we give."
>
> —H.G. "Sonny" Hunter, Jr.
> Kingston
> Roane County

Tennessee Volunteer Heroes 2001

> **If every Tennessean were to volunteer for one day a month, we could…**
> accomplish so many things for our great state. There would not be any "Tennessee Trash" on highways. With some of these volunteer hours, it would disappear. Every organization could provide more services. Hospitals, nursing homes and assisted living homes could provide many more hours of personal contact for those patients who do not receive that support from family and friends. Schools could probably benefit as much if not more than any other singular organization.
>
> —Mayor Cherry Jackson
> Thompson Station, Williamson County

the comfort and treatment as well as enhancing the patient's dignity and self respect.

Gerry Lonsway
From: Franklin, Williamson County
Years of Service: 9
Volunteering Highlights:
Salvation Army
Meals on Wheels
Ronald McDonald House
Special Notes: Mr. Lonsway's consistent willingness to help "wherever I'm needed" on behalf of those less fortunate qualifies him as a Tennessee Volunteer Hero. Often going beyond the call of duty, Mr. Lonsway has generously donated many hours to the Salvation Army Angel Tree Program for several years and has made himself available to fill a variety of volunteer opportunities with the Salvation Army when there was a need for extra manpower. Though possessing leadership and organizational skills, no job is ever too small. His primary interest is always in helping those in need. His belief in the mission of the Salvation Army and his advocacy on behalf of that mission has led many in the community to understanding and supporting the work that our organization does.

Judy Lonsway
From: Franklin, Williamson County
Years of Service: 9
Volunteering Highlights:
Salvation Army
Meals on Wheels
Ronald McDonald House
Hendersonville Hospital
Second Harvest Food Bank
Special Notes: Mrs. Lonsway's compassion for those in need and her ability to creatively translate that into "volunteer work" qualifies her as a Tennessee Volunteer Hero. Mrs. Lonsway has helped in volunteer projects from sorting and pricing items for resale in Salvation Army Thrift Stores to working directly to applicants for the Salvation Army Angel Tree program. One of her unique contributions as a volunteer is her ability to inspire others to give of their time to benefit those in need. Her generosity in giving her time whenever needed and her ability to work harmoniously with both staff and volunteers have made a lasting impact on the Salvation Army's programs.

Jeff C. Lovejoy
Special Notes: Special recognition from the Governor and First Lady of Tennessee for excellence in volunteer service.

Nellie Loyd
From: Christiana, Rutherford County
Years of Service: 20
Volunteering Highlights:
Community Care of Rutherford County
Boulivard Terrace
National Health Corporation
American Red Cross
Peachtree Nursing Home
Special Notes: She serves unselfishly, giving of her time and resources to care for elderly in our nursing homes, hospitals, and those homebound.

> **If every Tennessean were to volunteer for one day a month, we could…**
> we could make a major difference in a lot more situations and better the lives of many more citizens living in our communities throughout Tennessee.
>
> —Martha Jamison
> Memphis, Shelby County

Tennessee Volunteer Heroes 2001

Thomas H. Lynch
From: Greeneville, Greene County
Years of Service: 20
Volunteering Highlights:
Greeneville-Greene County Community Ministries
J.C. Penney Golden Rule Award Nomination
Greeneville-Greene County Community Ministries Food Bank: helped establish
FEMA Board: Chairman
Special Notes: Rev. Lynch's concern for his fellow man, his volunteer spirit to go the extra mile without pay or recognition and his business acuity were all important building stones of the Greeneville-Greene County Community Ministries Food Bank, which today is an umbrella agency providing food, shelter, utilities, heating, medications, advocacy and other necessities of life, as needed in an emergency situation. There is also a broad base of partnerships with other community agencies and organizations which Rev. Lynch fostered during the initial organization and which he promotes daily in his volunteer work.

Sonya Madison
From: Chattanooga, Hamilton County
Years of Service: 2
Volunteering Highlights:
Orange Grove Center
J.C. Penney Golden Rule Award Nomination
Girl Scouts of America
Special Notes: As a senior in high school, Sonya had the opportunity to design a Girl Scout Project that would benefit the community. Orange Grove is a center for mentally challenged individuals, most of who have Down's Syndrome. Sonya and a fellow scout decided to design a prom for the clients of Orange Grove. To prepare for the big event, Sonya taught classes ranging from table etiquette to dancing. The clients were very excited about the prom and the parents were happy that their children were having the opportunity to attend a prom, something they never thought would happen. One parent stated she never thought she would see her son in a tuxedo and she was happy that Sonya allowed her this moment. Sonya secured community support for the prom obtaining donations of balloons, food, flowers, a photographer and even a band. From the punch bowl to the picture backdrop, the event was a night the children and their families will never forget. The joy in their eyes as they danced and ate in their formal attire was proof that Sonya had more than achieved her goal of providing an opportunity for the clients of Orange Grove to experience a prom. Sonya has realized the true meaning of love and friendship as each of the clients and their families befriended her in a way that is beyond words.

Ed Market
From: Chattanooga, Hamilton County
Years of Service: 8
Volunteering Highlights:
J.C. Penney Golden Rule Award Nomination
Family and Children's Services of Chattanooga, Inc.
Special Notes: Mr. Market has been a volunteer "Mr. Fixit" since 1992, repairing homes and home equipment for low-income seniors and disabled persons who are clients of Family and Children's Services of Chattanooga. As a volunteer, Mr. Market has repaired everything from leaky pipes to leaky roofs, enabling those with few financial resources to maintain their homes in good repair. Since he began, Ed Market has logged more than 2,000 volunteer hours helping with over 300 projects.

> If every Tennessean were to volunteer for one day a month, we could… provide a mentor for each child and teenager. The rate of suicide could be reduced from one every 15 minutes. The needs of the elderly would be better met. Tennessee would become the healthiest, wealthiest, most informed state. Each volunteer would share his or her own talents. We would become a state of great resources— our people!
>
> —Judy Johnson
> Smyrna
> Rutherford County

> If every Tennessean were to volunteer for one day a month, we could… mentor at-risk students, show them others care, and help them with self-esteem. We could have more city recreation choices, more flowers and trees along our streets. We could lift pride in our city and county with improved aesthetics, and having a long-term plan for what we want our county to look like and be like. We could achieve a higher level of our local quality of life.
>
> —Jack Jennings
> Tullahoma
> Coffee County

Tennessee Volunteer Heroes 2001

> If every Tennessean were to volunteer for one day a month, we could...
>
> # ensure that every child reaches his or her full potential.
>
> —Michele Johnson
> Nashville
> Davidson County

Jessie Marks
From: Nashville, Davidson County
Years of Service: 58
Volunteering Highlights:
St. Thomas Hospital
Hillwood Presbyterian Church
Special Notes: Jessie's smile and ability to stay calm and caring in stressful situations are two of many talents that make her so very valuable to St. Thomas Hospital.

Betty Martin
From: Greeneville, Greene County
Volunteering Highlights:
J.C. Penney Golden Rule Award Nomination
Appalachian Girl Scout Council: Service Unit Manager for Service Unit 81, Greene County
Special Notes: Mrs. Martin single-handedly got a room and furniture donated in a renovated school building. The room will be used for a Girl Scout Resource Library. Mrs. Martin also recruited a resource librarian, and then got several girls working on their Gold and Silver Awards to use their service hours helping to get the library established.

Corinne R. Martinez
From: Tullahoma, Coffee County
Years of Service: 47
Volunteering Highlights:
Trinity Lutheran Church
Historic Preservation Society of Tullahoma
Tullahoma Women's Club
League of Women Voters
Literacy Council
Special Notes: Ms. Martinez has a long history of sharing her time and talent to help folks in need, and to assist non-profit organizations. She has added much to the quality of life in Tullahoma.

Maryville College Bonner Scholars Program
From: Maryville, Blount County
Years of Service: 9
Volunteering Highlights:
Maryville College Families
Boys and Girls Club
Good Samaritan Clinic
Asbury Acres Habitat
Food Banks
Special Notes: The Maryville College Bonners are 55 college students who provide Maryville and surrounding communities with more than 28,600 hours of community service each year!

Maryville College Student Literacy Corps
From: Maryville, Blount County
Years of Service: 7
Volunteering Highlights:
Maryville College Families
Blount County Jail
Blount County Children's Home
Adult Basic Education Center
Martin Luther King Center
Special Notes: This group of 60 + college students is committed to helping children and adults learn to read.

Clint Mathis, Jr.
From: Memphis, Shelby County
Years of Service: 12
Volunteering Highlights:
Manna Outreach
Junior Achievement
Boys and Girls Club
Mississippi Christian Boulevard Church, teacher/leader
BellSouth Pioneer Volunteers
Special Notes: Clint is the very essence of volunteerism.

> If every Tennessean were to volunteer for one day a month, we could...
>
> # pass on the joy and fulfillment we receive when we are helping others. If a smile or hug were passed on to another person, we would enrich lives of those we touch.
>
> —Brenda Joines
> Maryville, Blount County

On the Manna Outreach program, he works three Saturdays a month, every month. Clint has been actively involved with Junior Achievement for the past 10 years, not only working in the classroom, but spearheading the program for fellow employees where he is employed.

Ross Matlock
From: Nashville, Davidson County
Years of Service: 5
Volunteering Highlights:
Nashville CARES

Special Notes: Although Cerebral Palsy physically limits Ross, it has never stopped him from helping others live as comfortably and with as much dignity as possible, no matter what the circumstance. Ross's volunteer activities include: providing all manner of services to clients in "high-risk" areas; befriending clients without families and supplies whatever service they might need; offering physical and emotional assistance and support to client's families; utilizing his own vehicle to provide all manner of transportation needs; and facilitating meal delivery to agency and then to clients.

Bettye May
From: Memphis, Shelby County
Years of Service: 7
Volunteering Highlights:
Memphis In May — Chairman of the Year- 1999 and BBQ Judge (Sylvia Bradshaw Award)
J.C. Penney Golden Rule Award Nomination
Friends of the Orpheum, Top Ten Usher
Wonders Series — worked at five exhibitions
Rock & Soul Museum — assist with tours
Daughters of the Nile — associated with Shrine Hospital support

Special Notes: Bettye has given generously of her time and talents as a Memphis in May Volunteer Leader. She devotes many hours to other community service projects as well. As Chairman of the Office Resource Committee, Bettye is responsible for organizing all support activities related to every mailing leaving the Memphis In May office. Typical duties include copying, filing, preparing bulk and first class mailings, telephone calls and many other non-glamorous but essential functions. She is the point of contact for all of our staff as well as other volunteer leaders who need office resource support. It is her task to determine the size and scope of the work based on the information we provide. Then, she decides how many other volunteers from her committee she will need to assist her. She also selects those volunteers best suited for the specific task as she is well aware of the skills and talents of her group members.

Dori Mayfield
From: Chattanooga, Hamilton County
Years of Service: 1
Volunteering Highlights:
Family and Children's Services
Family Violence Service Shelter: fundraising
Valley Brook Community Club: luncheon speaker
Youth Action Council
J.C. Penney Golden Rule Award Nomination
Family Career and Community Leaders of America: 2nd place

Special Notes: It is difficult to describe Dori's activities because they are so numerous. Dori began her volunteer work with Family and Children's Services through the Service Learning Center and as a requirement of Hixson High School, which required community service hours. She began by stuffing envelopes. She was soon making presentations to her class about domestic violence and

---

If every Tennessean were to volunteer
for one day a month, we could...

create a reservoir of talent, energy, experience and creativity that could produce limitless benefits. Our state could be cleaner, greener and richer. Our people could enjoy a better quality of life with improvements in the environment, health care and community services. Economically, the state could only profit from a population that is more content and has greater pride and confidence in its community.

—Lorraine Kaufman
Memphis
Shelby County

If every Tennessean were to volunteer
for one day a month, we could...

improve the status of the poor, homeless, parentless and all others in need.

—Virginia Jones
Nashville, Davidson County

Tennessee Volunteer Heroes 2001

> If every Tennessean were to volunteer for one day a month, we could…
>
> accomplish a great deal. Volunteering helps those who give to others by keeping them active and healthy. Volunteering helps the community by saving money that would have to be spent otherwise to help those in need.
>
> —Helen Kelley
> Chattanooga
> Hamilton County

sexual assault. Dori also assists at Health Fairs and mall events. She volunteers weekly providing childcare for children living in the Domestic Violence Shelter. And, if that is not sufficient to keep a teenage girl busy, Dori also acts in the Family and Children's Services of Chattanooga, Inc. Springboard Productions called Fairy Tale, a play about domestic violence.

Pat Maynard
From: Cookeville, Putnam County
Volunteering Highlights:
Stevens St. Baptist Care Center
J.C. Penney Golden Rule Award Nomination
Special Notes: Pat works very hard to keep the Care Center clean. She works in the food room and also keeps the clothing area neat and clean. She also counsels people who come in for help. Pat is always ready to listen. So many people come into the Care Center without hope. She ministers to them not only physically and spiritually, but also by supplying them with everyday needs.

Holly McAmis
From: Greeneville, Greene County
Years of Service: 2
Volunteering Highlights:
Camp Creek Care Bears, founder
Greene Valley Development Center
Camp Creek Elementary School, A Honor Roll
J.C. Penney Golden Rule Award Nomination
Special Notes: Holly interacts remarkably well with both children and adults and she is extremely helpful. One of her most impressive traits is her concern and interest in her community and for people in need. She has always made time, even with her busy schedule of school, athletics, and music, and to devote herself to others. Holly co-founded a youth service organization called the "Care Bears." At the age of 10, Holly has already devoted over 370 hours to her community. Holly exemplifies the well-rounded student, athlete, and leader of tomorrow.

Donna McBride
From: Celina, Clay County
Years of Service: 10
Volunteering Highlights:
American Cancer Society
Clay County Partnership
Secured grant for restoration of Courthouse
Halloween in the Park; Organizer
Committee member, creation of Tourism brochure for county
Special Notes: She is very active with student involvement. She helps organize community events, charity events, and volunteers many hours to those events.

Carla Flatt McCauley
From: Old Hickory, Davidson County
Years of Service: 15
Volunteering Highlights:
DuPont Elementaty School, PTO Volunteer
Hunters Lane Parent Advisory Committee
Old Hickory United Methodist Church
Tom Joy Elementary School, Classroom Mentor
Lakewood Theatre company board of Directors
Special Notes: I am passionate about making a difference for all children. My hope is to pass this quality on to the next generation.

> If every Tennessean were to volunteer for one day a month, we could…
>
> accomplish what no other state, nation, region or community has ever achieved before— total unity.
>
> —Randall Killman
> Celina, Clay County

Edwin E. McClure
From: Johnson City, Washington County
Years of Service: 50
Volunteering Highlights:
American Red Cross of Johnson City/Washington County
Civitans of Johnson City
Habitat for Humanity
Winner JC Penney Golden Rule Award
Winner Tennessee Conference on Social Welfare Volunteer Award
Special Notes: Ed is always there to help meet the needs of our community, whether by donating blood, comforting a disaster victim or building a house. We can count on Ed!

Lois McComb
Special Notes: Special recognition from the Governor and First Lady of Tennessee for excellence in volunteer service.

Bill McCord
From: Chattanooga, Hamilton County
Years of Service: 25
Volunteering Highlights:
BellSouth Pioneer Volunteers: Past Chapter President
Chattanooga Ronald McDonald House: Board; fundraising; weekend manager
Chattanooga Exchange Club
March of Dimes: Chattanooga; Columbia; Nashville
Special Notes: Bill and his family spend at least four weekends a year as weekend managers at the Chattanooga Ronald McDonald House. It has been the family custom to spend Christmas Eve with families at the RMH for the past several years. He also has held various local and state offices with the BellSouth Pioneer Volunteers.

> If every Tennessean were to volunteer for one day a month, we could...
>
> ## provide every senior citizen with one good meal and a friendly visit each day.
>
> —Rita Kittrell
> Charlotte, Dickson County

> If every Tennessean were to volunteer for one day a month, we could...
>
> ## reach out to alleviate much of the avoidable suffering and add to the quality of life of our fellow Tennesseans— every needy adult and child, our neighbors.
>
> —Eva L. Knabb
> Chattanooga, Hamilton County

Martha V. McCord
From: Dyersburg, Dyer County
Years of Service: 15
Volunteering Highlights:
Area Agency on Aging, Advisory Board
American Red Cross, Dyer County Chapter: Outstanding Volunteerism by a Board Member, 2000
Methodist Hospital — Dyersburg, ICCU Hostess; ICCU Hostess of the Year, 1999
Crime Stoppers — Dyer County, Board
International Friends, Board of Directors
Special Notes: Martha McCord is a Tennessee Volunteer Hero not only because she volunteers her time, but also because she makes a personal impact on people in need by giving a piece of her heart in the process. While volunteering, if she notices an extra need, she raises money and goes the extra mile to fulfill that need.

Danny McCorkle
From: Gallatin, Sumner County
Years of Service: 10
Special Notes: For years Danny has dedicated his time, energy, and talent to entertaining people of all ages, from all walks of life. He volunteers his services and asks neither recognition nor pay for his great work.

Frank McDonald (Deceased)
Years of Service: 40
Volunteering Highlights:
United Way Campaign Chair (93), Endowment Committee Chair (97)
Chamber of Commerce Board Chair (95)
Rotary Club President (94-95)
University of Chattanooga Foundation Trustee
Dismembered Tennesseans Founding Member
Special Notes: Frank's entire life embodied the spirit of the

Tennessee Volunteer Heroes 2001

> If every Tennessean were to volunteer for one day a month, we could... truly change the quality of life of each resident and visitor. The wealth of society is not measured in tax revenues, but by the quality of the citizens that make a difference in each other's lives. I have been blessed with family and the community in which I live. I was fortunate to obtain a formal education and volunteering is my way of paying back the debt to those who inspired me and helped me achieve my goals.
>
> —Kent E. Koederitz
> Johnson City
> Washington County

criteria for Tennessee Volunteer Heroes. He cared deeply about people and translated his caring into actions that made life better in the Chattanooga community.

John McGonagle
From: Nashville, Davidson County
Years of Service: 30
Volunteering Highlights:
St. Thomas Hospital
Sales and Marketing Executives of Nashville
Nashville Invitational Golf Association
Special Notes: Whenever John volunteers in St. Thomas Gift Shop, the customers pour in just to visit with him! He is an absolute joy.

Clifford and Ruth McKinney
From: Bristol
Years of Service: 6
Volunteering Highlights:
Big Brothers and Big Sisters of Greater Tri-Cities
Central Elementary School
J.C. Penney Golden Rule Award Nomination
Special Notes: Cliff and Ruth have served our agency and the students at Central Elementary by working one-on-one with students who have needed extra attention and help with schoolwork. They have served as mentors and friends to the many students they have served.

Laura McLaughlin
From: Nashville, Davidson County
Volunteering Highlights:
Second Harvest Food Bank
Julia Green Elementary School
Nashville Community Foundation
West End United Methodist Church
Harpeth Hall School
Special Notes: Families from miles around recognize Laura as an outstanding mother and teacher, community builder and activist. Laura, with two children, has made positive handprints all across our community. Neighborhood children are at her house every afternoon, she does countless hours of volunteer work at her church, she fights community hunger and is especially interested in supporting children's education.

Sue R. McLaughlin
From: Memphis, Shelby County
Years of Service: 8
Volunteering Highlights:
Lifeblood Mid-South Regional Blood Center
J.C. Penney Golden Rule Award Nomination
Special Notes: Sue McLaughlin is a longtime dedicated blood donor with Lifeblood Mid-South Regional Blood Center. She has donated red blood cell/plasma, whole blood and platelets — gallons of blood and blood components. Sue is one of those volunteers you can really count on. Every week, like clockwork, she comes into the center and spends six hours helping out the staff, hands out refreshments to donors, keeps supplies in stock, decorates for the holidays, fills out donors' reminder magnets, she even cleans and straightens up the center!

Corinne McLerran
From: Celina, Clay County
Years of Service: 20
Volunteering Highlights:
Clay County Museum Board Member
Soil Conservation Board Member
United Daughters of the Confederacy
Local Historian
Clay County River Run: event organizer
Special Notes: Corinne has donated many hours

> If every Tennessean were to volunteer for one day a month, we could... change the future of our state and our communities. The most important volunteering we can do is within our own families, going the extra mile to do something to help a family member, such as not going to the game in order to help Johnny with his homework, or not going to the dance in order to help Mom with the housework and the younger children.
>
> —Larry Kuka
> Harrison, Hamilton County

Tennessee Volunteer Heroes 2001

of service through the years planning our annual Homecoming Days celebration, Clay County Tour of Homes event, and many fundraisers to help fund the operations of the Clay County Museum.

Robert E. McNeilly, Jr.
From: Nashville, Davidson County
Years of Service: 30
Volunteering Highlights:
United Way Executive Committee of the Board
American Red Cross, Board Member
Senior Citizens, Inc., Advisory Committee
The Salvation Army, Advisory Board
Metro Action Commission, board Member

Carolyn R. McPherson
Special Notes: Special recognition from the Governor and First Lady of Tennessee for excellence in volunteer service.

Linda Meador
From: Portland, Sumner County
Years of Service: 3
Volunteering Highlights:
Ruth P. Carter Senior Center, Volunteer of the Year — 1999
Special Notes: "I began volunteering after having a heart attack and quadruple bypass, July 1, 1997. I have a deep understanding of the position the elderly and injured are in. I am comfortable with going to the Emergency Room and comfortable visiting critical care. I am very prayerful and careful about how I go about my mission. In my heart, I do this as my work for God."

Metropolitan Inter-Faith Association
From: Memphis, Shelby County
Years of Service: 32

If every Tennessean were to volunteer for one day a month, we could...

have a world, not measured by gold, but one where caring and giving is the treasure of a lifetime.

—Nickie Louise Lancaster
Hermitage
Davidson County

 If every Tennessean were to volunteer for one day a month, we could...
become the model for change from a culture that has habitually fallen asleep to the needs of others and forgotten the true essence of what it means to be a part of a society or group. When you give of your time and heart, you share in a true healing process. You help heal the wounds of another, be it human, animal, or mother earth, and in many unexpected ways you heal yourself. One cares for oneself by caring for another. The state of Tennessee would be like one huge barn-raising!

—Reneé LaRose
College Grove, Williamson County

Volunteering Highlights:
MIFA is recognized as delivering the largest home-delivered meals program in Tennessee
Hands-On Memphis Agency of the Year Award in 1999
MIFA's Estival Communities was recognized with a City Beautiful Award in 2000
Vox Award, Public Relations Society of America, Memphis Chapter in 2000 for design of a holiday card
HUD Best Practices Award, 2000
Special Notes: Diverse groups working together under the umbrella of the Metropolitan Inter-Faith Association (MIFA) have proven the ability to develop lasting solutions to complex individual and community problems. MIFA's programs touch the lives of hundreds of thousands of people in need with a strong volunteer base providing more than 200,000 community service hours annually. MIFA's history is based on segments of the community coming together to help all people; and the dedication of so many volunteers continues today. Our goals are fulfilled through uniting all ages, faiths and cultures.

MIFA Ombudsman Program
From: Memphis, Shelby County
Years of Service: 5
Volunteering Highlights:
Metropolitian Inter-Faith Association (MIFA)
Aging Commission of the Mid-South
Tennessee Commission on Aging
National Coalition for Nursing Home Reform
Finalist, 2000 JC Penney Golden Rule Award
Special Notes: The Metropolitan Inter-Faith Association (MIFA) VOR group of over 40 volunteer Ombudsman have volunteered 3,900 plus hours in the last 2 years. They are dedicated and caring volunteers who advocate for the rights of Nursing Home residents.

> If every Tennessean were to volunteer for one day a month, we could...
>
> do so very, very much more to alleviate the suffering and poverty of our fellow Tennesseans. The many agencies that assist those less fortunate so often work with limited budgets. They need not only our financial support, but our physical presence as well.
>
> —John Lavecchia
> Memphis, Shelby County

Brandy Miller
From: Germantown, Shelby County
Years of Service: 20
Volunteering Highlights:
Germantown High School PTSA: Past Pres.; Ex Board Member; Honorary Lifetime Achievement Award
City of Germantown Environmental Commission: Recycling Chairman, youth
Germantown Garden Club: Past Pres.; named Worker of the Year by District 1, TN Fed. of Garden Clubs
J.C. Penney Golden Rule Award Nomination
Germantown Middle School Band Booster Fundraising Chairman
Dogwood Creek Homeowners Association: Secretary
Special Notes: "I have been active in my city as a volunteer for some time, but so have many others. We are fortunate to have a city like Germantown where there are many fine, involved individuals."

Mary A. Miller
From: Memphis, Shelby County
Years of Service: 3
Volunteering Highlights:
Norris Elementary
Special Notes: Mrs. Miller willingly gives of her time to help do many tasks at Norris. She helps to make the halls bright and cheerful by displaying our students' work; she monitors teachers classes when they have to be away, attends field trips assisting in monitoring; helps set up class parties at holiday time; helps teachers organize papers and file in their classrooms when necessary; monitors the cafeteria to help with breakfast duty; tutors students in small groups who are experiencing difficulty. Schools need more parents like Mary Miller!

Pat Miller
From: Springfield, Robertson County
Years of Service: 8
Volunteering Highlights:
Springfield Baptist Church
Springfield High School Show Choir
American Cancer Society
Special Notes: Pat is an outstanding example of volunteering at its best. Convinced that Relay For Life would go over well in her community, she began the daunting task of pulling the community together to support the event. As chairman, she pulled together a fantastic committee of volunteers who raised over $95,000 for the first event in Robertson County, the second largest total for a 1st year event in Tennessee. Their relay won national recognition from the American Cancer society, placing 5th in the nation in their population group. The past 2 years, the Relay has continued to grow, raising almost $127,000 last year and over $140,000 this year. Her dedication to providing the very best possible services to cancer patients and her willingness to use her own story as an example continue to inspire others. She is a true "Volunteer Hero!"

Bonnie Harris Moore
From: Nashville, Davidson County
Years of Service: 30
Volunteering Highlights:
Hume-Fogg: Fund-raising Committee/Chair
Meigs Magnet School: Fund-raising Chair, directory, classroom
Eakin Elementary: library and classroom help
St. Bartholomew's Church: youth volunteer; fund-raiser; Room in the Inn; music
Metro Schools: various committees
Special Notes: "I don't consider myself a hero, but doing

> If every Tennessean were to volunteer for one day a month, we could...
>
> enhance the lives of our fellow countrymen by giving an incredible 72,000,000 people days of human excellence in volunteer service.
>
> —Rip Lebkuecher
> Hendersonville
> Sumner County

for others is an important part of my life. I'm grateful to have the time and opportunity to serve where I can."

Mary Viuna Moore
From: Parsons, Decatur County
Years of Service: 65
Volunteering Highlights:
American Red Cross
Family, Community, Education Clubs
Friends of Parsons Public Library
Area on Aging — Meals on Wheels
W.M.U. First Baptist Church
Special Notes: Ms. Moore has been volunteering since the age of 10, beginning her volunteer experience running errands for neighbors. She also has been volunteering for the American Red Cross for 45 years. Her reliability is demonstrated with 46 years perfect attendance in F.C.E. Clubs.

Chasity Morris
From: Norris, Anderson County
Years of Service: 2
Volunteering Highlights:
AmeriCorps — Emerald Youth Foundation
Whittle Springs Middle School: Mentor
Emerald Avenue United Methodist Church
Andersonville Elementary School — America Reads Program
Special Notes: Chasity has overcome great obstacles in her life. She is rearing a 4 year old daughter alone with determination to complete college yet finds time to do AmeriCorps service and other volunteer activities.

Rev. Larry Morris
From: Memphis, Shelby County
Years of Service: 22
Volunteering Highlights:

If every Tennessean were to volunteer for one day a month, we could...

make Tennessee a better place to live, ease racial tensions and help those who need help the most— the young, the old and the ill.

—Paul LeBlanc
Cordova, Shelby County

If every Tennessean were to volunteer for one day a month, we could...

set the tone for the nation. We could build stronger communities and set good examples for our children. If every Tennessean would volunteer, we would have less need in our community and more pride in our state.

—Martha Leiper
Signal Mountain, Hamilton County

United Way
YMCA
J.C. Penney Golden Rule Award Nomination
Job Corps
Special Notes: Rev. Morris counsels troubled teens and their families, including spiritual and employment counseling. He has been active in every phase of his endeavor to seek new avenues in assisting the youth and teens of this community and our city.

Roland and Eleanor Morton
From: Ashland City, Cheatham County
Years of Service: 7 (each)
Volunteering Highlights:
Sudan Interior Mission
World Vision
Assembly Church, Gateway
World War II Veteran
American Red Cross
Special Notes: Mr. and Mrs. Morton are quite elderly, but they keep on giving! Even though they live outside Nashville, they will go anywhere to help out. Mr. Morton also works every Saturday in the Blood Center without fail.

Peggy Moss
From: Nashville, Davidson County
Years of Service: 64
Volunteering Highlights:
The Salvation Army
Election Precinct
Special Notes: For Peggy Moss, volunteering has been a way of life, beginning when she was 10 years old. Giving her time to help others in some way has been as natural as breathing. The young, the elderly and those who are ill have always had a special place in her heart, and her empathy is translated into practical acts of help and

> If every Tennessean were to volunteer for one day a month, we could... see and understand each other's problems. We could help stop poverty, hunger and illiteracy— it would make us all feel closer and give us a desire to put forth a great effort to help mankind. The world would be a better place if we had more consideration for our neighbors.
>
> —Frank and Ruby Leslie
> Nashville
> Davidson County

kindness. Though an active volunteer in several organizations for many years, for the last 10 years Mrs. Moss has devoted all her time to programs of The Salvation Army. She gives many hours each week in support of the men in The Salvation Army Adult Rehabilitation Center. This program shelters men struggling with substance abuse and helps them achieve self-sufficiency through counseling, work therapy and spiritual and emotional support. Mrs. Moss accepts the men as they are, acknowledging their dignity as human beings and offering support and encouragement for those successes. For years, she has supplied five cakes each month for their sobriety birthday parties. Mrs. Moss has helped to raise thousands of dollars by generously donating her time and skills in jewelry repair for The Salvation Army Thrift Store jewelry sales. She has recruited many friends as fellow Salvation Army Volunteers over the years and enlists them to help with projects such as the annual Christmas luncheon and wrapping Christmas gifts for the men in the program. During the holiday season, Mrs. Moss spends two to three weeks working full time (thirty to forty hours per week) taking application information from families applying for aid through the Angel Tree Program. Once the application portion of the Angel Tree is finished, she is a daily volunteer at the Christmas warehouse working wherever needed. Her generosity in giving her time and her concern for others make her a Tennessee Volunteer Hero for The Salvation Army and those it serves.

Dr. Joe P. Moss, Jr.
From: Chapel Hill, Williamson County
Volunteering Highlights:
Williamson County Jail
A.A.A.
Special Notes: Dr. Moss is a true Tennessee Hero. He understanding and compassionate, and has touched many lives. He looks at you the same and treats you with respect if you have millions of dollars or nothing. If every patient he has seen over the years could have paid him, he would have been retired a long ago.

Howard and Barbara Moulton
From: Knoxville, Knox County
Years of Service: 23
Volunteering Highlights:
J.C. Penney Golden Rule Award Nomination
Knoxville/Knox County Mobile Meals Program
Special Notes: For over 2 decades, Howard and Barbara have given of themselves and their resources on a regular basis to the frail, homebound senior citizens living in Knoxville, TN. More than 15,960 meals have passed through their caring hands. They have driven over 23,940 miles using their own vehicle and gas without reimbursement. Their level of consistency has been incredible. They have never missed a scheduled day since they began delivering meals!

Mt. Pleasant UMC Youth Group
From: Greeneville, Greene County
Years of Service: 5
Volunteering Highlights:
Greeneville/Greene County Community Ministries — Food Bank
Greeneville/Greene County Gifts for Kids
Johnson City Melting Pot Soup Kitchen
United Methodist Volunteers in Mission
Holston Conference Traveling Youth Choir — Salt and Light
Special Notes: The Mt. Pleasant UMC Youth Group is very active in both their church and community. They assist others in daily routine tasks, as well as work for various volunteer organizations in the area.

> If every Tennessean were to volunteer for one day a month, we could... staff health clinics in all schools. We could brighten the day of nursing home residents through recreation/visitation. We could teach health/safety courses to all school children K-5. We could offer free swim classes for children in the inner city and safety courses for adults every weekend. We could provide programs of recreation for mental health hospital residents.
>
> —Peg LeVan
> Knoxville
> Knox County

Tennessee Volunteer Heroes 2001

Robert Mullins, Sr.
From: Smyrna, Rutherford County
Years of Service: 20
Volunteering Highlights:
United Way of Rutherford County, Board Member and various committees
Town of Smyrna; elected Mayor and Councilman, youth Program
Greater Nashville Regional Council
Metropolitan Planning Organization
Regional Transportation Authority
Special Notes: Robert excels in leadership. He is very caring and outgoing in his community.

George and Mary Murphy
From: Memphis, Shelby County
Years of Service: 15 and 18
Volunteering Highlights:
Ladies of Charity
J.C. Penney Golden Rule Award Nomination
Knights of Columbus
Holy Rosary Church
St. Peter Villa
Special Notes: George and Mary attend St. Peter Villa every Monday and Tuesday. They facilitate the daily functions of the Pastoral Department by making sure the chapel is always clean and neat, flowers are watered, communion supplies are well stocked, the priests robes are dry-cleaned or laundered, and they provide one on one visits to the residents and arrange special events and for volunteer entertainers to play music on holidays, etc. These two have gone over and above the call of duty when they could just transport residents to the chapel area.

> If every Tennessean were to volunteer for one day a month, we could...
>
> *Energize Tennessee!!!!* There is a place for each of us to volunteer; carpenters, tutors, answering the phone, mentoring, cleaning up an area, reading to a child... What do you like to do? There's a need waiting for you. Try a day... bet you can't stop at one!!!
>
> —Lucille Shattuck Lewis
> Hixson, Hamilton County

> If every Tennessean were to volunteer for one day a month, we could...
>
> **help alleviate many of the current problems, primarily those associated with the homeless and those unable to care for themselves.**
>
> —Gerry Lonsway
> Franklin, Williamson County

Rick Murphree
From: Knoxville, Knox County
Years of Service: 20
Volunteering Highlights:
Foothills Land Conservancy: Board Member
Ijams Nature Center: Chairman of the Board
Tennessee Conservation League: Board Member; Executive Committee; Treasurer
United Way: First TN Campaign Co-Chair; Allocations Panel Chair; Allocations Task Force
Habitat for Humanity: Building Coordinator for First TN's home building project
Special Notes: Rick's work with organizations that help to promote the preservation of our natural resources shows the value he places on educating the public, as well as taking an active role in conservation. Not only does Rick serve on the boards of these organizations, he takes the time to participate in the events they coordinate, such as river cleanups and training seminars. In addition, he chairs one of ten United Way Allocations Panels, and successfully led First Tennessee's United Way 2000 campaign, which exceeded its fundraising goal of $180,000. Earlier this year, Rick devoted extensive time to Habitat for Humanity as the Building Coordinator of First Tennessee's first home building project.

Lori Murphy
From: Cookeville, Putnam County
Years of Service: 17
Volunteering Highlights:
MS Walk Site Coordinator, most successful walk to date as of 4/8/00
Self-Help Group Leader, Coordinates speakers and monthly meetings
First Christian Church, member/leader
Mission trip leader to Mexico to an orphanage with 23 teenagers

Tennessee Volunteer Heroes 2001

> **If every Tennessean were to volunteer for one day a month, we could...**
>
> help so many people in need. There are so many worthwhile programs out there and so few people who are willing to do their share. We would really find the true meaning of loving in the Volunteer State.
>
> —Judy Lonsway
> Franklin
> Williamson County

Sunday School Teacher, 3 & 4 year olds
Special Notes: Lori is superhuman. She has multiple sclerosis, a life-long neurological disease that has a multitude of symptoms. Lori is not daunted by the fact that she has this disease and never lets it run her life — she is far too tough and stubborn! She surpasses all boundaries! For the MS Walk, Lori obtained underwriting, organized volunteers and met with corporate sponsors. As the Self-Help Group Facilitator, she is sometime the only link between the National MS society and the client. Lori arranges for speakers, spends her own money on snacks for attendees, sends out agendas and reminders monthly, and becomes a friendly listener who people can always rely on. Lori is a Tennessee Volunteer Hero.

Diomede Musigaro
From: Nashville, Davidson County
Years of Service: 3
Volunteering Highlights:
Catholic Charities, Refugee and Imigration Services
Special Notes: He has been a wonderful volunteer helping so many new arrival refugees assimilate to American culture — many, many hours. He understands what it is like to be a stranger in a foreign land.

Nashville Youth PULSE
From: Nashville, Davidson County
Years of Service: 3
Volunteering Highlights:
Over 2,000 teens performed over 10,000 service hours
3 annual, city-wide youth volunteer days
Published a highly popular directory of youth volunteer opportunities
Provided opportunities for youth and adults to work in partnership
Developed dozens of teens into volunteer leaders

Special Notes: PULSE helps create hundreds of young "Volunteer Heroes" by providing monthly volunteer and leadership opportunities.

Jerry Nass
From: Clarksville, Montgomery County
Years of Service: 7
Volunteering Highlights:
St. Bethlehem Civitan Club
Special Olympics Director, Montgomery County
Montgomery County Historical Society, L&N Train station
Montgomery County Parks Commission
Christian Missionary Alliance Men's Group, President
Special Notes: Jerry dedicates countless hours to special needs children and the TN Special Olympics. He also plays Santa for the local handicapped classes and works with the Civitan and Historical Society whenever heeded.

C. Cella Neapolitan
From: Cookeville, Putnam County
Years of Service: 20
Volunteering Highlights:
The Clean Commission: volunteer; board member
UNICEF: volunteer; local committee member
Putnam County Schools: volunteer
City of Cookeville: Volunteer of the Month, August 2000 for creating environmental education program
Putnam County Library of BPW: Volunteer Awards
Special Notes: "For the last 20 years I have volunteered an average of 1-2 hours a week in service of children, mostly in public education."

> **If every Tennessean were to volunteer for one day a month, we could...**
>
> bring joy and happiness to those who are less fortunate than ourselves. I can bring a ray of sunshine to those who are so lonely.
>
> —Nellie Loyd
> Christiana, Rutherford County

Stephen R. Neff
From: Tazewell, Clairborne County
Years of Service: 30
Volunteering Highlights:
Lions Club
Heart of Appalachian Tourism Authority
Boy Scouts of America
Special Notes: Steve was chairman of the Daniel Boone Tri-State Visitors Center Golf Tournament. He worked countless hours, spent his own money and raised $18,000.

Deener D. Newberry
From: Memphis, Shelby County
Years of Service: 7
Volunteering Highlights:
AmeriCorps Hamilton Neighborhood Initiative
Junior Achievement Bowl-a-Thon
Summer Care Camp
Y.E.S.S. After School Program
Community First-Aid and Safety
Special Notes: She is a person who loves to serve as a volunteer who has great commitment. She is reliable and dependable for Tennessee, and that makes her a Tennessee Volunteer Hero!

Thuc Nhu Nguyen
From: Nashville, Davidson County
Years of Service: 4
Volunteering Highlights:
Oasis Center's Teen Outreach Program: various community agencies
Nashville Mayor's Youth Advisory Council
Designed and maintains a website to help international youth caught between two cultures
Teaches traditional Vietnamese dance to children in Nashville's Asian community

> If every Tennessean were to volunteer for one day a month, we could... revitalize the entire nation. The resulting spirit of neighborliness, friendship and caring which would envelop every community would cause the entire nation to take note of what was happening in Tennessee. The poor would be helped. The lonely would be comforted. The uncaring would begin to love. Every state would feel compelled to emulate Tennessee and the nation would be changed.
>
> —Ed Markert
> Chattanooga, Hamilton County

> If every Tennessean were to volunteer for one day a month, we could...
>
> # turn the world upside down!
>
> —Jessie Marks
> Nashville
> Davidson County

Instigated International Fair at her high school, highlighting over 20 different cultures.
Special Notes: Due in part to her own experiences as an immigrant, Nhu has a special affinity for people on the fringe of society. She is able to connect with others on a purely human scale. As Nhu herself says, "being happy is more than just going out and having fun. I'm happy when I see other people happy, laughing and having fun."

Mary Nichols
From: Nashville, Davidson County
Years of Service: 60
Volunteering Highlights:
St. Thomas Hospital
St. Henry's Church, Golden Agers
Vanderbilt Children's Hospital
Harpeth Highlands Women's Club
South Carolina Club
Special Notes: Mary always goes above and beyond in her volunteer work. She positively affects hundreds of people with her efficiency and commitment.

Bryan I. Nishimoto
From: Germantown, Shelby County
Years of Service: 7
Volunteering Highlights:
Boy Scout Troop 368
Houston High School National Honor Society
Houston High School Beta Club
Baptist Health Shining Star
Houston High School Cross Country

Scott M. Niswonger
From: Greeneville, Greene County
Volunteering Highlights:
Greeneville/Greene County Area Chamber of

Tennessee Volunteer Heroes 2001

> **If every Tennessean were to volunteer for one day a month, we could…**
>
> provide more help in making life more tolerable for those in need. We could bring more cheer into the lives of those who are ill or depressed. We could reach more newcomers learning their way around our culture.
>
> —Corinne R. Martinez
> Tullahoma
> Coffee County

Commerce: Past President
United Way: Board of Directors
Junior Achievement of Greene County: Founding Director; Past President
Greater Tri-Cities Business Alliance: Board of Directors
U.S.S. Greeneville: Board of Directors

Mary Etta Nixon
From: Hickman, Smith County
Years of Service: 52
Volunteering Highlights:
Hickman Baptist Church: clerk; Sunday School teacher; Bldg Comm; Maint Comm; Pastor Search Comm; Nominating Comm
Smith County Family & Community Edcuation Clubs: FCE President; FCE Member of Year; FCE Family of Year
American Cancer Society: Relay for Life planning committee
Hickman Beautification Committee: Chair
New Salem Association of Baptists: clerk (group of Southern Baptist Churches in this area of TN)
Special Notes: "I am an Extension Agent with the University of Tennessee, and have had the privilege of working with Mary Etta in the Family and Community Education clubs (formerly Home Demonstration Clubs). I can hardly think of a time that she has turned down a request to assist in any endeavor that has risen in the community."

Edna M. Nojelm
From: Greeneville, Greene County
Years of Service: 6
Volunteering Highlights:
Religious Ed. Resource Center
Holston Home for Children
Notre Dame Catholic Church

J.C. Penney Golden Rule Award Nomination
Laughlin Memorial Hospital

Mary Nolen
From: Goodlettsville, Sumner County
Years of Service: 17
Volunteering Highlights:
NMH Auxiliary: Volunteer of the Year
Meals-on-wheels
Dr. Thomas Frist Humanitarian Award, 2000

Clara Nell Norwood
From: Camden, Benton County
Years of Service: 10
Volunteering Highlights:
Northwest Tennessee Economic Development Council
American Cancer Society
Camden Healthcare and Rehabilitation Center
Special Notes: Mrs. Norwood is a cancer patient who has never given up.

Meg Nugent
From: Nashville, Davidson County
Years of Service: 10
Volunteering Highlights:
TN Community Education Association
Nashville Volunteer Literacy: Volunteer Tutor; Tutor Trainer
Nashville Adult Basic Education
American Society for Training and Development: Chair; Professional Development Committee
TAACE: Program Committee
Special Notes: Outstanding leadership as a supervisor of Volunteers in Service to America (VISTA), trainer of hundreds of volunteers to teach reading, connecting professional training to non-profit community in middle Tennessee

> **If every Tennessean were to volunteer for one day a month, we could…**
>
> eliminate hunger among Tennessee's elderly. On any day, in any part of the three Tennessee Metros, you can drive ten minutes in any direction, from any starting point, and you will find an elderly person who has food needs that are either not met, or met only occasionally. After the initial mobilization of these volunteers, a much smaller number of volunteers would be required to manage an on-going effort to ensure that no one "falls through the crack."
>
> —Clint Mathis, Jr.
> Memphis
> Shelby County

Tennessee Volunteer Heroes 2001

Vicki Oglesby
From: Nashville, Davidson County
Years of Service: 14
Volunteering Highlights:
Buddies of Nashville: Board Member; Buddy of the Year; mentor and buddy
McNeilly Center for Children: Board Member; Past Chairman
Nashville's Table: Founding Board Member
Comprehensive Care Center: volunteer and fundraiser (AIDS Clinic)
Tennessee Leadership: Board Member
Special Notes: "I really care about the individuals served by an organization — I have compassion and respect for them."

Maurine "Bunnie" Olivere
From: Germantown, Shelby County
Volunteering Highlights:
Germantown Arts Alliance: Board, Vice President
Memphis Area Race for the Cure: Chair 97 Race; President of Board 1998
Memphis Tour for the Cure: Board Member; Administrator
Subsidium, Memphis Oral School for the Deaf; former Board Member
Pegasus: Past President; Chair Fundraiser

Richard Osgood
From: Nashville, Davidson County
Years of Service: 11
Volunteering Highlights:
American Red Cross, Nashville Area Chapter and Regional Council
Children's Center
Junior Achievement

If every Tennessean were to volunteer for one day a month, we could…

take a lot of people's pain away!

—Ross Matlock
Nashville, Davidson County

If every Tennessean were to volunteer for one day a month, we could… make it possible for events and cultural exhibits to succeed and flourish financially by supplying manpower. Help neighbors and friends across Tennessee through service to MIFA, Boys and Girls Clubs, Big Brothers and Sisters, etc. In general, we could make life a little richer for all citizens and enrich our own lives.

—Bettye May
Memphis, Shelby County

Belle Meade United Methodist Church
Community Care Fellowship
Special Notes: His proven record of 11 years of service in a leadership role, two as Chapter Chair of the American Red Cross Nashville Area Chapter Board, Chair of the Rhapsody in Red fundraiser, and accepting a variety of other assignments. He works well with people.

Our Lady of Perpetual Help Senior Youth Group
From: Germantown, Shelby County
Years of Service: 1
Volunteering Highlights:
J.C. Penney Golden Rule Award Nomination
Habitat for Humanity
Special Notes: The youth of Our Lady of Perpetual Help (OLPH) raised $5,000 toward sponsoring the construction of a Habitat for Humanity Home and actually constructed the home themselves. The OLPH youth were an inspiration to everyone at the Habitat for Humanity worksite because of their attitudes, work ethic and commitment to improving the community through numerous volunteer activities. During the actual construction of the home, the youth of OLPH braved rain, mud, snow and cold winter days… but nothing could dampen their spirits or deter them from completing the house. The OLPH youth also: work at local soup kitchens; volunteer at Ronald McDonald House; attended 3 Catholic Heart Summer Work camps.

Mike Palazzolo
From: Germantown, Shelby County
Years of Service: 10
Volunteering Highlights:
Chairman Germantown Area Chamber of Commerce
Board Member AXA / Liberty Bowl
Board Member Leadership Germantown

Tennessee Volunteer Heroes 2001

> If every Tennessean were to volunteer for one day a month, we could...
>
> # improve the quality of life for all Tennesseans.
>
> —Donna McBride
> Celina, Clay County

Treasurer Leadership Germantown Alumni Association
Volunteer Rhodes College
Special Notes: Mike qualifies as a Tennessee Volunteer Hero because of his involvement in the community he calls home.

Parents As Support System (PASS)
From: Greeneville, Greene County
Volunteering Highlights:
Volunteer Center, Cookeville High School
J.C. Penney Golden Rule Recognition
Years of Service: 1
Special Notes: The most important goal that Parents As Support System (PASS) has accomplished is the increased awareness of the need for parent and community involvement within the schools. Even though there were already several volunteer parents working in various areas of the school, there was still the need for more parents and other people working in the community to get involved with the students.

Raven Parris
From: Oak Ridge, Anderson County
Years of Service: 1
Volunteering Highlights:
J.C. Penney Golden Rule Award Nomination
Doris A. Walker Academy
Special Notes: The Doris A. Walker Academy was without a reading library when Raven came there at the beginning of the year. She has purchased and donated hundreds of books to establish the library. She also bought bookcases to hold the books. She spends many evenings going through local used bookstores looking for bargain classics for the academy.

David Brown Parrish
From: Gallatin, Sumner County
Volunteering Highlights:
Meals on Wheels; Sumner Regional Hospital; Ramsey Hospice Volunteer
Board Member: Gallatin Sr Housing; Sr Citizens; Greater Nashville Agency on Aging
Advisory Board of Youth Alive and Free
Grand Masters Service Award; Key of City of Gallatin 2000
Humanitarian of the Year, 1996; Citizen of the Year, 1996
Special Notes: Year after year, David Brown Parrish has unselfishly devoted his time and energy, and wealth of expertise to serving the people of Gallatin and Sumner County in any and all capacities concerning volunteerism.

Mary Parsley
From: Murfreesboro, Rutherford County
Years of Service: 8
Volunteering Highlights:
American Red Cross
Meals on Wheels Program
Special Notes: "I just want to do anything I can to help someone."

Ronnie Parsons
From: Celina, Clay County
Years of Service: 10
Volunteering Highlights:
Clay County Industrial Board
New Hope Church of Christ
Clay County Commission
Jr. Pro Basketball league
Special Notes: He goes above and beyond his duties as

> If every Tennessean were to volunteer for one day a month, we could...
>
> change the lives of children in the communities in which they live. In the eyes of a child I see the importance of a positive role model. The children fuel my fire.
>
> —Carla Flatt McCauley
> Old Hickory, Davidson County

Solid Waste Director of Clay County. He volunteers many hours to see that Clay County is a litter-free community and has helped to educate schools on recycling in Clay County.

Nikoo Paydar
From: Memphis, Shelby County
Years of Service: 15
Volunteering Highlights:
Metropolitan Inter-Faith Association
Bridge Builders
March of Dimes: Walk America
WKNO (Public Television)
Church Health Center
Special Notes: "I have an interest in and commitment to helping recruit and organize young volunteers who will support charitable programs in the Memphis community."

Wesley Joe Penn
From: Germantown, Shelby County
Years of Service: 7
Volunteering Highlights:
Boy Scouts of America: Eagle Scout; Thane Smith Award
Germantown Youth Commission: Chairman
Key Club
DECA: voting delegate to National DECA Convention
Houston High Marching and Concert Band: Section leader, 1st Chair
Special Notes: He is a volunteer hero because of his dedication and volunteering in the City of Germantown. His seven years in scouting have taught him the value of service in the community, and the importance of always helping other people.

If every Tennessean were to volunteer for one day a month, we could...

instill volunteerism as a core value of our young people. I believe that when people give of their time, they are less likely to make poor decisions about using drugs, drinking or controlling their tempers.

—Edwin E. McClure
Johnson City
Washington County

If every Tennessean were to volunteer for one day a month, we could...

save organizations across Tennessee millions of dollars and provide much needed services. It would also bring us all closer together as we work for the common goal of our communities.

—Bill McCord
Chattanooga, Hamilton County

Jo Ann Perry
From: Friendship, Crockett County
Years of Service: 7
Volunteering Highlights:
American Cancer Society: Board of Directors; Relay for Life Chair
Chamber of Commerce: Ambassador for Crockett County
Crockett Memorial Library: Board of Trustees Chair: Friends of Library, Founding Member; Book Sales Chair
American Association of Univ. Women: State Treasurer; Past President
FCE Club: Secretary and Reporter
Special Notes: since relocating to Tennessee in 1993, she has become involved in community and county.

Lois H. Pezdirtz (deceased)
From: Collierville, Shelby County
Volunteering Highlights:
Wings Volunteer Program: Founder
Carpe Diem Retreat group: Ambassador
Special Notes: Lois was diagnosed with breast cancer in 1995, and her disease recurred in 1997. While in treatment at the West Clinic in Memphis, she was inspired to help patients cope with the disease. Together with a retired Baptist Minister, she founded what is now the "heart and soul" of Wings, a nonprofit organization, which collaborates services to provide hopeful relationships of caring and support to anyone touched by cancer in the greater Memphis community. Lois loved life and she loved people. "Hugs Heal" was Lois's favorite slogan. The idea was to give hugs, encouragement and hope to cancer patients and their families and friends. She lived to give hugs and personal attention to everyone she met at West Clinic and beyond. Her husband Karl says,

> If every Tennessean were to volunteer
> for one day a month, we could...
> change the course of our state's future. As volunteers, we have the opportunity and capability to use our talents and gifts to improve the quality of life for every Tennessean! With our expertise in various area of service, we can energize the economy of our great state, freeing monies for research and other areas where time alone cannot solve the problem. Motivation is the key; volunteerism is the catalyst!
>
> —Martha V. McCord
> Dyersburg
> Dyer County

"she touched the hearts of everyone she has met. She had great empathy as well as the ability to communicate with people who were ill. And even when she was dying, she felt that a day as a volunteer made her feel like the lucky one — a day she didn't have cancer." Lois shared what she believed in. She still lives on in our hearts and will live in countless others' hearts in the future. Lois had a wonderful, positive outlook and a joy for life that radiated from her like a light. On June 6th, 2000 Lois passed away, but she left a legacy of love and caring for others. Everyone who comes to the West Clinic is the recipient of Lois's love.

Ruth Phillips
From: Kingsport, Sullivan County
Years of Service: 7
Volunteering Highlights:
DOVIA of Greater Tri-Cities: Secretary
RSVP Project Director for 74 worksites in 8 counties of Northeast TN
Foster Grandparents Program
VISTA program
Special Notes: Ruth is a Volunteer Hero because of her outstanding leadership as the project director of a Tennessee Senior Volunteer project. 945 volunteers provided 156,777 hours of service in 1999-2000.

Rachael N. Pickett
From: Cleveland, Bradley County
Years of Service: 38
Volunteering Highlights:
BellSouth Pioneer Volunteers
March of Dimes: Mothers March and Walk America
IRS: Volunteer Income Tax Asst. Program
Muscular Distrophy & Muscular Schlerosis: Neighborhood Collector
Citizens Police Academy: Alumni Association
Special Notes: Whether volunteering in the community or caring for her 96 year old mother-in-law, Rachael is an inspiration to Tennessee Volunteers across the state.

Beth Pickler
From: Germantown, Shelby County
Years of Service: 12
Volunteering Highlights:
Houston Middle PTA: Treasurer
Farmington Elementary PTA: President; Treasurer: Programs: Ways and Means
Girl Scouts: Daisy and Browne Leader
Subsidium
Shelby County Education Associations Friend of Education Award
Special Notes: "Over the years I have been an advocate for children. Our children should be our priority. I have treated my role with PTA as a full time job spending time almost every school day to help in any way needed."

Chris Pickler
From: Germantown, Shelby County
Years of Service: 11
Volunteering Highlights:
Boy Scouts of America: Eagle Scout; over 80 merit badges: Senior Patrol Leader
City of Germantown: Youth Commission; Germantown 2000 Steering Committee
Order of the Arrow: Chapter Chief; Lodge Vice-Chief
Houston High School: HOBY delegate; Beta Club; Honor roll; Presidential Scholar
Houston High School Band: marching, concert and jazz
Special Notes: Chris has been very active in youth service organizations all his life. His Boy Scout Eagle project took over 2½ years to complete and transformed a

> If every Tennessean were to volunteer
> for one day a month, we could...
> make the world a better place to live. For instance, when a person volunteers their time and/or talents, they receive more than they give, so both parties benefit. Doing things for others brings smiles to people's faces and reduces some of their loneliness, if only for a moment.
>
> —Danny McCorkle
> Gallatin
> Sumner County

Tennessee Volunteer Heroes 2001

large center courtyard at Farmington Elementary School in Germantown from an unused, community eyesore, into a spectacular Educational Garden and Outdoor Classroom.

David Pickler
From: Germantown, Shelby County
Years of Service: 35
Volunteering Highlights:
Shelby County Government: Ad Hoc Committee on Public Education & Long Term Financing
Leadership Germantown: Inaugural Class, 1996; President, Alumni Association 1998-00
Leadership Memphis, Class of 2000
Germantown Youth Athletic Association: Coach 1990-99
Boy Scouts of America
Special Notes: "I have committed my life to community service. I believe volunteerism is an integral part of the American experience as one neighbor reaches out to help another. I have attempted to be a good friend, good neighbor and good citizen."

Katie Pickler
From: Germantown, Shelby County
Volunteering Highlights:
Yearbook Staff
Dance, jazz, tap, ballet
Chorus
Band
Girl Scouts
Special Notes: "I am 11 years old and have helped younger children and special needs children with reading and math. I also helped build a garden at my school, helped with the carnival and ran errands. I support the St. Jude Children's Hospital with my piggy bank."

If every Tennessean were to volunteer for one day a month, we could...

not only fill all of the present needs for volunteers, but also create new volunteer positions to serve the ever increasing needs of our communities.

—John McGonagle
Nashville
Davidson County

If every Tennessean were to volunteer for one day a month, we could...

preserve our past, improve our present, and prepare a brighter future for generations to come.

—Corinne McLerran
Celina
Clay County

Patricia Ann Pierce
From: Nashville, Davidson County
Years of Service: 25
Volunteering Highlights:
CABLE, Past President, Board of Directors
YWCA: Past Pres. & Board Member; Affordable Housing Taskforce; Mentoring Program; Domestic Violence
American Council on Education's TN Network: Past President; Board Member
Association on Higher Disability: Past International President & Board Member; Past Conference Chair
Women in Higher Education: Founding Member; Past President and Executive Committee
Special Notes: She graciously and unselfishly gives her time and energy to many worthy groups and organizations. Her compassion for humankind can be seen in her community service to groups focusing on promoting equity for women, empowering young women, and promoting the rights of individuals with disabilities. Pat not only gives of her time, she shares her expertise. She has assisted groups and agencies with strategic planning, fund raising, and training. Many consultants charge large fees for services of this nature, but Pat provides her time and skills with a smile.

Rictrell L. Pirtle
From: Memphis, Shelby County
Years of Service: 3
Volunteering Highlights:
United Cerebral Palsy
Beta Club
Voted most likely to be in the CIA by my 9th grade class
Special Notes: "I think I have demonstrated the qualities of a true volunteer. I have proved that you can be young and still make a difference in the lives of other people."

> If every Tennessean were to volunteer for one day a month, we could...
>
> almost guarantee that every child graduates prepared for success in college or a meaningful career because we intervened early for those at risk.
>
> —Robert E. McNeilly, Jr.
> Nashville
> Davidson County

Dianne K. Polly
From: Memphis, Shelby County
Years of Service: 25
Volunteering Highlights:
Girl Scouts
TN Dietetic Association: Board of Directors; Program Chair CPI
Memphis in May: Volunteer; Judge, BBQ Admissions
Council on Aging: Board of directors 1994-98; 2000 Day Volunteer Fair Day Expo
Lord of Life Lutheran Church: Chair Staff Support
Special Notes: "I love my adopted state of 10 years! I am committed to making Memphis and Tennessee a better place to live by volunteering to help others improve their lives."

Porter-Leath Youth Advisory Council
From: Memphis, Shelby County
Volunteering Highlights:
Porter-Leath Children's Center
Youth Retreat
Back to School Bash
Annual Teen Christmas Party
Awards Banquet
Special Notes: "Porter-Leath Children's Center has been in existence since 1850. Since then, we have added a number of programs to address the ever-changing needs of children and families within our community. Among those programs are Employment Training for Teens and After Care Project whose ultimate goal is to provide youth with job training, independent life skills and counseling relating to everyday situations the teenagers must face. To assist us in our endeavors, the Youth Advisory Council was added as a core component of these programs. The council provides staff with innovative ideas as a way of enhancing the program and increasing youth involvement from the current program participants. These young people have been invaluable to the Center.

Sam Powell
From: Signal Mtn., Hamilton County
Years of Service: 35
Volunteering Highlights:
River Park Advisory board
Signal Mtn.: Parks Board
Shackleford Ridge Park of Hamilton County/Mountain Rec., Inc.
Tennessee Conservation Commission
Tennessee State Parks and Greenways Foundation, Tennessee River Gorge Trust
Special Notes: Mr. Powell was a leader in the development of the Cumberland Trail, originally a state scenic trail which in 1998 was designated as the new Cumberland Trail State Park. This is a linear park running 280 miles from Signal Point on Signal Mountain, to Cumberland Gap National Park on the Kentucky-Tennessee border. Starting with the trail segment running through the town of Signal Mountain, Mr. Powell was able to interest the Town of Signal Mountain in allowing him to develop an adjoining 550-acre tract into the Rainbow Lake Wilderness Area. It includes several trails. He presently is working on trails in the Hamilton County Shackleford Ridge Park on Signal Mountain, which will connect with the Cumberland Trail. His interest in building these trails has been to create access to the wilderness environment for many generations to come.

> If every Tennessean were to volunteer for one day a month, we could...
>
> greatly enhance the lives of countless numbers who desperately need *someone* to really *care*.
>
> —Linda Meador
> Portland
> Sumner County

Mrs. Mattie Jean Pressley
From: Nashville, Davidson County
Years of Service: 11
Volunteering Highlights:
Mary Catherine Strobel Award, finalist
Room-In-The-Inn
Community Care Fellowship
Adult Literacy
Assistance to immigrant families
Special Notes: "I enjoy volunteering. We carried six people from an immigrant family from Yugoslavia to get shoes yesterday and we have to go again today to purchase shoes for others in the family. I like to make other people happy — that is why we should volunteer."

George Price
From: Athens, McMinn County
Years of Service: 40
Volunteering Highlights:
Meridian Sun Lodge, Member
Chilhowee Shrine Club, President
Athens Municipal Planning Commission, Member for 34 years, Chairman for 32 years
Athens Optimist Club, Charter Member, Past President, Lt. Governor, Bulletin Editor
BellSouth Pioneer Volunteers
Special Notes: George truly loves people. He is involved with all people, young and old. He passes along his Christian values and encourages all to keep busy. George lives what he says!

James E. (Jim) Queen
From: Chattanooga, Hamilton County
Years of Service: 15
Volunteering Highlights:

> *If every Tennessean were to volunteer for one day a month, we could...*
>
> have better schools, cleaner parks, and support services for all in need. In this way, the citizens would augment the fine work done by the governmental employees of Tennessee.
>
> —Brandy Miller
> Germantown, Shelby County

> *If every Tennessean were to volunteer for one day a month, we could...*
>
> bring hope to the hopeless of the world. By taking a stand against homelessness, poverty, illiteracy and disease, what an impact we could make on the world's problems, and what a blessing we would receive by giving of ourselves.
>
> —Pat Miller
> Springfield, Robertson County

Volunteer Construction Manager for original Ronald McDonald House
Volunteer Construction Manager for RMH Family Room in TCTCH
J.C. Penney Golden Rule Award Nomination
Volunteer Construction Manager for 12-bedroom expansion to RMH
Chairman of the RMH Building, maintenance, and safety/crisis committees
Ronald McDonald House Board Member, 15 years
Special Notes: Jim has been a dedicated volunteer at the Ronald McDonald House in a variety of capacities. The incredible gift of his time to oversee construction and maintenance issues at the House has been nothing less than record-setting.

Queen of Peace Catholic Church Ladies Auxiliary
From: Olive Branch
Years of Service: 8
Volunteering Highlights:
Special Kids and Families, Inc., Memphis, TN
J.C. Penney Golden Rule Award Nomination
Special Notes: The Queen of Peace Ladies Auxiliary approached Special Kids and Families, Inc. with an offer to help in whatever way was needed. Special Kids and Families, Inc. identified the need to establish a Resource Library or Center that would house adaptive toys, specialized equipment, and varied reading/AV materials to loan to families in the Memphis — Delta community who had children with disabilities. The Queen of Peace Ladies responded to the idea with a resounding "yes!" The Queen of Peace Ladies designed, planned, initiated, executed, and further developed their project to create "The Special Kids and Families Adaptive Resource Center." Beginning in 1990 and through 1998, they held annual fundraisers. In 8 years,

> If every Tennessean were to volunteer
> for one day a month, we could...
> have a practical and life-enriching effect on anyone associated with the volunteer group and others. When you are excited about volunteering, it is easy to bring others into that circle of volunteering and watch it grow.
>
> —Bonnie Harris Moore
> Nashville
> Davidson County

the Queen of Peace Ladies Auxiliary has donated over $8,000 to make the Special Kids and Families Adaptive Resource Center a reality.

Kay Dillon Ramsey
From: McMinnville, Warren County
Years of Service: 30
Volunteering Highlights:
Girl Scouts: Troop Leader; Day-camp Director at Camp Walling Woods
Good Neighbors: helped start program which delivers a hot meal on Thursday evenings to needy
Families in Crisis: Board Member
Warren County Cancer Fund: radio broadcast of annual auction
Habitat for Humanity: Chairman for Warren County
Special Notes: Kay Ramsey is a person of creative vision and common sense. Decisive and compassionate, she shares her time, energy and resources generously. She has a terrific sense of humor. Her high standards and good judgment contribute to her excellent leadership skills.

David Ray
From: Memphis, Shelby County
Years of Service: 30
Volunteering Highlights:
Shelby County Mayor's Office on Aging
J.C. Penney Golden Rule Award Nomination
Junior Achievement
International Paper West
Special Notes: David Ray epitomizes what a great volunteer should be. He is always willing to help in any way needed, and he seems to have an uncanny knack of knowing when to call to help with any aspect. He asks nothing in return and is tireless in his efforts. I believe he is completely tuned in to the Fans for the Needy Program and feels deeply that the people he is helping to serve are at great risk. He wants to make sure that every person who needs a fan gets one. Before David began helping with this program, the largest number of fans delivered in one summer was 450. The first year David volunteered, we delivered 1289 fans! Over half of those were purchased, donated, or delivered by David and his recruits. This past summer we again broke the 1200 mark with his help. We have been able to triple the numbers of fans going to the homes of needy seniors due to the efforts of David Ray.

Cleve Redus
From: Jacksboro, Campbell County
Years of Service: 10
Volunteering Highlights:
Kids Say America
Rotary Clubs of Campbell County
Food Life Services of Campbell County
Roane State Community College Foundation of Campbell County
Campbell County Health Council
Special Notes: Dr. Redus is a true community leader. He consistently promotes good health, healthy lifestyles and often provides screenings as a public service. He "makes a difference" and has a true "volunteer spirit."

Cheryl Reed
From: Brentwood, Williamson County
Years of Service: 2
Volunteering Highlights:
Nashville CARES
Woodmont Hills church of Christ
Nurse-Baptist Hospital Neonatal
Special Notes: Cheryl is a member of the inter-Faith team at Nashville CARES. She provides rides to many

> If every Tennessean were to volunteer
> for one day a month, we could...
> change our community, our county and our state, and our country would also change. I quit a paying job so I would have more time to volunteer. Some people say, "Mary V., you are going to have to slow down," and I tell them "Don't you think I will know when I have to quit?" So many people just say, "let someone else do it." The world would be a better place if everyone would just hold out a helping hand. If you say you can't make a difference, you won't.
>
> —Mary Viuna Moore
> Parsons
> Decatur County

medical appointments, laundry, grocery shopping to the homebound, sick and dying.

Vernon Reed
From: Memphis, Shelby County
Years of Service: 15
Volunteering Highlights:
Brooks Museum: Docent; Speakers Bureau
Theatre Memphis: Scene Shop
Bowld Hospital
Wonder Series: Docent; Speakers Bureau
Metal Museum: Docent; Speakers Bureau

Zenia Revitz
From: Memphis, Shelby County
Years of Service: 20
Volunteering Highlights:
Women in Community Service
Haddasah
Special Notes: For three years, she has been successful as a mentor to women being released from the Shelby County Division of Corrections. She has helped them lead productive lives and get back on track during periods of relapse.

Clark Reyes
From: Knoxville, Knox County
Years of Service: 2
Volunteering Highlights:
AmeriCorps — Emerald Youth Foundation: Mentor, Teacher; Leader
Whittle Springs Middle School: Mentor
Special Olympics: peer tutor
Youth of Knoxville Evangelism: Mentor
Emerald Ave. United Methodist Church
Special Notes: Clark Reyes grew up in urban Knoxville, the son of Filipino immigrants. He has done well overcoming obstacles. He is a very intelligent young man whose passion is to give back to urban youth what was given to him by Emerald Youth Foundation, an inner city youth ministry. Thus, he served as an AmeriCorps member while attending college and is now working part-time with the Boys and Girls club.

>
> If every Tennessean were to volunteer for one day a month, we could...
>
> ## reach troubled teens, both boys and girls, all across the state, as well as the elderly, homeless, and adult men and women inmates.
>
> —Rev. Larry Morris
> Memphis, Shelby County

> If every Tennessean were to volunteer for one day a month, we could...
>
> make a difference in people's lives. The hierarchy of basic needs, e.g., food, clothing, and shelter, does not include relationships with people. Yet, people need people! When we work together to accomplish a common goal, we not only accomplish the goal, but we also impact each other.
>
> —Chasity Morris
> Norris
> Anderson County

George Rhea
From: Nashville, Davidson County
Years of Service: 7
Volunteering Highlights:
American Red Cross
Special Notes: Mr. Rhea drives thousands of miles each year for the American Red Cross. His duties include: picking up blood at Bloodmobiles in the 80 Tennessee counties served by the Red Cross, and rushing it back to Nashville for processing; transporting boxes of life-saving blood to hospitals in Tennessee and Kentucky; picking up people who need a ride to the Red Cross Blood Center, making it possible for them to donate blood and return to work in a timely manner; transporting our education speaker, Mr. Baker who is visually impaired — Mr. Rhea has taken Mr. Baker as far as southern Illinois and eastern Missouri. Mr. Rhea is truly an inspiration to others.

Elbert N. Rich, Jr.
From: Memphis, Shelby County
Years of Service: 5
Volunteering Highlights:
Barksdale/Cloverdale Neighborhood Association
David Street Block Club
J.C. Penney Golden Rule Award Nomination
Alcy-Ball Neighborhood Watch
MANW

Tennessee Volunteer Heroes 2001

> If every Tennessean were to volunteer for one day a month, we could... help young people out of poverty. We could help improve our schools and help keep children from a life of crime. We could send a message to politicians that volunteers are interested in their legislation and are aware of what they are doing. We could spend time with the elderly and ill people who are often forgotten.
>
> —Peggy Moss
> Nashville, Davidson County

Special Notes: The services Mr. Rich provides help keep the community safe, focused and aware of crime. He strengthens communication among neighbors, helps maintain property value, assists with senior citizens, and gives a sense of security. He has affected thousands of Memphis residents. He speaks to many groups all over the city. He has been mentioned many times in the Commercial Appeal for his outstanding contribution to this community and city. Mr. Rich faces many challenges such as being criticized often by citizens who are involved in drug activity, those that don't participate in maintaining their property, and is sometimes in the bad eye of city officials because he doesn't take no for an answer when it comes to the well being of a neighborhood or citizen. His life has been threatened by dealers, and much more. He continues the fight and stands for the youth, seniors, and all of Memphis. He is a village-raised child protecting the village as an adult.

Mrs. Marjorie Evans Rios
From: Cookeville, Putnam County
Years of Service: 43
Volunteering Highlights:
American Red Cross, Putnam County: Past Chair; member Tennessee's first state council
International Community Hospitality Association: Past President
TN Tech University Chapter of Phi Delta Kappa and Pi Lamba Theta: Past President
First Presbyterian Church, Cookeville: Deacon
Cookeville Refugee Committee
Special Notes: She has volunteered all her life, from delivering Meals on wheels, to helping resettle Vietnamese and later Bosnian refugees in her community.

Virginia Rippee
From: Nashville, Davidson County
Years of Service: 30
Volunteering Highlights:
The Salvation Army: Band; Women's Auxillary
Nashville Symphony Association
YWCA
Nashville Humane Association
March of Dimes
Special Notes: Mrs. Rippee qualifies as a Tennessee Volunteer Hero because she quietly lives the true spirit of volunteerism, generously giving of her personal gifts of time, leadership and organizational skills for the benefit of others. Very much a "hands-on" volunteer in all that she undertakes, Mrs. Rippee has personally spent thousands of hours from October through December during the last eight years working alongside community volunteers in The Salvation Army Angel Tree program. Her greatest contributions have been her leadership, administrative skills and planning that have helped shape this Nashville holiday tradition into an efficient and effective means for providing much needed material help and hope to over 14,000 needy children, disabled people, and senior citizens each year. Her dedication to this program as a volunteer leader has had a lasting positive impact on the well being of thousands of underprivileged citizens of her community.

David A. Robb, Jr.
Years of Service: 24
Volunteering Highlights:
J.C. Penney Golden Rule Award Nomination
CONTACT of Chattanooga: Board of Directors: Training Committee
Special Notes: Dave's excitement and involvement has

> If every Tennessean were to volunteer for one day a month, we could... help people sign up for social services such as health and housing; form planning groups to define problems, to volunteer.
>
> —Dr. Joe P. Moss, Jr.
> Chapel Hill
> Williamson County

certainly brought in many new recruits. His remarkable ability in training volunteers has produced top quality individuals who are capable of handling the multiplicity of problems presented by callers, whether it's a young girl contemplating abortion or someone threatening to end their life by suicide. Dave has exhibited a remarkable devotion to his ministry as well as compassion and empathy for the callers, and he has been doing this for almost 25 years.

Billie Henard Roberts
From: Greeneville, Greene County
Years of Service: 16
Volunteering Highlights:
Nathanial Greene Museum; Founder
1983 Greeneville/Greene County Bicentennial Celebration: Co-Chair
J.C. Penney Golden Rule Award Nomination
Roby School: Past President of the PTA
Appalachian Council Girl Scouts of America
Greene County Republican Women
Special Notes: Billie has given tirelessly of her time and talents to create a place for all citizens of Greeneville and Greene County to realize their heritage, accept their ancestry, and preserve our history for future generations through the Nathanial Greene Museum. In addition to all her work at the museum, she still finds time for the elderly, handicapped and youth. Billie volunteers to drive neighbors to the doctor, to the grocery store, the drug store, or anywhere lese they might need to go.

Pam Roberts
From: Nashville, Davidson County
Volunteering Highlights:
Nashville Family shelter: Volunteer Coordinator; Interim Administrator; volunteer overnight stay

---

If every Tennessean were to volunteer for one day a month, we could…

have a cleaner and greater Tennessee by removing all litter and by improving the living conditions for seniors on "fixed" incomes, and those struggling with low incomes. We could improve the quality of life for all Tennesseans.

—Robert Mullins, Sr.
Smyrna, Rutherford County

 If every Tennessean were to volunteer for one day a month, we could…

ensure that residents of nursing homes are happier. If someone visited them at least once a week, even if it was just for twenty minutes it would make such a difference. Our reward would be much greater than what we put into visiting them. We receive love and affection.

—George and Mary Murphy
Memphis, Shelby County

Tennessee Special Olympics: Opening Ceremonies committee; former coach
Hands on Nashville
Walk for the Homeless

Shirley Robinson
From: Antioch, Davidson County
Years of Service: 8
Volunteering Highlights:
The Salvation Army: Angel Tree Mall Captain
Special Notes: Shirley Robinson is modest and would certainly never consider herself a hero. She is, however, a Tennessee Volunteer Hero to the staff of The Salvation Army. For the last eight years she has worked as a Salvation Army Angel tree Volunteer. Her volunteer career began when she offered to fill some volunteer shifts at an area mall. When an urgent need arose for a mall captain, a volunteer to coordinate and help supervise the 60 to 80 volunteers needed to man each Angel Tree during a holiday season, Shirley agreed to take the job. She has been the mall captain ever since. With an unabashed love for the holidays and the Angel Tree program, Shirley has worked thousands of hours over the past eight years, often filling in when other volunteers are not available. She frequently works just because she enjoys meeting people, sharing the purpose of the Angel Tree with them, and letting them share their stories of what Christmas means to them. Each holiday season for the past eight years, Shirley has planned her Christmas around her commitment to the Angel Tree program. She has taken this commitment very seriously, serving as a goodwill ambassador for Angel Tree, explaining that her Angel Tree operated efficiently and for the best benefit of those it serves. Many Angels can thank Shirley for helping ensure that their Christmases have been brighter.

> **If every Tennessean were to volunteer for one day a month, we could...** have a better understanding of how great the needs are. If people volunteer and have firsthand experience with others who are in need, then they would have a greater appreciation of the difference that their time and efforts can make.
>
> —Rick Murphree
> Knoxville, Knox County

Joe M. Rodgers
From: Nashville, Davidson County
Years of Service: 35
Volunteering Highlights:
American Red Cross
Boy Scouts of America: Middle Tennessee Council
YMCA of Nashville and Middle Tennessee
National Law Center for the Protection of Children and Families
National Football Foundation and College Hall of Fame, Inc.
Special Notes: Ambassador Rodgers was honored in 1999 by the American Red Cross with "Volunteer Fundraiser of the Year." This award is presented to a volunteer who has demonstrated exceptional leadership in successfully completing fund raising efforts for the American Red Cross. After the tornado hit the Nashville area, in April 1998, Ambassador Rodgers was contacted and he agreed to come into the Chapter. He was here for many hours and made telephone calls to every friend and CEO he knew, obtaining pledges of more than $700,000. In response to his calls, the presidents of area banks opened a special tornado relief account to which their customers could make donations. This netted an additional $200,000.

Jennifer Rodriguez
From: Cordova, Shelby County
Years of Service: 1
Volunteering Highlights:
AmeriCorps National Service Organization
Memphis City Council, Awarded Outstanding Service to the Community
Court Appointed Special Advocate
Memphis In May volunteer; Hands On Memphis volunteer
Special Notes: Jennifer goes beyond the call of duty and never asks for anything in return. She puts her heart into all the work she does and is always willing to help others do the same.

Heber Rogers
From: Nashville, Davidson County
Years of Service: 20
Volunteering Highlights:
Catholic Charities
American Red Cross

Peter C. Rousos
From: Brentwood, Williamson County
Years of Service: 20
Volunteering Highlights:
American Red Cross
United Way
March of Dimes
U.S. Chamber of Commerce
Rochester Institute of Technology
Special Notes: He is a very successful businessman, cherishes his family, and is eager to make a contribution to his community. He is the current Chairman of the Nashville Red Cross Chapter.

Kay and Guy Rowland
From: Memphis, Shelby County
Years of Service: 15
Volunteering Highlights:
Friends of Orpheum Theater: Star Award; Office: Usher
Memphis in May: Office Resource; Debut Award
Theater Memphis: Usher
Davies Manor Association: Directions Chair; Finance Committee Chair; VP: Board
Memphis/Shelby Library Friend: Satterfield Award
Special Notes: "We volunteer as a team and want to help causes that we feel improve the quality of life in the community."

> **If every Tennessean were to volunteer for one day a month, we could...** have no hunger and a cure for every disease. The possibilities are limitless.
>
> —Lori Murphy
> Cookeville, Putnam County

Denis Rozier
From: Memphis, Shelby County
Years of Service: 20
Volunteering Highlights:
The Crisis Center
Special Notes: Denis responded to an ad for volunteers because he knew he enjoyed helping others. He often helped his friends and co-workers so crisis counseling volunteer work was a natural. Like all volunteers with some experience, Denis has helped many, many callers find their way through dark and difficult times.

Marguerite Rubel
From: Clarksville, Montgomery County
Years of Service: 70
Volunteering Highlights:
Montgomery County Historical Society
Montgomery County Republican Women
Advisory Council for the Postal Service
Clarksville Chamber of Commerce
Friends of Dunbar Cave Group
Special Notes: She is a walking history book and I have never known her to say "no" when asked to participate in helping promote the Clarksville/Montgomery County community or the state of Tennessee. She is always enthusiastic and motivates people . She continues to amaze me with her energy and caring for others.

Audrey Russell
From: Greeneville, Greene County
Years of Service: 3
Volunteering Highlights:
J.C. Penney Golden Rule Award Nomination
Family Resource Center
Special Notes: Audrey instructs a weekly ballet class for the Family Resource Center, held at Highland

> If every Tennessean were to volunteer for one day a month, we could…
> be more and more efficient in helping others, especially those in need, disabled persons, elderly persons and all people looking for assistance in health education, employment, housing and transportation. Union makes power, and more Tennessee Volunteers are needed to accomplish the noble mission of helping others.
>
> —Diomede Musigaro
> Nashville, Davidson County

> If every Tennessean were to volunteer for one day a month, we could…
> take care of many of the needs of our citizens. It would eliminate many government departments, programs and taxes. It would improve the quality of life for everyone. We could create a great sense of self-worth, self esteem and accomplishment in the volunteers.
>
> —Jerry Nass
> Clarksville, Montgomery County

Elementary School. She plans the curriculum, supervises all support staff, choreographs the program, plans and chaperones field trips to performances by professional ballet companies. Audrey's impact is not only on the students, but also on each individual who has seen her interaction with children and her leadership ability.

Barbara S. Russell
From: Memphis, Shelby County
Years of Service: 30+
Volunteering Highlights:
PTA — 30+yrs serving on 2 local PTA boards (2 terms as president), City PTA Council Training
Citizens Against Busing Board, then community contact for the Superintendent's office
City Beautiful Commission — 14 years promoting clean-up, paint-up, fix-up & an environmental curriculum
School Partnerships — raised $44,000+ to promote local school partnerships in several cities & states
Teen Job Service (City Slickers) — served 15yrs on this board (2 terms as president)
Special Notes: For the PTA, she trained other members to volunteer citywide and promoted many activities for involvement. She also sat on the State PTA board, raising funds and promoting programs to benefit children and youth. For the Citizens Against Busing Board, when the judge ordered the desegregation of the Memphis City Schools, she served as a community contact for the Superintendent's office to help quiet the fears of the community; she organized buses to bring black parents into her neighborhood school and white parents into the black community school; she encouraged white parents to keep their children in public schools; and she also met the buses of black children before and after classes to help ensure their safety. All four of her chil-

> If every Tennessean were to volunteer for one day a month, we could...
>
> not only dramatically improve our social and environmental structures, but also enjoy the dividend of camaraderie to give new meaning to our being the Volunteer State.
>
> —C. Cella Neapolitan
> Cookeville, Putnam County

dren attended public schools through the desegregation plans A and Z, and each graduated from a Memphis public school. For the City Beautiful Commission, she organized volunteers to judge in the competitions held by the schools. For the Teen Job Service, she raised funds, planned youth activities, recruited worksites, and encouraged students to stay in school.

Lynn Russell
From: Memphis, Shelby County
Volunteering Highlights:
J.C. Penney Golden Rule Award Nomination
Junior Achievement
Special Notes: Susan has given over 16 years of her time and talent, used her resources and is committed to her belief that Junior Achievement is a very worthwhile way in which she can give back to the community. But, most of all, she gives to children a strong sense of self-worth and a motivation to stay in school and succeed in the future. The lives of over 1,500 children have been touched through Susan's unselfish commitment.

Susan D. Russell
From: Memphis, Shelby County
Years of Service: 17
Volunteering Highlights:
Junior Achievement; Classroom Consultant
Habitat for Humanity: Builder and financial supporter
J.C. Penney Golden Rule Award Nomination
Christian Brothers High School: Chair Auction Operations 2000
St. Jude's Children's Research Hospital
Special Notes: A "volunteer" disposition — both as an example and advocate, and many years of volunteer work.

The Volunteers of Saint Patrick's Center
From: Memphis, Shelby County
Years of Service: 22
Volunteering Highlights:
Provided thousands of meals yearly to the homeless, homebound and needy families
Provided better housing by building and renovating homes in impoverished areas
Provided educational opportunities to youth, adults and those in prison
Provided financial training to needy families seeking to secure home loans or file taxes
Provided healthy, positive recreational opps for young people living in high-crime, impoverished areas
Special Notes: The Volunteers of St. Patrick's Center are a role model for compassionate service, diversity and the acceptance of all people regardless of race, religion or socio-economic condition. Their doors, hearts, and minds are open to all. They have literally made dreams a reality by refusing to accept defeat no matter how great the challenge! Not only have they changed the lives of those they serve, but they have inspired others to serve as well.

Edward Salinas
From: Nashville, Davidson County
Years of Service: 2
Volunteering Highlights:
1999 Gore Family Reunion — Families and Community
Nature Center and Creative Discovery Museum
Dismas House (halfway house for parolees)
Oasis Center Teen Outreach Program Advisory Committee, affecting program design
Worked with other youth writing anti-violence skits aimed at Middle School students
Special Notes: Edward is a tireless volunteer. During his

> If every Tennessean were to volunteer for one day a month, we could...
>
> change Tennessee. We could make it a better, more peaceful place to be. Crime in Tennessee would decrease and it would be a better place for teens.
>
> —Thuc Nhu Nguyen
> Nashville
> Davidson County

Tennessee Volunteer Heroes 2001

8th grade and 9th grade years, he volunteered over 265 hours in the community. As Edward puts it, "Volunteering doesn't pay in the pocket, but it does in the heart. It makes me proud of who I am and what I do."

Tracy L. Salmon
From: Lexington, Henderson County
Years of Service: 15
Volunteering Highlights:
United Methodist Youth Counselor
Special Olympics
United Way, Chairperson for Henderson County Campaign
Habitat for Humanity
Ducks Unlimited
Special Notes: Tracy really has the spirit of a volunteer. He has seen the different problems facing people and he gets involved. He gives freely of his time to make an impact in areas he's committed to. His enthusiasm is contagious and he excites people he's working with.

Salvation Army Women's Auxiliary
From: Nashville, Davidson County
Years of Service: 13
Volunteering Highlights:
Kare for Kids
Magness Potter Tutoring Program
Angel Tree Program
Transitional Housing
Adult Rehabilitation Center Support
Special Notes: The members of the Salvation Army Women's Auxiliary are Tennessee Volunteer Heroes because of their dedication to changing lives and caring for those less fortunate through the gift of their volunteer time. This group of Salvation Army volunteers has, over the past 13 years, repeatedly marshaled both manpower and community resources to benefit individuals and families in need who are served through a variety of Salvation Army programs. These programs serve underprivileged children, elderly, disabled homeless and those struggling with alcohol and drug abuse. Auxiliary members have served as volunteer daycare workers, youth tutors and Angel Tree volunteers. They have, as a group, planned, executed and hosted major fundraising events. They have helped inner-city children experience the joy of nature by providing a summer camp experience for those in Salvation Army programs. They have nurtured and encouraged those struggling with homelessness and substance abuse by providing home-like touches such as curtains and furnishings for transitional housing apartments and the fellowship of social events, holiday parties and sobriety birthday parties. By enthusiastically and articulately communicating both the mission and programs of the Salvation Army and the needs of those living in poverty in the Nashville community, the Salvation Army Women's Auxiliary volunteers have been responsible for bringing about and sustaining positive changes in the lives of thousands of Nashville residents.

Dorothy Sanders
From: Dickson, Dickson County
Years of Service: 15
Volunteering Highlights:
Piney FCE Club, Past President
AARP, Volunteer of the year
Breast Advocate
Senior Citizens, Past Secreatry and Board Vice President
Health Board

If every Tennessean were to volunteer for one day a month, we could…

wipe out hunger, poverty, illiteracy, litter, or other ills prevalent in our society. It would foster understanding between people of different backgrounds and promote feelings of good will. A little helping hand goes a long way, so if everyone pitched in our society will be much improved.

—Bryan I. Nishimoto
Germantown
Shelby County

If every Tennessean were to volunteer for one day a month, we could…

share the blessings that volunteering brings to both the giver and the receiver.

—Mary Nichols
Nashville, Davidson County

Tennessee Volunteer Heroes 2001

> If every Tennessean were to volunteer for one day a month, we could...
>
> feed the hungry, cheer up the sick and lonely, make friends, give smiles and reach so many people in need.
>
> —Mary Nolen
> Goodlettsville, Sumner County

Mark Schempp
From: Tullahoma, Coffee County
Years of Service: 17
Volunteering Highlights:
Historic Preservation Society of Tullahoma, Past President and Director
Tennessee's Backroads Heritage, Inc., Director
Alzheimer's Association, Director
Tullahoma Historic Zoning Commission
Coffee County Senior Citizen's Center, Director
Special Notes: Mark is a native of Connecticut, but has a warm Tennessee heart. When he sees someone in distress, or an opportunity to improve the looks and amenities of Tullahoma, he is always ready to help when asked. He has donated thousands of his hours. He is very bright and kind, so his input is always helpful and appreciated.

Jo Sanders
From: Goodlettsville, Davidson County
Years of Service: 35
Volunteering Highlights:
NMH Auxiliary: Volunteer of the Year, 1988; Board President 1982-84
Memorial Foundation
Connell United Methodist Church: Board of Trustees
THA Award of Excellence in Volunteerism, 1999
Special Notes: She is incredibly devoted to helping other people and to supporting causes that she believes in. Also, her smile is like pure sunshine!

Florence Schillinger
From: Greeneville, Greene County
Years of Service: 24
Volunteering Highlights:
Retired Senior Volunteer Program
J.C. Penney Golden Rule Award Nomination
Roby Senior Center
Special Notes: Dedication to service others, has volunteered since 1976 at senior meal site delivering meals, then later serving meals, cleaning meal site and assisting other elderly persons at meal time. Mrs. Schillinger has overcome 2 major surgeries for cancer.

Richmond Savage
From: Memphis, Shelby County
Years of Service: 20
Volunteering Highlights:
Tennessee School of Religion: Board
Oakville Health Care Center
MIFA
Mississippi Valley State University
Christian Aid Mission
Special Notes: I have been blessed with the gift of help and because of this gift I have seen a special need for the elderly, children, churches and/or individuals and responded.

Kim Sawvell
From: Ashland City, Cheatham County
Years of Service: 1
Volunteering Highlights:
Pathways of Cheatham County
Creates beautiful ceramics for family and friends
Special Notes: Kim is pleasant and always eager to help.

> If every Tennessean were to volunteer for one day a month, we could...
>
> touch many lives in many thoughtful ways. Each small kind deed brings cheer to others. There is work we can all do.
>
> —Clara Nell Norwood
> Camden, Benton County

Elma Schnapp
From: Memphis, Shelby County
Years of Service: 15
Volunteering Highlights:
Josephine Circle; Les Passers Circle
Race for the Cure
Counceling Dept at White Station High School — provides services
St. Jude's Hospital; Temple Israel; Jewish Community Center
Gramhood School
Special Notes: "I came to America unfamiliar with its customs and language, but I have a love for mankind and I know I could make a difference, regardless of my difficulties."

Mildred Schwartz
From: Memphis, Shelby County
Years of Service: 50
Volunteering Highlights:
Women in Community Service (WICS)
National Council of Jewish Women
The Seymour-Schwartz Scholarship Fund for successful WICS graduates was named after her.
Special Notes: Ms. Schwartz was instrumental in starting Women in Community Service Programs in Memphis. She has been involved with National Council of Jewish Women, both on a national and local level. Before volunteerism became popular, Ms. Schwartz was at the cutting edge, especially helping those in the community less fortunate than she.

Oscar Scott
From: Ooltewah, Hamilton County
Years of Service: 30
Volunteering Highlights:
GIVE A HOOT FOR KIDS, Inc.: educated 3,000 children, teachers and volunteers

> If every Tennessean were to volunteer for one day a month, we could... change the life of every Tennessean who is struggling to meet basic needs. From the adult education perspective, it is a fact that no amount of money can pay for the time, talent and expertise that volunteers offer every day. The most profound changes in society are made one person at a time, one person teaching another person, and so on. Tennessee could truly be "The Volunteer State" if all Tennesseans volunteered one day per month.
>
> —Meg Nugent
> Nashville
> Davidson County

> If every Tennessean were to volunteer for one day a month, we could...
>
> ## be more compassionate and understanding. We all need to be kinder to one another.
>
> —Vicki Oglesby
> Nashville
> Davidson County

100 Black Men of Chattanooga: mentoring, school activities, role model
River City Football Classic: Scholarship fundraising
Farm Service Agency: Board Member, assist with loans to farmers
United Negro College Fund: donor and fundraiser for scholarships
Special Notes: Oscar Scott, a lifetime farmer, was amazed that most children believed food came from the local grocers and was in no way related to a farm. His vision was to educate them regarding agriculture, conservation and farm life. He initiated the GIVE A HOOT FOR KIDS program 16 years ago, which is held annually the 1st week of May on Mr. Scott's farm.

Patricia E. Scott
From: Memphis, Shelby County
Years of Service: 3
Volunteering Highlights:
National Dean's List Member, 2000
Crichton College, Honor student
Memphis Leadership Foundation
Urban Youth Initiative, Class of 2001
Golden United Methodist Church
Special Notes: Patricia is a Tennessee Volunteer Hero because of the compassion she has for our youth, education and commitment to change our world.

Tricia Seubert
From: Memphis, Shelby County
Years of Service: 6
Volunteering Highlights:
Memphis Child Advocacy Center
Member First Families of Tennessee # 6496
Neshoba Unitarian Universalist Church
Special Notes: "I don't think of myself as doing very

> If every Tennessean were to volunteer for one day a month, we could...
>
> set an example for the rest of the states in caring and concern for others, and set a precedent for strong support for community projects.
>
> —Maurine "Bunnie" Olivere
> Germantown, Shelby County

much. In fact, I have been doing all my volunteer work at home while recovering from a stress fracture on my femur. The Child Advocacy Center doesn't have an elevator and I cannot get up stairs yet. They have been kind enough to send me work that I can do at home."

Kate Sevier
From: Nashville, Davidson County
Years of Service: 4
Volunteering Highlights:
University of Kentucky Alumni Association
Kappa Kappa Gamma Alumni Association
Saddle Up!
St. Henry CYD
Nashville Diocese Youth Program
Special Notes: Enthusiasm and dedication to Saddle Up! and the community's children are what qualify Kate as a Tennessee Volunteer Hero.

Eva Babb Sexton
From: Newport, Cocke County
Years of Service: 21
Volunteering Highlights:
Newport Rescue Squad, Board of Directors
Stokley Memorial Library, Chairman
Pisgah Presbyterian Church Memorial Garden
First United Methodist Church Sunday School Teacher
City Beautification Director
Special Notes: As a result of Mrs. Eva volunteering her time and expertise to our town and community, Newport and Cocke County have become a much more enjoyable place to reside or visit. Some of the projects this volunteer has pioneered are restoring an abandoned cemetery, developing a city memorial garden and planting a dogwood for deceased city employees. She was instrumental in obtaining a retired train caboose, but has also planted flowers at the City Hall and other areas around town. She provides Christmas decorations for the City Hall. Her latest project was turning an eyesore along the Pigeon River into a park, which can be enjoyed by all citizens.

Mary Lee Seymour
From: Memphis, Shelby County
Years of Service: 6
Volunteering Highlights:
Coalition of 100 Black Women: Board; Lifetime Honorary Member
Jefferson Award
MIFA
Bethany Maternity Home
Women In Community Service, Inc.
Special Notes: Ms. Seymour was instrumental in starting Women In Community Service (WICS) programs in Memphis. She can be called on with a minute's notice to provide inspirational speaking, mentoring, fundraising and program development ideas. She has led in empowering over 2,000 Memphis women and children.

Sue Shafer
From: Knoxville, Knox County
Years of Service: 7
Volunteering Highlights:
J.C. Penney Golden Rule Award Nomination
Tennessee Aquarium
Special Notes: Sue has been a dedicated volunteer diver at the Tennessee Aquarium since the fall of 1992. She lends her excellent diving skills to help provide the proper habitat and necessary diets for the fish that reside at the Tennessee Aquarium. Sue has a keen eye for detail and good observation skills for detecting unusual animal/fish behavior. Sue also created and developed

> If every Tennessean were to volunteer for one day a month, we could...
>
> have the resources to solve every social ill that exists today. The world that would result from such a condition would be one that mankind has never before seen, one that would reflect the amazing synergies of "being our brother's keeper."
>
> —Richard Osgood
> Nashville, Davidson County

a program curriculum called the "Day in the Life of a Diver." The program leads children aged 8 to 12 years old through a day of exploration in and out of the water.

Bobbie Shainberg
From: Memphis, Shelby County
Years of Service: 4
Volunteering Highlights:
J.C. Penney Golden Rule Award Nomination
Bethany Home: Board of Directors
Special Notes: Three years ago, she and her daughter decided to sell their business, Delectables. They donated to Bethany their fudge recipe, fudge making machine, and trademark. Bobbie has continued to work with us, teaching others how to make, package and ship the fudge that made Delectables famous. Last Christmas, we sold over $9,000 of fudge. This new source of income can be used where it is most essential. It is a tremendous gift that will keep growing year after year. Bobbie's efforts in providing both the wherewithal and the instruction to help Bethany Home "learn to fish" is exactly the kind of life-changing effort needed to transform the non-profit sector.

George Shane
From: Germantown, Shelby County
Years of Service: 11
Volunteering Highlights:
Germantown Senior Citizen Advisory Commission: President, member
St. Francis Hospital: volunteer
General Motors Greater Memphis Retiree Club: President
Duntreath Homeowners Association: Past President and Treasurer
Germantown Methodist Church: ushering, etc.

If every Tennessean were to volunteer for one day a month, we could...

have the best state in the nation.

—Mike Palazzolo
Germantown, Shelby County

 If every Tennessean were to volunteer for one day a month, we could...

stamp out want, need, and loneliness. We could generate such a feeling of comfort, of wellbeing, in both the served and the serving, that the long looked for Golden Day of Brotherhood would have arrived.

—David Brown Parrish
Gallatin
Sumner County

Kathryn Shanks
From: Jonesborough, Washington County
Years of Service: 4
Volunteering Highlights:
People to People Student Ambassador Program — 2000 Ambassador to the British Isles
Bays Mountain Park Association Volunteer
National Storytelling Center Volunteer
Celtic Air — A Celtic music performance band
Rocky Mount Museum: Youth Volunteer of the Year in 1998; JC Penney Golden Rule Youth Award 2000
Special Notes: Kathryn has served as a volunteer for Rocky Mount Museum since she was just 11 years old, and has donated 1,065 hours since becoming a volunteer. Kathryn dresses in historic costume and portrays Eliza Cobb, daughter of William Cobb, Jr. and granddaughter of the builder of Rocky Mount. She gives tours for the general public, plays the fiddle, and helps with school tours, instructing them in period craft projects during their visits. Kathryn is home schooled, thus she is able to give valuable time during the weekdays. Thousands of visitors, both adults and children have been impacted by Kathryn's volunteerism. She has set a standard of commitment and generated hours that continue to serve to challenge other youth volunteers.

Crystal Sharp
From: Trenton, Gibson County
Years of Service: 1
Volunteering Highlights:
People Who Care
United Way of the Mid South
Liberty Place Outreach Center
The Gobson County Inner-Agency
Bellingham
Special Notes: Crystal is a young person with a positive

Tennessee Volunteer Heroes 2001

> If every Tennessean were to volunteer for one day a month, we could...
>
> # help anyone in need.
>
> —Mary Parsley
> Murfreesboro, Rutherford County

mind, willing to work and help her community in any way she can.

Charlene Shelton
From: Kingsport, Sullivan County
Years of Service: 25
Volunteering Highlights:
Tennessee Resource Conservation & Development Council
J.C. Penney Golden Rule Award Nomination
Rascals Teen Center: Founding Member; Board President
Clean Kingsport: recycling events; public land's day events; litter-free events
Kingsport Tomorrow — Greenbelt Task Force: Past Board Member
Appalachian RC&D: Secretary/Treasurer
Special Notes: "I have the ability to 'hold my community in trust.' I have a desire to serve and to lead, a healthy sense of self, respect for diversity and a deep commitment to my community."

Ken Shipp
From: Murfreesboro, Rutherford County
Years of Service: 6
Volunteering Highlights:
MTSU Blue Raider Athletic programs
Boy Scouts
Chamber of Commerce
Boys & Girls Clubs of Rutherford County
Local high school football
Special Notes: Coach Ken Shipp is totally dedicated to the 1,000 children of the Boys and Girls Clubs of Rutherford County. His speaker's bureau meets with club members once a month to share their personal stories and encourage worthy life goals. Helicopter visits, a planetarium, fire safety house, magicians and a gym-sized whale are just a few of the many extra experiences that he has organized. Coach Shipp always has the best interest of the community's children in mind and is its best club promoter and supporter!

Betty Short
From: Nashville, Davidson County
Years of Service: 17
Volunteering Highlights:
Illiteracy Program
Chamber of Commerce
Easter Seals
American Red Cross
Special Notes: Betty volunteers every Thursday in the Blood Center where she serves refreshments to the donors. She always makes the donors feel welcome and appreciated.

Rosetta Shotwell
From: Nashville, Davidson County
Years of Service: 18
Volunteering Highlights:
Clover Bottom Developmental Center
The Post 88
Veterans Hospital in Murfreesboro and Nashville
Metro Government Senior Citizens Nutrition Program
Special Notes: I have has an opportunity to be associated with various volunteer programs, in which I gave 110% of my time and effort. The smiles, the happiness in each face I found was worth every minute I volunteered.

> If every Tennessean were to volunteer for one day a month, we could...
>
> # experience the true meaning of life itself.
>
> —Ronnie Parsons
> Celina, Clay County

Tennessee Volunteer Heroes 2001

Connie Siemanski
From: Nashville, Davidson County
Years of Service: 26
Volunteering Highlights:
St. Henry Parish Emmaus Program Coordinator: four major outreach programs
St. Henry Parish Women's Council: Treasurer; Hospitality Chair; Co-Chair Sunshine Club; Henrietta Award
St. Thomas Hospital: Family Waiting Room Chair; Vol. Board of Directors, Past Pres: Strobel Nominee
St. Henry Parish and St. Thomas Eucharistic Minister
Nashville Cursillo Movement: Rector; Team Leader; Kitchen Crew
Special Notes: "My family, my church and my community— these are my life. Whatever I can do for the persons in these areas, I have tried to do. I love people and any faith leads me to reach out to others and be involved."

Kathy Simon
From: Readyville, Cannon County
Years of Service: 10
Volunteering Highlights:
Cannon County 4-H Clubs
West Side School Volunteer
West Side Volunteer Fire Department
Cannon County Caring for Youth
Angel Tree Volunteer
Special Notes: You can depend on Kathy Simon — fundraising, recruiting — she can do it all. People who work with her are in awe of what she can accomplish with few resources.

If every Tennessean were to volunteer
for one day a month, we could...

provide unlimited resources for service projects throughout the state of Tennessee.

—Wesley Joe Penn
Germantown, Shelby County

If every Tennessean were to volunteer
for one day a month, we could...

have the best services and public facilities possible. By volunteering and getting involved, one learns what is available and appreciates the efforts required for success. It is too easy to criticize when one "knows not of what they speak."

—Jo Ann Perry
Friendship, Crockett County

Teri R. Simon
From: Nashville, Davidson County
Years of Service: 16
Volunteering Highlights:
Our Kids Center: Leader of Community Education Program on Child Abuse: founder, Birthday Giving Program
Gilda's Club Volunteer
Congregation Micah: Religions School Teacher
Parent volunteer at children's school
Special Notes: Terri's commitment to serving others and inspiring people to serve permeates her life. Her vision and determination make her a great leader. She has installed this dedication in her children and countless others.

Rev. Tony Sirten
From: Old Hickory, Davidson County
Years of Service: 4
Volunteering Highlights:
Church of the Living Water
Madison Healthcare
Nurse
Chaplain
Fulltime single parent and student
Special Notes: Rev. Tony is a full time pastor who is not paid. He also works a fulltime job as a nurse and still makes time for anyone in need.

Siskin Re-Entry Volunteers
From: Chattanooga, Hamilton County
Years of Service: 3
Volunteering Highlights:
Chattanooga Area Food Bank
American Cancer Society
Willows Creek/North Jackson County Exceptional

> **If every Tennessean were to volunteer for one day a month, we could...**
> gain a new set of eyes to see the world. To look at others with compassion and deep empathy makes us students and teachers in this arena called life. In giving, we absorb and retain light that we reflect back to others, an eternal cycle that keeps going, a cycle that cannot end. The fruits of this give-and-take then double, triple and magnify as we become more open-hearted and more loving as parents, sons, daughters and citizens of our chosen communities.
>
> —Karl Pezdirtz
> Collierville
> Shelby County

Children Olympics
J.C. Penney Golden Rule Recognition
Special Notes: This is a very special group of volunteers. They are not only special because they volunteer, but because of the difficulties they must endure just to show up at our doorstep each week. All of these volunteers have suffered from acquired brain injuries. They have undergone extensive rehabilitation, suffered through numerous major surgeries, and continue to struggle to regain control of their bodies. All of these trials just seem to harden their resolve to work. Some must also contend with physical problems they have suffered through due to their accidents. They never say, "It's too difficult", or "I can't do it". They say, "Yes, I can!"

Dorothy B. Skinner
From: Harriman, Roane County
Volunteering Highlights:
General Federation of Women's Clubs: Charter Member; Past President
State Federation of Women's Clubs: Past Executive Committee; awarded Tribute of Honor, 1992
Roane County Association for Retarded Persons: co-founder
Michael Dunn Center and Dunn Diversified Industry
Girl Scouts of America
Special Notes: Since 1949 she has served her church in Oak Ridge as Sunday School Teacher many times, been on the Building Committee of a new edifice, chaired two Vacation Bible Schools and served as Altar Guild Chairman for six years. After moving to Roane County in 1952, she has served as PTA officer, Girl Scout leader for 20 years, operated a Girl Scout Uniform Exchange in her home, and served on the Regional Girl Scout Council for 15 years. After the birth of a son with Downs Syndrome in 1959, within two months, she had, with three other local citizens, founded the Roane County Association for Retarded Persons. She has worked tirelessly for this organization for forty-one years. This organization first searched for any retarded citizens who had been hidden because of the shame of their families. A nursery was set up and gradually the work was expanded to be an accredited rehabilitation center, The Michael Dunn Center and Dunn Diversified Industry. At present this organization operates eight residences, a handicap apartment, a pre-school program, a nursery school, a sheltered workshop as well as adult services for the handicapped. At present, the Michael Dunn Center and Dunn Diversified Workshop serves over 300 clients each day and employs 260 persons in Roane County!

Martin J. Skinner, Sr.
From: Harriman, Roane County
Years of Service: 45
Volunteering Highlights:
Episcopal Church: Vestry; Lay Chalice Bearer & Lector; Area VP of Episcopal Church of TN Keyman
Lions Club: Past President: various club officers and committees; Awarded Lion of the Decade, twice
Volunteer Michael Dunn Center and Dunn Diversified Industries
Tennessee Inventors Association: co-organizer and officer
City Council; County Industrial Studies Committee; City Planning Commission & Park & Recreation Board
Special Notes: Mr. Skinner has actively volunteered and participated in many phases of work in his church, community, and service organizations throughout the past 45+ years.

> **If every Tennessean were to volunteer for one day a month, we could...**
> make a difference in Tennessee that would make all of America want to visit Tennessee. Children and adults of all ages would be learning to read. The disabled homebound would not feel so lonely or isolated and would receive a nutritious meal every day. The countryside would be cleaner and every person would feel the great satisfaction that comes from "helping get the job done."
>
> —Ruth Phillips
> Kingsport, Sullivan County

Tennessee Volunteer Heroes 2001

Coleman Smith
From: Adamsville, McNairy County
Years of Service: 50
Volunteering Highlights:
United Way: beginning 12th year as Chair of McNairy County campaign
Adamsville First United Methodist Church: Sunday School Teacher — 50 years
Past Adamsville Mayor for over 20 years
Past McNairy County Commissioner for 32 years
Adamsville Lions Club for 50 years
Special Notes: Mr. Smith gives of himself totally and unselfishly. Whenever there is a need in the community, he doesn't allow himself the option of doing nothing— he acts.

Dixie Smith
From: Belden, Tennessee
Years of Service: 2
Volunteering Highlights:
Make-A-Wish Foundation, Memphis
Special Notes: As a wish-granting volunteer for the Make-A-Wish Foundation for the past two years, Dixie has gone above and beyond the call of duty. For example, Dixie has helped grant wishes for 8 children who were medically qualified to receive a wish. Each wish can take from 20 to 30 hours of work over a 2 to 3 month period. She and a partner interviewed each child and his or her family to determine the child's one true wish. Interviewing families in the midst of a medical crisis takes an equal measure of diplomacy and compassion. She shows true compassion for each child and turns in complete paperwork on each wish. All of Dixie's wish children were able to enjoy their wishes quickly thanks to her thoroughness and attention to detail.

> If every Tennessean were to volunteer for one day a month, we could...
>
> ## ease the pain of millions of people while making our world a much safer, more peaceful and beautiful place to live.
>
> —Rachael N. Pickett
> Cleveland, Bradley County

> If every Tennessean were to volunteer for one day a month, we could...
>
> enrich our society and our communities. Our children would be so blessed if volunteers would read, care, love and assist monthly. When a group gathers for a common goal, anything is possible. An asphalt courtyard at a local school was envisioned by a few as a garden. With many volunteers hours, that dream is now a reality and children and parents learning and benefiting from what volunteers can do.
>
> —Beth Pickler
> Germantown, Shelby County

Dora Smith
From: Bartlett, Shelby County
Years of Service: 37
Volunteering Highlights:
Youth Villages: Fundraiser; Supporter
Boy Scouts of America: fundraiser; Den Mother
Hispanic Business Alliance: Board member
American Heart Association: fundraiser; supporter
American Cancer Society: fundraiser; supporter
Special Notes: "I have volunteered most of my life and will continue to do so. If I have or will change one person to better themselves, it will all be worthwhile."

Helen C.T. Smith
From: Greeneville, Greene County
Years of Service: 10
Volunteering Highlights:
Appalachian Girl Scouts Council: troop leader; Service Unit Manager
Opportunity House of Greene County: Past President Board of Directors
Greeneville Schools in Action: Past Treasurer and President; fundraiser
J.C. Penney Golden Rule Award Nomination
Sequoyah Boy Scout Council: Den Leader
Asbury UMC: Board of Directors; legal counsel for Asbury Child Enrichment Center
Special Notes: Contributions and participation in a wide variety of community organizations, financial support also.

Holiday H. Smith
From: Kingsport
Volunteering Highlights:
Shepherd Center
Special Notes: Because of Holiday's strong belief in

Tennessee Volunteer Heroes 2001

> If every Tennessean were to volunteer for one day a month, we could...
>
> ## eliminate poverty and illiteracy, improve the quality of public education, empower citizens to strive for personal achievement while caring for their neighbors.
>
> —Chris Pickler
> Germantown
> Shelby County

servitude, his leadership in recruiting, and his personal work with the Shepherd Center, hundreds of Kingsport's senior-adults have been able to remain in their homes, and their family members have had much needed assistance in caring for their loved ones.

James Smith
From: Brighton, Tipton County
Years of Service: 5
Volunteering Highlights:
1st Baptist Church, Deacon
Baptist Hospital
Exchange Club
Chamber of Commerce
Carl Perkins Prevention of Child Abuse Center
Special Notes: James is a Tennessee Volunteer Hero because of his work refurbishing the Carl Perkins Prevention of Child Abuse building — 4,400 square feet.

Rev. Joanne P. Smith
From: Germantown, Shelby County
Years of Service: 4
Volunteering Highlights:
Shelby County Republican Women
Presbytery of Memphis: Committee on Church and Development and Mission Planning
Leadership Germantown Alumni Association
Memphis Cotton Patches: Chair Memphis Family Shelter; Christmas Devotional
Memphis Literacy Council
Special Notes: "I have faithfully gone to the Criminal Justice Center twice a week to work with women and young male prisoners to help and encourage them to obtain their GED, study and apply Biblical truths."

Justine Smith
From: Nashville, Davidson County
Years of Service: 3
Volunteering Highlights:
The Salvation Army: Magness Potter Community Center
Boys and Girls Club and summer program
Cheerleading squad
Sports events
Special Notes: Justine Smith is a true Tennessee Volunteer Hero. Her selfless reflex act of caring is the essence of the volunteer spirit — she saw a need and without even thinking of it as volunteering or giving herself — simply stepped in to meet that need. For the past 3 years, Ms. Smith has been the cheerleading coach for 40 to 50 six to twelve year old girls at The Salvation Army Magness Potter Community Center. This began quite by accident when her children were participants in an after school program at Magness Potter. When the cheerleading program for girls, a companion to the boys after school sports program, suddenly found itself without coaches, Ms. Smith stepped in without hesitation to provide that adult leadership and keep the program going. This is significant because of the importance of these kinds of programs to children growing up in the inner city where wholesome activities and worthy role models are so important. Mrs. Smith gave this gift of her time from a life already full with the responsibilities of raising her own children and being employed at night in a full time position. She describes her volunteering as "a great and joyful experience" and this joy is translated both to the children she mentors and The Salvation Army staff members with whom she works. Beside the gift of her time, her example in giving back to her community is a priceless gift to the children in her care.

> If every Tennessean were to volunteer for one day a month, we could...
>
> ## revitalize communities, reestablish the family as the core to our future, and create a sense of interdependency to achieve cooperative growth.
>
> —David Pickler
> Germantown
> Shelby County

Tennessee Volunteer Heroes 2001

Michelle Smith
From: Brighton, Tipton County
Years of Service: 5
Volunteering Highlights:
Big Brothers and Big Sisters of Memphis
Make A Wish Foundation
Hands On Memphis
Smith and Nephew: Cultural Awareness Program
Ducks Unlimited
Special Notes: "I don't consider myself a hero. I consider myself blessed with a great family, friends, home and job. But, one day I could be in need, and I hope that someone would care enough to volunteer for me. Volunteering brings a great sense of joy to my heart and enriches my life. But, I never do things alone — I have wonderful family and friends who help me with any project that comes up. My co-workers and I started adopting families at Christmas, that is what started the wonderful friendship with Big Brothers and Big Sisters. They are wonderful! They are the real heroes, they spend every day of their lives working to make things better, a huge achievement compared to my achievements. Thank you for this nomination."

Rachel Smith
From: Shelbyville, Bedford County
Years of Service: 7
Volunteering Highlights:
Action Counts for Teens in Society, Bedford County
Tennessee Commission on National and Community Service: Board of Trustees
Chamber of Commerce, Bedford County
Tennessee Youth Action Council: Founding Member
Points of Light Foundation
Special Notes: As a junior, Rachel organized a community blood drive that led to a county record-breaking collection of blood. She started an elementary school tutoring program in 3 middle Tennessee schools. She painted a mural on a cultural arts building in Shelbyville. When she began college at Davidson College, she developed a database of service opportunities for fellow college students.

Henry Smithson
From: Nashville, Davidson County
Years of Service: 12
Volunteering Highlights:
American Red Cross
Special Notes: Henry has been volunteering in the Blood Center for years. He is always willing to jump in and help any way he can. The only thing he asks for is a hug! He volunteers at least twice a week and often more when someone calls off.

Kevin A. Snider
From: Germantown, Shelby County
Years of Service: 6
Volunteering Highlights:
Germantown Chamber of Commerce
Germantown Library and Youth Commissions
Memphis Humane Society and Germantown Animal Shelter
Shelby County Bar Foundation
Germantown Performing Arts Center
Special Notes: "I believe I was chosen for this honor because of the extensive community involvement that our law firm tries to make in the Germantown community."

If every Tennessean were to volunteer for one day a month, we could…

make a tremendous impact on the lives of people in need of a helping hand. It is so important to give back to our community and society. If everyone would volunteer just a minimal amount of their time to work with children, elderly individuals, or people with disabilities they would experience the joy of giving.

—Patricia Ann Pierce
Nashville
Davidson County

If every Tennessean were to volunteer for one day a month, we could…

make a difference in so many people's lives. The little children, handicapped, and older people all could use just a friendly word and a little help. Anyone can do that, even a kid!

—Katie Pickler
Germantown, Shelby County

Tennessee Volunteer Heroes 2001

> *If every Tennessean were to volunteer for one day a month, we could...*
>
> show the younger generation that helping people makes you feel good inside. We could show the whole country why they call us the Volunteer State.
>
> —Rictrell L. Pirtle
> Memphis
> Shelby County

Norma Jean Soloff
From: Chattanooga, Hamilton County
Years of Service: 35
Volunteering Highlights:
Siskin Foundation: Points of Light Volunteer; Auxiliary Historian & Program Chair; Past President Fundraising Committee; Point of Light Winner, 1992
American Lung Association, Woman of Distinction: Table Hostess; Auction
J.C. Penney Golden Rule Award Nomination
Alterra Sterling House Assisted Living
Health House Festival of Trees Committee
Chattanooga Golf & Country Club: Chair Fashion Show & Luncheon; Chair Gingerbread Display
Big Brothers-Big sisters Association Golf Benefit: Golf Benefit Committee
American Cancer Society: Golf Benefit
March of Dimes Golf Benefit: Auction Committee
Special Notes: Mrs. Soloff is a volunteer who goes the extra mile. She devotedly works innnumerable hours a week and many times on through the night creating and designing new ways to promote the Siskin Foundation Auxiliary 365 Benefit for the Siskin Children programs. She gives back to the community on a daily basis whether it is civic or charitable organization. She thinks of others before herself. "As long as I am physically able, I will always give back to the community. My mother passed away at 37, when I was 11 months old. My heart works for everyone. The greatest gift of all to receive is to give of yourself. This is my reward. It is felt by warmth in the heart, satisfaction and gratitude. It's an opportunity to helping others. To see those smiling faces makes it all worthwhile."

Ronnie Sowards
From: Nashville, Davidson County
Years of Service: 40
Volunteering Highlights:
St. Thomas Hospital Advocates
United Way
American Red Cross
Hands on Nashville
Habitat for Humanity
Special Notes: Whatever the volunteer need is, Ronnie is willing to fill it. He works tirelessly helping the less fortunate and makes it fun.

B.D. and Marcella Spence
From: Lewisburg, Marshall County
Years of Service: 30
Volunteering Highlights:
State Committee of Volunteer Leaders
Outstanding Leader District II (A.B. Harmon Award)
Citizen of the Year Marshall County
4-H Alumni Marshall County
Silver Award presented by Dairy Show each year in appreciation
Special Notes: The Spences have installed and reinforced the ethical values and character traits that children need to live meaningful lives. They exemplify the true spirit of volunteerism; thousands of campers, judging-team members, school children and workshop participants have benefited from their endless knowledge, energy, kindness and devotion. The Spences have been volunteer leaders for more than 30 years. Their volunteer efforts range from hosting county 4-H clubs to being camp leaders, outdoor classroom teacher and leader trainers.

> *If every Tennessean were to volunteer for one day a month, we could...*
>
> truly make our community a better place to live. Walking in another person's shoes helps break down barriers and prejudices that often exist due to ignorance of the unknown. By helping others, we truly help ourselves live fuller lives.
>
> —Dianne K. Polly
> Memphis, Shelby County

Gayle P. Spence
From: Memphis, Shelby County
Years of Service: 24
Volunteering Highlights:
Metropolitan Inter-Faith Association (MIFA)
Calvary Episcopal Church
Family Award Winner of the 1999 Best of Hands On Memphis Volunteer Recognition Awards
MIFA's nominee for the 1999 Jefferson Awards
Girls Scouts
Special Notes: Weekly, for over 24 years, five generations of the Partridge/Spence Family have delivered meals together to frail, homebound individuals, strengthening their own family ties as they have strengthened their community.

Harold Spillars
From: Olive Branch, Shelby County
Volunteering Highlights:
Aviation Explorer Scout Post 924 and Post 2645: Founder
Wooddale Aviation Advisory Board
Memphis Boy Scout Chickasaw Council
ACE Camp for Rhodes College
St. Luke's Lutheran Church: education and property committees
Special Notes: Harold realized if we are going to have pilots, somebody had better start training them. Harold's ambition in life is to help young people fly. Through scouts, he makes Ground School free every Tuesday night. Harold solicits help from flight instructors, and gives of his services for free, so youth can afford to fly. Videos and flight simulator time are made available. Through Douglas aviation, Harold provides the building, meeting room, utilities and planes. Then he supplies the teachers, guest speakers

---

If every Tennessean were to volunteer for one day a month, we could... at today's population and minimum wage save all Tennessee citizens some $1,640,000,000. This labor applied to the Tennessee Greenways Program would be more than enough to tie all cities, counties, state parks and other lands together. We could have a state with environment second to none. Tennesseans could surely be proud of such an accomplishment.

—Sam Powell
Signal Mtn., Hamilton County

If every Tennessean were to volunteer for one day a month, we could... help the homeless; feed the hungry; clothe the naked; comfort the ill and aging; encourage citizens to return to Christian principles which we once enjoyed. We could eliminate those things that have placed our state in disrepair, spiritually, morally and financially.

—George Price
Athens
McMinn County

---

and field trips. Open House is provided every fall. Flyers are sent to all students identified as interested in flying. His openness and crusty friendliness makes flyers want to soar to his expectations. Children seek his approval— he is a positive experience in the life of his pilots.

Hal T. Spoden
From: Kingsport, Sullivan County
Years of Service: 33
Volunteering Highlights:
Past Member, Tennessee Commission for the Restoration of the State Capitol
Past Member, Tennessee State Library and Archives Commission
Past President, Greater Kingsport Area Chamber of Commerce
Past Chairman and member, Tennessee State Board of Architectural and Engineering Examiners
Past Chairman of The Netherland Inn Steering Committee
Special Notes: Mr. Spoden's historical preservation activities date back to 1967 when he and 3 other interested citizens initiated action to purchase, save and restore The Netherland Inn. His tireless work since that time continues to this day. The Inn would not have the distinction it currently possesses if it were not for Mr. Spoden's adherence to historical detail.

Spring Hill Police Dept.
From: Spring Hill, Maury County
Volunteering Highlights:
Library
Rotary Club
Bike Safety Program
Middle TN Survivors of Violent Crimes
Special Notes: "On October 23, 1995, my daughter Stacey

Tennessee Volunteer Heroes 2001

> If every Tennessean were to volunteer for one day a month, we could...
>
> ## provide comfort to those who may need help to get through troubled times.
>
> —staff at Franklin Memorial Chapel
> Franklin, Williamson County

Dale Grissom was murdered. The Spring Hill Police Dept. has been there for me. Most people don't know the department like I do. Reggie Pope, Chief of Police, goes to church with me. He tries to reach out to kids and goes the extra mile if it saves that child from drugs or jail. I am so very thankful God allowed me to meet this man. I believe God has special plans for him. Sgt. Ron Coleman has listened to me and cared about me since 1995. He has made a great impact on my life and that of my daughter Shannon. When Stacey died, Shannon was holding her in her lap. Sgt. Coleman has talked with Shannon many, many times. We are truly blessed this man is in our life. Sgt. Kordell McKissock has also shared our heartache since 1995. All of the staff of the Spring Hill Police Dept. are the finest people I know."

Sara Brianne Stacy
From: Kingsport, Sullivan County
Years of Service: 6
Volunteering Highlights:
University of Tennessee: travel & Recreation Committee; Team VOLS; Collegiate Club
JC Penney Golden Rule Award, 1999
Kodak Young Leader Award, 1997
World Changers, 1997, 1998, 1999

Ida Starkey
Volunteering Highlights:
Nashville Metropolitan Bordeaux Hospital

STARS MVPs
From: Chattanooga, Hamilton County
Years of Service: 4
Volunteering Highlights:
STARS (Students Taking A Right Stand)
Family and Children's Services
Teddy Bear Round-up
J.C. Penney Golden Rule Award Nomination
Domestic Violence Task Force
Special Notes: STARS MVPs are members of the STARS Team Executive Council, a multi-school advisory group that plans and implements STARS programs and events. These students volunteer their time and talents improving the environments of their schools. Each student has undergone a three level training process that includes serving as a peer helper, cross-age mentor and/or peer mediator and serving on the executive council. To advance through the required training, students spend numerous hours of time and energy. In fact, several current MVPs have participated in specialized training and have served on a STARS Team in excess of four years.

Lelan A. Statom
From: Nashville, Davidson County
Years of Service: 15
Volunteering Highlights:
UT & TSU Agricultural Extension Service — State Advisory Board
Davidson County 4-H Volunteer, Camp, Public speaking, etc.
North West YMCA: Board of Directors and Advisory Board; Black Achievers Program
Boy Scouts, Middle Tennessee Advisory Board
Lee Chapel African American Methodist Episcopal Church: Steward Board; Trustee Board

Connie C. Steere
From: Kingsport, Sullivan County
Years of Service: 25
Volunteering Highlights:
Who's Who in Education (Missouri)
Washington Elementary, Kingsport City Schools, PTA

> If every Tennessean were to volunteer for one day a month, we could...
> within the 21st century, banish ignorance, intolerance, hopelessness, soothe suffering and sorrow, resolve that pain will be contested through progress and dedication, and that no one's twilight years will be endured alone. Tennesseans' common virtue is that they never consider what they give as great or that the reward they receive in return is small. The "Volunteer State" is Tennessee's proud legacy and "Tennessee is America at its best!"
>
> —James E. (Jim) Queen
> Chattanooga
> Hamilton County

President
LINK House (runaway and homeless youth): Executive Director
CASA of Sullivan County, Inc.: Executive Director
Who's Who in Professional Management
Special Notes: An advocate for children through PTA, my church, United Way and through my careers, I believe I have made a significant difference for over 1,000 troubled teenagers, and helped expedite services and safety for another almost 1,000 alleged abused/neglected children in Tennessee.

Caitlin Steiger
Volunteering Highlights:
Baptist Health Care Shining Star Award
The Jefferson Award
Prudential Insurance Spirit of Community Award, Nominee

Elsie Steiner
From: Nashville, Davidson County
Years of Service: 60
Volunteering Highlights:
American Red Cross
Senior Citizens, Inc.
Council on Aging
National Conference of Caring and Concern
Congregation Micah
Special Notes: She has been giving of herself for 60 years through all kinds of agencies to help people in need. She has held a variety of volunteer roles — leadership and direct service.

Debra E. Stewart
From: Shelbyville, Bedford County
Years of Service: 8
Volunteering Highlights:

> If every Tennessean were to volunteer for one day a month, we could...
> have such a significant effect on the lives of everyone in the state. Both volunteers and the people their efforts benefited could be much richer in ways too numerous to mention and all could share in the joy of giving of themselves.
>
> —Kay Dillon Ramsey
> McMinnville
> Warren County

> If every Tennessean were to volunteer for one day a month, we could...
> see a drastic change for the better in the quality of life for all. The disabled, elderly and children are ideal candidates for volunteering services. Bored with nothing to do? Been there, done that? Poor in spirit? Volunteer to help someone else. It's a guaranteed picker-upper!
>
> —David Ray
> Memphis
> Shelby County

Bedford County Association for Exceptional Students
Special Olympics: volunteer local and state events
Shelbyville/Bedford County Youth Football League: Board of Directors
Leadership Bedford: Graduate and Board Member
Bedford County Election Commissioner

Susie Stewart
From: Memphis, Shelby County
Years of Service: 5
Volunteering Highlights:
J.C. Penney Golden Rule Award Nomination
Salvation Army
Leadership Council of Magnolia elementary
Special Notes: "I come everyday to school to help out the teachers that need my assistance. I volunteer from 7:15 — 2:15 pm."

Vernon Stewart
From: Memphis, Shelby County
Years of Service: 17
Volunteering Highlights:
Metropolitan Inter-Faith Association (MIFA): Senior Volunteer of the Year 1989 and 1999
JC Penney Golden Rule Award: 1999 Senior Volunteer of the Year; Judge for 2000
Fixodent Denture Cleaner Role Model Search Finalist, 1999
Daily Points of Light Award (#1692 for July 28, 2000)
Special Notes: Mr. Stewart's exceptional dedication to the Memphis Community is exemplified by his 17 years and over 12,000 hours of volunteer service, delivering meals to the homebound elderly, giving the frail, isolated individuals genuine concern and emotional support as well as hot nutritional meals.

Tennessee Volunteer Heroes 2001

> If every Tennessean were to volunteer for one day a month, we could...
>
> ## make Tennessee the number one state in the United States in every facet of life— education, business, recreation and quality of everyday life.
>
> —Cleve Redus
> Jacksboro
> Campbell County

Floyd Stewart, Jr.
From: Nashville, Davidson County
Years of Service: 10
Volunteering Highlights:
Technology Access Center: Chairman of the Board
Willow Trace Homeowners Association: Chairman
Journeys (Television Show): Host
Consortium on Disability Issues: Treasurer
Tennessee Commission on National and Community Service: former Commissioner
Special Notes: He is committed to making life better and more complete for individuals with disabilities.

Viola Tribble Street
From: Memphis, Shelby County
Years of Service: 5
Volunteering Highlights:
Highland Heights Methodist Church
Memphis Family Shelter
J.C. Penney Golden Rule Award Nomination
Transportation for 2 ladies to the bank, the grocery store, shopping, doctor, etc.
Special Notes: "After 35 years with the Memphis Board of Education in nutrition services, I can't sit and read and watch television. I have to help people who need me."

Lottie M. Strupp
From: Nashville, Davidson County
Years of Service: 10
Volunteering Highlights:
Council of Community Services: Board Member
Council on Aging: Board Member; Past Chair
Planned Parenthood: Advisory Committee; works weekly in clinic
The Temple: 5-6 hours weekly doing clerical work; various committees
Whitsett Elementary: teaches ESL children, one-on-one

Nancy Surber
From: Knoxville, Knox County
Years of Service: 2
Volunteering Highlights:
AmeriCorps — Emerald Youth Foundation: Mentor and Leader
Christenberry Elementary School
Emerald Avenue United Methodist Church
Oakwood-Lincoln Park Neighborhood Association
Special Notes: Nancy has had to face some tough hurdles in her growing up years. After her parents divorced and a cousin committed suicide, her grades dipped and she needed support. She found it at Emerald Youth Foundation and, in 1998, returned to serve as an AmeriCorps member there. After completing 2 years, she is now on the staff at this urban ministry in Knoxville.

Takoma Adventist Hospital Volunteers
From: Greeneville, Greene County
Years of Service: 3
Volunteering Highlights:
Greeneville City Schools
J.C. Penney Golden Rule Award Nomination
Greene County School System
Takoma Adventist Hospital
Special Notes: The Volunteers of Takoma Adventist Hospital have presented a program called "Making Bubbles" to the kindergarten children in the 15 schools of the Greeneville City and the Greene County School systems for the past three years. This program teaches the importance and mechanics of handwashing to the children. The Volunteers first teach the three important times to wash hands: before meals and snacks; after using the bathroom; and after

> If every Tennessean were to volunteer for one day a month, we could...
>
> ## bring everybody together in a spirit of love and understanding. With love, everything is possible.
>
> —Cheryl Reed
> Brentwood
> Williamson County

playing with or handling pets. The children are given a liquid to rub on their hands, which glows in ultraviolet light. The children wash their hands to see if all the liquid has been washed away. The Volunteers then teach the mechanics of handwashing. The Volunteer "makes bubbles" with a bubble maker to emphasize the point that the children should make a lather of warm water and soap. The Volunteer then demonstrates that these areas: the fronts and backs of hands; between fingers; around the nails should be washed throughly for the length of time it takes to sing two verses of "Mary Had A Little Lamb." The Volunteers present the children with a coloring book, which highlights good health habits, a package of crayons, and a bar of soap.

Luther Carol Tanley, Jr.
Special Notes: Special recognition from the Governor and First Lady of Tennessee for excellence in volunteer service.

Lois H. Taylor
From: Memphis, Shelby County
Years of Service: 13
Volunteering Highlights:
Foster Grandparent Program
Foster Grandparent Advisory Council
J.C. Penney Golden Rule Award Nomination
Retired Senior Volunteer Program (R.S.V.P.)
Support Older Women Network (S.O.W.N.)
Senior Leaders, Inc.
Special Notes: "As a retired person, I have time to give, anyway I can."

Richard Taylor
From: Chuckey
Years of Service: 10
Volunteering Highlights:

> If every Tennessean were to volunteer for one day a month, we could...
>
> teach all children to read and excel. We could bring art and theatre to citizens. We could cut back on a lot of government funding and save tax monies.
>
> —Vernon Reed
> Memphis
> Shelby County

> If every Tennessean were to volunteer for one day a month, we could...
> have an open mind about what we really need in Tennessee. For example, we are too caught up fixing our major highways when we forget about some of the most important people in our state, the children! So many kids are crying out for attention and many parents are not able to provide for them. Children need love and undivided attention. Thus, if every Tennessean were to volunteer one day a month, they could change a young person's life!
>
> —Clark Reyes
> Knoxville
> Knox County

Boys and Girls Club of Greeneville and Greene County, President and Chairman
J.C. Penney Golden Rule Award Nomination
West Pines Ruritan Club; Governor of Davy Crockett District Boys and Girls Club. Outstanding Member of the Board, 1999
Special Notes: As a member of the Boys and Girls Club Board, Rick has appeared at many community functions representing the Boys and Girls Club and spreading the word about the Club's importance and its needs.

Teen Outreach Program (TOP)
From: Nashville, Davidson County
Years of Service: 8
Volunteering Highlights:
Since 1992, over 900 youth have given an est. 11,000 hours of volunteer work to the Nashville Community.
TOP youth regularly tutor local elementary school children.
Second Harvest Food Bank
United Cerebral Palsy
Dismas House
Special Notes: TOP is a unique pregnancy prevention program that uses service-learning as its methodology. TOP engages youth ages 14-18 in meaningful volunteer work which is tied to "real life" issues, such as decision-making, respect for self and others, and job readiness.

Robert M. Teeples
From: Celina, Clay County
Years of Service: 40
Volunteering Highlights:
Celina Lion's Club
Organized construction of Clay County Recreational Complex
As a County Court Member, worked diligently to build Celina K-8 school
Celina High School

Tennessee Volunteer Heroes 2001

> If every Tennessean were to volunteer for one day a month, we could...
>
> # change lives from despair to hope. By helping others, we enrich our lives.
>
> —Mrs. Marjorie Evans Rios
> Cookeville, Putnam County

Celina Methodist Church, Chairman of the Board
Special Notes: He has always worked for the community with the best interests of the county at heart. His service to Clay County has brought progress in education and community development.

The Ten Mile Singers
From: Ten Mile, Meigs County
Years of Service: 13
Volunteering Highlights:
Shriners
East Tennessee Children's Hospital
Knoxville Area Reserve Ministry
Toys for Tots Program, Roane, Meigs and Rhea Counties
Operation Reach
Special Notes: This members of this group are Tennessee Volunteer Heroes because of the unselfish sacrifices they make as they travel doing concerts to raise money for Tennessee's non-profit organizations to assist children and the homeless.

Dennis Tennant
From: Baxter, Putnam County
Years of Service: 25
Volunteering Highlights:
Girls Softball League
J.C. Penney Golden Rule Award Nomination
Baseball Leagues in Baxter, Cookeville and Algood
YMCA
Relatives as Parents Program (RAPP)
Shriners
Special Notes: Dennis has selflessly devoted his time, resources, influence, organizational skills and hands-on efforts towards improving the lives of many people in the community — most especially young people. During the past 25 years, Dennis has coached in many sports leagues. Many schools, clubs and organizations call on Dennis to play Santa Claus. He willingly obliges as many as possible, and always has a smile and a kind word for each child. Dennis also has a special fondness for veterans' activities, and is one of the most active members of the local VVA (Vietnam Veterans of America).

Tennessee National Guard
From: Nashville, Davidson County
Years of Service: 220
Volunteering Highlights:
CADCA/Nashville Prevention Partnership
100 Black Men
Tennessee Safe and Drug Free Schools
Tennessee Commission on National and Community Service
"Bee Like Me" Drug Awareness Program
Special Notes: Since 1780 at King's Mountain, Tennessee National Guard Volunteers have answered the call of their state. That tradition continues with today's Tennessee National Guard.

Lucia Thomas
From: Franklin, Williamson County
Years of Service: 4
Volunteering Highlights:
Williamson County Hospital Medical Center
Manor at Steeplechase
Special Notes: She is dedicated to the Williamson County Hospital Medical Center.

> If every Tennessean were to volunteer for one day a month, we could... change the lives of our fellow citizens significantly. There are so many needs in our communities that could be alleviated by caring people donating six to eight hours per month. We could tutor children and adults, feed the homeless, build homes, help the needy at Christmas. The possibilities are endless!
>
> —Virginia Rippee
> Nashville, Davidson County

Tennessee Volunteer Heroes 2001

Amy Thomason
From: Johnson City, Washington County
Years of Service: 5
Volunteering Highlights:
Tri-Cities Baptist Church, Kingsport, TN
Special Olympics Volunteer (15 years)
2000 Mission trip — Navajo Indian Reservation
Special Notes: Amy volunteers her time regularly to a group of senior citizens with mental retardation. In addition to her hands-on involvement with these special people, Amy coordinates fundraisers to provide money for recreational/leisure activities otherwise not attainable. Amy works tirelessly and enthusiastically for the improvement of their quality of life.

Christa K. Thompson
From: Smyrna, Rutherford County
Volunteering Highlights:
Rape & Sexual Abuse Center

Elisa Thompson
From: Celina, Clay County
Volunteering Highlights:
Clay County Partnership: Board Member
Clay County Museum: Board Member
American Cancer Society
Clay County Home and Beauty Showcase: co-organizer
Helped organize fundraisers for restoration of courthouse
Special Notes: Elisa volunteers her time weekly to help various organizations improve our community. She is a tremendous asset to Clay County.

Shelley Thompson
From: Crossville, Cumberland County
Years of Service: 2
Volunteering Highlights:

If every Tennessean were to volunteer for one day a month, we could...

lower poverty, reduce homelessness, and raise awareness. There are pockets of people that volunteer. By increasing the variety of volunteers, by resources and financial ability, greater awareness would take place. An awareness would be raised about just what is out there and how great the need really is.

—Pam Roberts
Nashville, Davidson County

If every Tennessean were to volunteer for one day a month, we could...

perhaps ease pain, anxiety and hopelessness. We could create a wider understanding of others' lack of fortune and opportunity. We could enhance private aid, thereby reducing dependence on government.

—Heber Rogers
Nashville
Davidson County

Battered Women, Inc.
Criminal Justice Club, Tennessee Tech University
Omega Phi Alpha member, Tennessee Tech University
Cumberland County High School Graduate
Special Notes: Shelley is a Criminal Justice student at Tennessee Tech University who has lived with cerebral palsy since birth. For the past two years, she has dedicated her summers to Battered Women, Inc. She is willing to perform any task asked of her and is a true Tennessee Volunteer Hero.

Mrs. Ruth Thorsberg
From: Germantown, Shelby County
Years of Service: 34
Volunteering Highlights:
Heritage Woman's Club of Germantown: President; Secretary; Scholarship Committee Chair
Germantown Heights Homeowners: Past President; Secretary
Germantown Beautification Committee
Germantown Heights Garden Club: held all offices
Germantown Church of Christ
Special Notes: "With the Heritage Women's Club behind me, I worked 8 years to save the Depot. It was saved, renovated, and Depot Park is a jewel in Old Town."

Joyce Tidwell
From: Burns, Dickson County
Years of Service: 6
Volunteering Highlights:
The Renaissance Center
Adult Education Center
American Association of Retired Persons
Bon Aqua United Methodist Church
Centerville Nursing Home
Special Notes: Her willingness to be a part of new

Tennessee Volunteer Heroes 2001

>
> If every Tennessean were to volunteer for one day a month, we could…
>
> # accomplish almost everything we need to do in Tennessee.
>
> —Peter C. Rousos
> Brentwood
> Williamson County

initiatives and her generous spirit to serve others make her a true Tennessee Volunteer Hero.

Larry Tifverman
From: Memphis, Shelby County
Years of Service: 8
Volunteering Highlights:
New Zionfield M.B. Church
Alpha Omega Veterans' Services
Choice, Inc.
Spirit, Soul and Body Ministries
Vance Avenue Child Development Center
Special Notes: Outstanding leadership as a supervisor of Volunteers in Service to America (VISTA). This team did 21 projects with 24 VISTA Volunteers serving West Tennessee.

Grace Tomkins
From: Gallatin, Sumner County
Years of Service: 33
Volunteering Highlights:
Citizen of the Year Award, 1986
Volunteer of the Year: Sumner Regional Auxiliary; United Way of Sumner County; Sertoma; YMCA, Sumner
Gallatin Junior Service League: Founding Member
Sumner Foundation of SRHS: Founding Member
Board Member: Chamber of Commerce; United Way; Volunteer State Community College Foundation
Special Notes: Grace Tomkins is a legend where volunteerism is concerned. She has given her time, energy, and self to nearly every community and state project that has needed assistance.

Dawn Tomlin
From: Hendersonville, Sumner County
Years of Service: 5
Volunteering Highlights:
Mid Cumberland Homebound Meal Program
Networking Medical Equipment to Seniors with limited funds
Spaying and neutering of 132 wild cats, to date
Special Notes: Dawn spends twenty hours a week volunteering delivering food, Doctor visits, government appointments, grocery store, drug store, the mall, banking, veterinarian visits, beauty shop, rides to the airport and just doing everyday things for people. She is a real Tennessee Volunteer Hero!

Jason R. Tomlin
From: Franklin, Williamson County
Years of Service: 11
Volunteering Highlights:
Williamson County Rescue Squad
Franklin Memorial Chapel
Williamson County Emergency Management Agency
Spring Hill Fire Dept: Past Member
Maury County Civil Defense: Past Member

Luanne Townsend
From: Madison, Davidson County
Years of Service: 30
Special Notes: For 30 years, Luanne has been the buyer for the Gift Shops, and has volunteered 20,000 hours. She's been to the Atlanta Gift Market 58 times — every January and July for five days and has never been paid a single penny for this service. She has missed only one board meeting 2 years ago during the time she was undergoing chemotherapy.

> If every Tennessean were to volunteer for one day a month, we could…
>
> # create a Utopia, with no need for governmental social programs. Most of these problems would be solved with the good work of volunteers.
>
> —Kay and Guy Rowland
> Memphis
> Shelby County

Donald Traylor
From: Germantown, Shelby County
Years of Service: 6
Volunteering Highlights:
Germantown Performing Arts Center: Organizes usher program; Usher Liaison Committee
First Evangelical Church
Ridgeway Baptist Church, former Bible teacher

Patricia Traylor
From: Germantown, Shelby County
Years of Service: 10
Volunteering Highlights:
Germantown Performing Arts Center: Organizes usher program; Usher Liaison Committee
First Evangelical Church: Women's Ministry Teaching Chairman
Germantown Methodist Hospital
Evangelical Christian Church

Robert Lee Truax, Sr. (deceased)
From: Cordova, Shelby County
Years of Service: 9
Volunteering Highlights:
J.C. Penney Golden Rule Award Nomination
J.K. Lewis Center for Senior Citizens
Special Notes: Prior to his death in 1999, Robert was involved daily in many activities at the Lewis Center. He began volunteering in 1991 and over the years assumed several volunteer leadership roles. He was appointed Chairperson of the Games Committee for 5 years, then elected as member-at-large among his peers for 2 years. As the staff at the center decreased due to budget reductions, Robert assumed many duties and responsibilities voluntarily. His initiative and willingness to help in any was greatly benefited the center. He was very serious about hanging the American Flag daily. In addition to calling the weekly bingo games, he and his wife shopped for prizes. He assisted with the setup of many activities and would do anything he could for the staff, from putting together a new piece of office equipment to hanging decorations for an upcoming holiday. Robert was a true Tennessee Volunteer Hero and he is sorely missed at Lewis Center.

Clinton N. Trusty
From: Memphis, Shelby County
Years of Service: 11
Volunteering Highlights:
J.C. Penney Golden Rule Award Nomination
LeBonheur Children's Medical Center
Special Notes: Mr. Trusty rocks and feeds babies for us in the Special Care Unit. He also serves as a "volunteer preceptor" in the unit because of his loyalty and expertise in the unit. The Medical Center considers him ancillary staff because he is so dependable and knowledgeable. He will do anything that needs to be done: fold laundry, rock or feed babies. He gets to know each baby's personality and cares for him or her regardless of race, nationality or color. Mr. Trusty has proven to be someone who can empathize and comfort.

Liz Turner
From: Nashville, Davidson County
Years of Service: 12
Volunteering Highlights:
The Salvation Army: Corporate Angel Tree Coordinator: Angel Tree: Project Help
The Salvation Army Adult Rehabilitation Center; assisted the Director of Social Services
Metropolitan Bordeaux Hospital: Bordeaux Advocates, VP; Information Desk Volunteer;

If every Tennessean were to volunteer for one day a month, we could...
improve the quality of life for every citizen. This would improve the education of every child, eliminate illiteracy, eliminate poverty housing, provide hope and comfort to our sick and aged, and provide a mentor for every child in need. The benefit would be incalculable, creating a population with immense self esteem, a workforce unsurpassed in readiness, a quality of life so rich that Tennessee would have its pick of investment. It is in giving that we receive.

—Susan D. Russell
Memphis, Shelby County

If every Tennessean were to volunteer for one day a month, we could...
Change the world because people would be more compassionate for the diverse population of our state. They would be more understanding of other people's problems and needs. They could bring joy into the lives of the ill or elderly. They could serve as mentors to children and perhaps turn their lives around. There would probably be fewer people on drugs. We would help to improve the education of our youth. We would diminish racism, reduce teen pregnancy, and help clean up the environment.

—Barbara S. Russell
Memphis, Shelby County

Tennessee Volunteer Heroes 2001

> If every Tennessean were to volunteer for one day a month, we could... clean up the community. More people want to live in clean communities, which is good for the economy. In a clean community, you don't have to smell trash. Clean communities are nice areas and are a lot safer than dirty places.
>
> —Edward Salinas
> Nashville, Davidson County

Alzheimer's Association of Middle Tennessee: office volunteer

Special Notes: Ms. Turner's diligent work as a volunteer with the Angel Tree, Adult Rehabilitation and Social Services programs has helped The Salvation Army in extending its services to those in need. She is always willing to work both with clients and behind the scenes. As a volunteer she has for several years coordinated the Corporate Angel Tree program, taking responsibility for contacting and soliciting businesses to adopt Angels and coordinating the delivery of their gifts. This is the equivalent of a full time job during Angel season. She has served as a volunteer assistant to the social services department and with Project Help program, answering phones and scheduling appointments. As a volunteer for the Adult Rehabilitation Center she helps regularly with the jewelry sale project which has become a major fundraiser for that program. Her willingness to take the responsibility for important volunteer positions and her thoroughness and attention to detail do much to enable The Salvation Army programs for which she volunteers to work effectively and efficiently. We feel her dedication to her volunteer work qualifies her as a Tennessee Volunteer Hero.

Mary Tuttle
From: Cookeville, Putnam County
Years of Service: 1
Volunteering Highlights:
Northeast Elementary K-4
Special Notes: How do you describe someone who gives their heart to education and others, and receives no pay? A blessing! Mary constantly gives of her time and talents to those around her, with only kind words. In the classroom, she helps students in small groups, cutting and assisting in art projects and making homemade cookies and treats. She often uses her own money to buy and make items for students. We call her "Mom of the Year" because she is one of those mothers the world sure could us a lot more of: loyal and always there for the children.

United Cerebral Palsy of Middle Tennessee
From: Nashville, Davidson County
Years of Service: 16
Volunteering Highlights:
Home Access
Weekly Sport Nights
Challenger League Baseball
Alternative Spring Break
Barry Dean Fulton Special Needs Fund
Special Notes: UCP's goal is to create volunteer opportunities that generate lifetime involvement in promoting the independence of people with disabilities. There are many ways in which interested persons can become involved with United Cerebral Palsy of Middle Tennessee. Volunteers are critical to the ongoing operation of all programs and services at UCP. Through a variety of programs, many individuals with cerebral palsy and similar disabilities participate in recreational activities. These programs stimulate self-confidence, self-esteem, and physical ability. Many volunteers participate in UCP's fundraising, education, administration, and public relations activities in roles that range from service on the volunteer Board of Directors to helping with fundraising events and newsletters.

Butch Valentine
From: Memphis, Shelby County
Volunteering Highlights:
Friends for Life AIDS Resource Center
Special Notes: Butch was the founder and principal par-

> If every Tennessean were to volunteer for one day a month, we could... all feel better about ourselves and our community. One of the reasons people volunteer is the intrinsic reward they receive. It is just as important to the volunteer to give of themselves as it is to be the beneficiary of the effort. If everyone would share in this, the generosity would foster a more loving and pleasant environment in our state.
>
> —Tracy L. Salmon
> Lexington, Henderson County

ticipant in organizing and developing the Hearth and Home Emergency Assistance Fund. The name for the program was also his idea, and he personally did all of the soliciting for support. The first occasion to use the Hearth and Home Emergency Assistance Fund (HOPWA) on a large scale was during July, August and September, 1997. The HOPWA housing funds were approved, but there was a delay between the award and the funding. During this quarter, Friends for Life was able to continue providing case management and housing/utility assistance to PWAs without interruption. Butch is a unique person who has faced devastating, life-changing circumstances. Stripped of career, personal goals, home and income, he has nevertheless redirected his time and energy to help others in Memphis. He has redirected himself to a new set of goals and personal objectives that give new meaning to his life.

Mary B. Vance
From: Gatlinburg, Sevier County
Years of Service: 28
Volunteering Highlights:
VISTA (Volunteers in Service to America)
United Way of Sevier County
Sevier County Health Improvement Council
Mountain Hope Good Shepherd Clinic
Nine Counties, One Vision
Special Notes: Mary is dedicated to community service and is concerned for others.

Tom D. Vance
From: Murfreesboro, Rutherford County
Years of Service: 20
Volunteering Highlights:
American Cancer Society, Former Director, President and Campaign Chair

>
> *If every Tennessean were to volunteer for one day a month, we could...*
>
> # help hold down the cost of health care while helping people who are lonely, sick and in need. We could also show people that by volunteering they could encounter friendly, caring people who become like an extended family.
>
> —Jo Sanders
> Goodlettsville
> Davidson County

United Way of Rutherford County, Director, Treasurer and Campaign Chair
Heartwalk Chair for Rutherford County 1997, $122M raised, 34th largest in the U.S.
American Heart Association of Rutherford County, President 1999-2000, $600M raised
Volunteer Trainer for American Heart Conferences in Dallas, D.C., Tampa, etc
Special Notes: Tom has shown a longtime commitment to the community through volunteer service and willingness to assume leadership roles to maximize the efforts of many.

Deborah G. Varallo
From: Mt. Juliet, Wilson County
Volunteering Highlights:
American Red Cross: Blood donor; Past chair, Blood Svcs. Board; volunteer public relations consultant
Center for Nonprofit Management: Exec. Board Member; Chair-elect for 2001; Volunteer Instructor;
Girl Scouts of Cumberland Valley: Board Member; Fundraising Chair; past Chair Nominations Committee
Nashville Area Chamber of Commerce: past Exec. Board Member; Committee Chair for Livability Index
Leadership Nashville: 25th Anniversary in 2001; former Program Chair; active member Alumni Assoc.
Special Notes: Deb Varallo exemplifies the spirit of volunteerism. Through her volunteer efforts, and her continuous encouragement of others to volunteer, she has had a tremendous positive impact on numerous organizations and communities.

Myra J. Vaughan
From: Crump, Hardin County
Years of Service: 12
Volunteering Highlights:

> *If every Tennessean were to volunteer for one day a month, we could...*
>
> # do a lot of good things for senior citizens in nursing homes and senior centers.
>
> —Dorothy Sanders
> Dickson, Dickson County
>

> If every Tennessean were to volunteer for one day a month, we could... educate young people on the long lasting effect of abortion, curtailing teen pregnancy. We could create a learning atmosphere within our schools, minimizing drug use, gang activities and alcohol use. We could prolong good health among the elderly by providing them assistance. We could create a safer environment in our schools and minimize illiteracy in our society.
>
> —Richmond Savage
> Memphis
> Shelby County

Created Crump Senior Citizens Program in 1996
Created annual Crump Santa visit, 1994
Creates, promotes needy holiday drives and programs
Established City Police/City Court in Crump, 1995
Elected Volunteer Mayor of Crump
Special Notes: The outstanding dedication to improving her community, senior citizens and youth programs, churches and schools.

Rick Vaughn
From: Memphis, Shelby County
Years of Service: 20
Volunteering Highlights:
The Crisis Center
Special Notes: When Rick started volunteering with the Crisis Center he knew he had a deep conviction about helping people. He had lost several friends to suicide, and he has been through crisis himself. One of Rick's favorite times to work is on Christmas Eve. Rick's effort to help others when most people are busy with their own lives is typical of his selflessness.

William J. Vaughn
From: Brentwood, Williamson County
Years of Service: 75
Volunteering Highlights:
Boy Scouts of America, Troop 1
Brentwood Methodist Church: Sunday School Teacher for 54 years
American Red Cross: 23 years
Junior Achievement: Board of Directors
Outlook Nashville
Special Notes: He has given his life to the Boy Scouts of America, to his church and to many civic organizations all of his life.

Nancy Wakeman
From: Memphis, Shelby County
Years of Service: 5
Volunteering Highlights:
J.C. Penney Golden Rule Award Nomination
Bridges, Inc.
Special Notes: In 1994, Nancy began to serve on the committee for the Annual Silent Auction for Youth Services. As she began her work on the mailings, she realized that many lists were used that led to duplications and serious omissions. She knew this was not only costly in terms of postage and materials, but ultimately in communications and fundraising. She had no computer skills but her many years of office experience taught her how to organize data. She undertook the task of manually putting all of the names into a single, corrected card file that eliminated duplications, corrected addresses and formed the basis for an extremely valuable database upon which BRIDGES could build its future.

Dr. Emily Walker
From: Knoxville, Knox County
Years of Service: 2
Volunteering Highlights:
Doris A. Walker Academy
J.C. Penney Golden Rule Recognition
Special Notes: Dr. Walker has committed her life to changing the lives of the young people around her. She works over 40 hours a week without pay (and often taking from her own savings) to establish a school for students who have been abandoned or rejected by our public school systems. She has opened her heart to these children and has helped them find a place in our society that is productive and long-lasting. She is saving lives one child at a time — can there be a greater gift?

> If every Tennessean were to volunteer for one day a month, we could...
>
> make sure that no one went a day without a hot meal and a smile to brighten their day.
>
> —Kim Sawvell
> Ashland City, Cheatham County

Tennessee Volunteer Heroes 2001

Thomas Walker, Jr.
From: Knoxville, Knox County
Years of Service: 3
Volunteering Highlights:
Knoxville Volunteer Emergency Rescue Squad, Inc.
J.C. Penney Golden Rule Recognition
Special Notes: Thomas Walker represents community service, partnership, and people helping people to the highest degree possible, with no regard to his own personal needs and no compensation for his time and effort. He is a great example to doing unto others what you would have them do unto you.

Grace M. Wallace
From: Memphis, Shelby County
Years of Service: 25
Volunteering Highlights:
Memphis Literacy Council Program
Lichterman Nature Center Program
Vollentine-Evergreen Community Association
University of Tennessee, Memphis, Retiree Association
Recycling Programs
Special Notes: "I chose to live in Tennessee. I am a native Canadian and a naturalized American citizen. I want to justify the privilege of belonging to the Volunteer State."

John R. (Robin) Wallace, Jr.
From: Cordova, Shelby County
Years of Service: 20
Volunteering Highlights:
J.C. Penney Golden Rule Award Nomination
Lifeblood Mid-South Regional Blood Center
Special Notes: Without dedicated volunteer blood donors like Robin Wallace, our community would not be able to save the lives of thousands of patients each year. In addition, he gives much of his time to help the blood program grow. In virtually every situation where he set out to accomplish something for Lifeblood, he has succeeded. He has given lots of blood, convinced dozens of others to raise the visibility of the blood program, and he has been responsible for Lifeblood receiving several grants totaling $8,000 each.

Walters State Service Learning Program
From: Greeneville, Greene County
Years of Service: 4
Volunteering Highlights:
Walters State Community College Service Learning
J.C. Penney Golden Rule Award Nomination
Special Notes: Early in November 1999 a group of Service Learning students from Walters State Community College began asking questions about the students in the Service Learning program and their needs. In a matter of days, these young people came up with a plan to adopt the families of our welfare reform program Families First. The students took great pride in getting the gifts for 23 children. Every gift on their wish list was acquired and Santa dropped by the special party. All who attended the party were surely blessed. These students gave much more than time, seeking out donations and food for these families. They gave of themsleves.

Sue Ward
From: Dickson, Dickson County
Years of Service: 8
Volunteering Highlights:
The Renaissance Center
First Baptist Church, Library
4-H club leader
Special Notes: Her gentle spirit, kindness to others and willingness to share her talents with others make her a real Tennessee Volunteer Hero.

If every Tennessean were to volunteer for one day a month, we could...

stand for the values of our flag and our constitution with pride.

—Elma Schnapp
Memphis, Shelby County

If every Tennessean were to volunteer for one day a month, we could...

have a better, prettier and cleaner state because citizens would take more pride in their community, and have a greater sense of ownership. This would be 40,000 hours of labor donated to the common good each month in Coffee County alone. What power! And all working together! Helping each other!

—Mark Schempp
Tullahoma, Coffee County

> *If every Tennessean were to volunteer for one day a month, we could...* enhance the quality of life of others, foster positive communication, strengthen community relations, increase self-esteem, and make a statement world-wide that Tennessee is a caring and sharing state. We could make a difference. We all have so much to give to others.
>
> —Oscar Scott
> Ooltewah
> Hamilton County

Doug Warner
From: Germantown, Shelby County
Years of Service: 14
Volunteering Highlights:
Habitat for Humanity
Mountain T.O.P. (Tennessee Outreach Project)
Germantown United Methodist Church: Missions Team
Special Notes: Doug is visible as a leader/organizer of work teams who do volunteer construction. "There are many people who work harder than me. I am just the initiator, recruiter, cheerleader and supporter."

Natalie F. Watson
From: Germantown, Shelby County
Volunteering Highlights:
Germantown Public Safety Education Commission
New Neighbors, Germantown Safety City
Germantown Community Theatre
Recording for the Blind, Oak Ridge, TN
Pi Beta Phi Settlement School, Gatlinburg, TN

Henry D. Wattenbarger
From: Kingston, Roane County
Years of Service: 60
Volunteering Highlights:
Kingston First Baptist Church: Sunday School Teacher; Church Clerk; Deacon
Kingston Lions Club: Past Secretary, Past President; Lion of the Decade: Secretary of the Year
Kingston Unions Masonic # 38 Lodge: Past Master; Secretary
Roane-Morgan Deacon's Union: President
TN Farm Bureau
Special Notes: He has used volunteerism of all his spare time as his "hobby" in lieu of golf, hunting, fishing, etc.

Mary Frances Watts
From: Nashville, Davidson County
Years of Service: 10
Volunteering Highlights:
Senior Citizen's Retired Senior Volunteer Program
Pencil Partner for Fall-Hamilton Elementary
Caring Committee for the First Unitarian Universalist church
McCann Elementary, Tutor
Vanderbilt Children's Hospital, Autistic and Retarded Children
Special Notes: Nominated for the Mary Catherine Strobel Award and the first winner of the Flora McKean Award for tutoring.

Wellmont Hospice Volunteers
From: Bristol, Sullivan County
Years of Service: 15
Volunteering Highlights:
JC Penney Golden Rule Award Winner
Bristol Cancer Advisory Council
Tri-City Nu-Voice Club
Holston Valley Medical Center
Bristol Regional Medical Center
Special Notes: Our dedicated volunteers have contributed over 5,250 hours in the past year serving terminal persons and their families. They are a *critical* component in completing the comprehensive services of caring for a terminal person. Providing services ranging from direct patient care, clerical tasks, to bereavement support. Hospice volunteers are able to provide compassion and comfort to persons as a very intimate time of their lives.

> *If every Tennessean were to volunteer for one day a month, we could...* change the world and make it a better place for all citizens. We are the heartbeat of the world and by giving of ourselves we will help others grow.
>
> —Patricia E. Scott
> Memphis
> Shelby County

Tennessee Volunteer Heroes 2001

Randy Wells
From: Harriman, Roane County
Years of Service: 10
Volunteering Highlights:
TC Thompson Cancer
Children's Miracle Network
Ronald McDonald House
American Cancer Society
Knoxville Area Rescue Ministry
Special Notes: Randy is a Volunteer Hero because of the encouragement and interest he shows in community service work along with inspiring others to follow along.

Larry R. West
From: Bon Aqua, Hickman County
Volunteering Highlights:
Meals on Wheels
Homeless Shelters — Room in the Inn Program
Battered Women's Shelters
Food Bank and delivering to seniors
DAV, VA programs
Special Notes: Being a disabled combat veteran doesn't stop Larry. Anytime and anything he can do he will. He never has to be asked. It just comes naturally to him. Even if he is in the hospital, he's always helping others.

Deborah White
From: Johnson City, Washington County
Volunteering Highlights:
Appalachian Girl Scout Council, former Leader and Board Member
Volunteer Johnson City, Board Member 10 years, Former President
East Tennessee Consortium for Service Learning, Project Director
America's Promise, currently Board Chair, Member task force to establish City — Community of Promise
ETSU, Asst. VP, helped create campus-wide culture of service & community outreach
Special Notes: Dr. White has been the initiator of service programs in higher education in Tennessee with the creation of Volunteer ETSU in 1985, to the establishment of service-learning programs in colleges across the state.

Jim White
From: Bristol
Years of Service: 3
Volunteering Highlights:
Healing Hands Health Center: original member Advisory Committee; Board of Directors
J.C. Penney Golden Rule Award Nomination
First Presbyterian Church
Special Notes: In his volunteer position as Volunteer Coordinator at Healing Hands, Jim accepts with enthusiasm any request for assistance and wholeheartedly embraces any project that he is asked to coordinate. He has served as Volunteer Coordinator of non-clinical volunteers as well as assisting in the coordination of building and grounds maintenance; coordinated with the Executive Director in writing effective position descriptions for each volunteer position that is available so that persons who inquire about volunteer opportunities will know what is available and what commitment is required.

Lillian White
From: Celina, Clay County
Years of Service: 25
Volunteering Highlights:
Tenntucky 4 Organization
TN Association Family Community Education, President

> If every Tennessean were to volunteer for one day a month, we could...
>
> eliminate at least 50% of crime, homelessness, truancy, teenage pregnancies, school dropouts, illness, and illiteracy.
>
> —Mary Lee Seymour
> Memphis
> Shelby County

> If every Tennessean were to volunteer for one day a month, we could...
>
> have a much cleaner place to live. The elderly and handicapped would not feel as lonely and neglected, and we would be a more positive example to our children and youth. Young people will not be involved if we do not set the examples they are to follow.
>
> —Eva Babb Sexton
> Newport, Cocke County

> If every Tennessean were to volunteer for one day a month, we could...
>
> ## enable the professionals to spend their time and resources much more efficiently. Also, we could save the healthcare providers, cities and states untold dollars!
>
> —George Shane
> Germantown, Shelby County

Leadership of Upper Cumberland, Secretary
Delta Cappa Gamma Alpha Upsilon Chapter, Treasurer
Clay County Library Board Member
Special Notes: She has always been a community-oriented person. She has been very active with local government and has volunteered many hours in writing grants for Clay County.

Lee Whitmore
From: Smyrna, Rutherford County
Years of Service: 31
Volunteering Highlights:
Smyrna Lions Club: Sight Chairman 21 years
Shrine Legion of Honor: Children's Hospital, 31 years
Alvin C. York Medical Center
Tennessee Rehabilitation Center
Meals on Wheels
Special Notes: Lee currently volunteers two full days and two to three partial days each week.

Lottie C. Whitmore
From: Smyrna, Rutherford County
Years of Service: 42
Volunteering Highlights:
Alvin C. York Veterans Administration Medical Center
GFWC Rutherford Women's Club, Past President
Order of the Eastern Star, Worthy Matron 1973
Smyrna LaVergne Assistance Coalition: Co-organizer
Friends of Smyrna Public Library: Co-organizer, board member
Special Notes: "I have been volunteering since my youngest child was two years old; scouts, Sunday School, Bible School, tutoring, working in hospitals transporting patients to area hospitals, delivering meals since 1976, volunteering in summer reading programs at the library and many other activities."

Frances Wiley
From: Lewisburg, Marshall County
Years of Service: 10
Volunteering Highlights:
American Red Cross: Blood Services; Volunteer of the Year, 1997
ARC Volunteer of the Year for Marshall County, 1997
Marshall County Outstanding Citizen of the Year, 1997
American Legion Auxiliary: Sergeant at Arms Volunteer with Poppy sale
United Daughters of the Confederacy
Special Notes: She is the backbone of MCARC. She gives to someone, someplace, every day. I have never asked Frances to help with any project that she didn't do — AND with a smile on her face — as if it were her pleasure to do so.

Virginia Dare Williams
From: Friendship, Crockett County
Years of Service: 60
Volunteering Highlights:
American Cancer Society
Regional Hospital volunteer
Officer in local PTA for 20 years
Past Matron, Order of Eastern Star
Chamber of Commerce Ambassador
Special Notes: She has spent all her adult years helping others. She served as chairman of the Red Cross Blood drive for three years. She is active in the Crockett County A.C.S., and is also the Recruitment Chair for the Relay For Life.

> If every Tennessean were to volunteer for one day a month, we could...
>
> ## help build community as well as personal wellbeing. I believe that volunteering not only helps the recipient, but also helps the person giving of their time and energy.
>
> —Kathryn Shanks
> Jonesborough, Washington County

Williamson County Sheriff's Dept.

From: Franklin, Williamson County

Special Notes: The Williamson County Sheriff's Dept. are the finest people I know. They have been there for me through thick and thin. On October 23, 1995, my life was torn apart when my daughter was murdered. These officers were there to try to ease my pain. They shared tears and let me know they were there for me and my family, and have been there ever sense. They risk their lives everyday they leave home. They face daily things that are very difficult to deal with emotionally. I honor them each year on my daughter's birthday, Oct 22. She lived one day into her 23rd year. God puts special people in places he wants them to be. The people in the Williamson County Sheriff's Dept are true Tennessee Heroes.

Williamson Medical Center Emergency Department

From: Franklin, Williamson County

Volunteering Highlights:
Tennessee Board of Nursing

Special Notes: One rainy night in 1995, my daughter Stacey was murdered. That night I really realized what the staff of the Williamson Medical Center Emergency Department meant to me. I can't and don't want to imagine what they have to face and how they take all this home with them. Whether it be a broken bone, car accident, heart attack, stroke, sick children, or murder — just imagine what they are faced with. They give you a kind word and a smile. In my darkest hour they were there for me. I didn't have to see what they did with my daughter. I thank God for our true Tennessee Heroes. It takes special people to have the job that they do. But, they do more than any amount of money can ever pay them. They do it with love, understanding, compassion and caring in the most upright way I know.

If every Tennessean were to volunteer for one day a month, we could...

decrease all the violence and build more activities for youth and senior citizens. There would be fewer people doing without basic needs. The environment would be a cleaner and safer place for my fellow brothers and sisters to live.

—Crystal Sharp
Trenton, Gibson County

If every Tennessean were to volunteer for one day a month, we could...

make changes that have a positive effect on families not just here and now, but an effect that crosses over to the next generation. The sky is the limit! We could eradicate illiteracy, provide proper, affordable housing, combat hunger, have a cleaner, more beautiful state and much, much more!

—Charlene Shelton
Kingsport, Sullivan County

Louise P. Wills

From: Nashville, Davidson County
Years of Service: 40
Volunteering Highlights:
The Salvation Army: Women's Auxiliary; The Salvation Army Humanitarian Award, 1999
West End United Methodist Church
Horticultural Society of Middle Tennessee
Cheekwood
Ballet Friends

Special Notes: For her dedication for helping inner city children at great risk for academic failure, Louise Wills is a Tennessee Volunteer Hero. In 1997, Mrs. Wills, through her work with the Salvation Army Women's Auxiliary, saw the need for academic support for children living in the East Nashville neighborhoods served by the Salvation Army's Magness Potter Community Center. A retired educator, Mrs. Wills planned and organized a tutoring program and recruited volunteer tutors to provide homework help and academic enrichment to children age 6 through 12 who attended the community center. Although the original intent of the program was to provide academic support, it quickly became evident that volunteer tutors could address other pressing needs as well. In a neighborhood with a high crime rate and many single parent families, the Magness Potter tutoring program began by Mrs. Wills has done much to boost children's self-esteem, their love of learning and their ability to make wise life choices. The promise of the tutoring program is seen in the many victories, both large and small that the children who participate have achieved. Many have improved grades, enthusiasm for learning and better behavior because of the work of Mrs. Wills and her volunteer tutors. The esteem with which the program is regarded is seen in the close working relationship between children's teachers and tutors in

Tennessee Volunteer Heroes 2001

> If every Tennessean were to volunteer
> for one day a month, we could...
> ensure that children have positive role models
> to assure them they are important and
> worthwhile and keep them motivated to finish
> their education, be good citizens, and
> contribute back to the community. As the
> youth of today become our community leaders
> of tomorrow, the tradition of volunteerism,
> family values and leadership would continue.
>
> —Ken Shipp
> Murfreesboro
> Rutherford County

the program. Tutors often receive communication from teachers about specific kinds of help their students need. Enrollment in the program has steadily increased, and Mrs. Wills and her corps of tutors have added academic enrichment two hours a week as a part of Magness Potter's summer day camp program.

Anne Wilson
From: Maryville, Blount County
Years of Service: 10
Volunteering Highlights:
MC Families
Blount County Literacy Council
Teen Pregnancy Prevention Action Team
United Way: Success-by-Six
Special Notes: Anne is dedicated to making a difference in the lives of children and families in East Tennessee.

Gary Wilson
From: Brentwood, Williamson County
Years of Service: 10
Volunteering Highlights:
American Red Cross/Nashville Area Chapter: Vice Chair, Board of Directors; Chair Board Development
American Red Cross/Nashville Area Chapter: Interim CEO
Urban League of Nashville: Board Member; Treasurer; Interim CEO; President
American Red Cross, TN Valley Blood Services Region, Board Chair
Family First Partners, Inc.: Vice President; Member Board of Trustees
Special Notes: His dedication and commitment to helping those in the community who are in need.

Judi H. Wilson
From: Chattanooga, Hamilton County
Years of Service: 35
Volunteering Highlights:
Ladies Oriental Shrine of North America, ASEBI Court # 36
Ladies Clown Unit
Hickory Valley Garden Club
Tennessee Federation of Garden Clubs, Inc
Epsilon Sigma Alpha International, Alpha Beta Chapter #163
Special Notes: Judi works with the children at the Shrine's Hospital, as well as T.C. Children's (Erlanger) Hospital in Chattanooga. She has also; worked with the March of Dimes, Gardens at Nursing Homes and Hospitals; Shakespeare Garden at UTC.

Deb Wofford
From: Germantown, Shelby County
Years of Service: 4
Volunteering Highlights:
Riverdale School
J.C. Penney Golden Rule Award Nomination
Special Notes: Mrs. Wofford and the Accelerated Reader Moms spend countless hours every month supplementing what the teachers and staff do in the classroom. There are not enough hours in the day to monitor, supervise and follow up on all the Accelerated Reader details. We have done the Accelerated Reader Program for about 12 years at our school, but until Deb organized the Accelerated Reader Moms group, the program was only partially successful. Recent test scores and the Accelerated Reader stats in the past four years show the results of this group on the program and the students in the school. At the present time, Deb is working with two other area schools in an effort to help them organize their parent groups, helping those schools become successful Accelerated Reader schools too.

> If every Tennessean were to volunteer
> for one day a month, we could...
> make differences in the lives that need
> various things, such as transportation,
> exercise, household needs, friendship. This
> would not only help people physically— the
> cost savings would also be very helpful.
> Volunteering is about sharing your time
> and effort with people with needs.
>
> —Rosetta Shotwell
> Nashville
> Davidson County

Tennessee Volunteer Heroes 2001

Jackie D. Wood
Special Notes: Special recognition from the Governor and First Lady of Tennessee for excellence in volunteer service.

Laurel Wood
From: Germantown, Shelby County
Years of Service: 5
Volunteering Highlights:
Germantown Youth Commission
Germantown Environmental Commission
Faith Presbyterian Church
Germantown High School Cross Country Team: Captain
Shelby County Metro Best Of Preps Cross Country Team, 3 years

Terry Woodard
From: Memphis, Shelby County
Volunteering Highlights:
Birthright of Memphis, Inc.
Special Notes: Birthright of Memphis helps any girl or woman who is experiencing a problem pregnancy and offers them an alternative to abortion. Because of Terry's joy for life and her willingness to share herself, many stressed women have been comforted. Many have chosen to have their baby because they knew that there was help from a caring, non-judgmental person. Terry has affected our office with her skills, and with her attitude of willingness and cheerfullness. Terry is a joy for life.

Betty Wolfe
From: White Bluff, Dickson County
Years of Service: 46
Volunteering Highlights:
The Renaissance Center

> If every Tennessean were to volunteer for one day a month, we could…
> not only enrich the lives of those around us, we could make ours better in the process. Volunteering is a two-way street. We receive much more than we give. What better way is there to make our families and our communities better than we already are?"
>
> —Connie Siemanski
> Nashville, Davidson County

> If every Tennessean were to volunteer for one day a month, we could…
> improve our schools. That is how I got started, volunteering for my daughter's kindergarten class. I was so badly needed, I just could not stop. If everyone did that, they would be more aware about what is going on in our schools and support our teachers. It makes you feel good to be needed, and volunteers are definitely needed in our schools.
>
> —Kathy Simon
> Readyville
> Cannon County

William James School
White Bluff United Methodist Church
Special Notes: She is particularly committed to children and in helping each one she comes in contact with feel loved and special.

Jane Work
From: Germantown, Shelby County
Years of Service: 16
Volunteering Highlights:
Le Bonheur Club: Headquarters Chairman; Baby Hugging
Our Lady of Perpetual Help Church Teen Spirit Ensemble: Adult Leader
Houston High School Swim team: Board Member; Assistant Manager
Kimbrough Woods Neighborhood Association: Block Captain: Garden Club
Germantown Swim Team: Board Member; Newsletter Writer/Editor
Special Notes: Jane works mostly for children, teens and community groups who make our world a better place to live. Her commitment to others while she works outside the home and nurtures three children is remarkable — she's a true Volunteer Hero for Tennessee.

Frank Wright
From: McEwen, Humphreys County
Years of Service: 1
Volunteering Highlights:
American Cancer Society
United Way
Pine Hill Church
Vanderbilt Children's Hospital
Individual children with spinal disease
Special Notes: In the fall of 1999 Frank Wright contacted

Tennessee Volunteer Heroes 2001

> **If every Tennessean were to volunteer for one day a month, we could...**
> solve most of the social problems facing our citizens. Today's technological advances threaten to move us deeper into an impersonal society. If we can encourage more face-to-face contact, we can maintain our humanity. The best way to do that is for each of us to use our unique talents in a volunteer setting, connecting with fellow Tennesseans, exchanging skills and ideas, and repairing what is broken, now, while we still care.
>
> —Teri R. Simon
> Nashville, Davidson County

staff at the American Cancer Society with his desire to start a Relay For Life fundraising event in his community, Waverly. The catch... staff would need to come to Vanderbilt Hospital because Frank was undergoing a stem cell transplant for lymphoma. Needless to say, Julie Campos and Deanna Carpenter were amazed. They met with Frank and knew immediately that this man was determined to not only beat his cancer, but to get this event started. Frank persuaded a small group to take leadership roles and the Relay For Life became a reality. Frank's role was Logistics Chair. He secured a location for the relay and created a detailed, strategic map of the facilities and layout, for the 1999 relay. He also planned for growth beyond the next couple of years. There were 17 teams of 8-10 people participating and countless volunteers. The first Waverly Relay For Life raised $41,000!

Catherine Wyatt-Morley
From: Nashville, Davidson County
Years of Service: 5
Volunteering Highlights:
Author of "Talk To a Junk Yard Dog"
Presented her book to Vice President, Al Gore
Works without a salary
Speaks at schools and universities, enlightening them on the effects of HIV
Speaker of Health Law Students at Tennessee State University
Special Notes: As an HIV positive individual, she founded W.O.M.E.N. to empower, enlighten and educate the urban community with families who are coming to terms with HIV/AIDS and the "true" devastating issues.

Rick Wyckoff
From: Germantown, Shelby County
Years of Service: 15
Volunteering Highlights:
Habitat for Humanity
Our Lady of Perpetual Help Church: Sr. High Youth Group; Knights of Columbus; Men's Club; Sports Coordinator
Lifeblood: Germantown Board
PTA Board: Houston Middle School Health & Safety; Dogwood Elementary Safety; PTA Honorary Life Membership
Farmington Meadows Homeowners Association: Board Member
Special Notes: "I enjoy helping others and being involved in the community. People close to me know that my involvement is not for tangible rewards. Helping others when needed is my responsibility to the community."

Howard "Posey" Young
From: Celina, Clay County
Years of Service: 40
Volunteering Highlights:
Founder of Clay County Reunion Celebration
Clay County C.B. Club, President
Pic Council
Clay County Fish Fry, music organizer
MC for community fundraisers
Special Notes: He has always volunteered his time to worthy causes and for people in need. He has worked for over forty years to make Clay County a more progressive and active community.

> **If every Tennessean were to volunteer for one day a month, we could...**
>
> ensure that no one in our state would be lonely, uncared for, or think they are unloved.
>
> —Rev. Tony Sirten
> Old Hickory, Davidson County

Tennessee Volunteer Heroes 2001

Youth Builders, Inc.
From: Greeneville, Greene County
Years of Service: 53
Volunteering Highlights:
Children's Theatre
Holston Home/Bewley Center
J.C. Penney Golden Rule Recognition
Nathanael Greene Musuem
School Assistance/Scholarships/Library Assistance
Special Notes: Youth Builders are Volunteer Heroes because they are a totally independent organization with no safety net. They have no outside affiliation or benefactors but rely solely on their own abilities to raise money or solicit contributions. More importantly, Youth Builders has been a leader in community service for over 50 years. A project doesn't have to be their idea to garner support, it only has to fulfill the objective of promoting the welfare of children and youth contributing needful service to the community.

William Laughlin Youree
From: Readyville, Rutherford County
Years of Service: 40
Volunteering Highlights:
4-H Volunteer leader for 35 years in livestock projects
Cripple Creek Presbyterian Church: member; Elder
Kittrell Volunteer Fire Department: Past President; founding member; firefighter
Rutherford County Cattleman's Association: Past President; Secretary and Treasurer
Kittrell Community Board
Special Notes: He is always there for his family and neighbors. His love for them keeps him striving to do his best for the community.

If every Tennessean were to volunteer for one day a month, we could... substantially raise the quality of education, increase the quality of life for low income families, and reduce the amounts of money spent by the state and federal government on assistance in these areas.

—Martin J. Skinner, Sr.
Harriman
Roane County

If every Tennessean were to volunteer for one day a month, we could... bring joy to every neglected elderly person. We could tutor slow-learning and underprivileged children. We could improve housing in poor neighborhoods, providing safer neighborhoods through volunteer patrols. We could make a clean environment a reality and have a beautiful state with no litter. In short, we could do anything we wanted to!

—Coleman Smith
Adamsville
McNairy County

If every Tennessean were to volunteer for one day a month, we could...

help our needy and handicapped citizens so that their quality of life could be much improved in every way— a most worthwhile endeavor!

—Dorothy B. Skinner
Harriman
Roane County

If every Tennessean were to volunteer for one day a month, we could... help non-profit organizations use all funds for the work intended to make a better and healthier society. The volunteer will feel better helping someone live a better life.

—Dora Smith
Bartlett, Shelby County

If every Tennessean were to volunteer for one day a month, we could…
help a child believe in achieving dreams, clean up the environment, rescue animals from the thoughtless, bring friendship to the lonely, give abused women and children a safe place to achieve, help wayward juveniles find love and direction, and encourage, by example, every community to care more about working together than competing against each other.

—Rev. Joanne P. Smith
Germantown
Shelby County

If every Tennessean were to volunteer for one day a month, we could…
make a difference in a child's life, especially the disadvantaged kids who need that the special attention of someone they can trust. Knowing that I touched *one* child was a success to me.

—Justine Smith
Nashville, Davidson County

If every Tennessean were to volunteer for one day a month, we could…
make Tennessee the best place to live! We could end hunger, clean the environment, stop violence, and help build lasting friendships by working together.

—Michelle Smith
Brighton
Tipton County

If every Tennessean were to volunteer for one day a month, we could…
work alongside each other and learn from one another. We could inspire young volunteers to come together to analyze the needs or problems of their local areas. We could teach all volunteers there are no financial rewards, but a real sense of satisfaction and gratitude. Volunteers are paid in six figures: S-M-I-L-E-S. We could promote racial equality and improve racial and religious harmony.

—Norma Jean Soloff
Chattanooga, Hamilton County

If every Tennessean were to volunteer for one day a month, we could…
help make the world a whole lot better place. 5.7 million volunteers at 8 hours a day for 12 days that equates to 547 million volunteer hours a year! WHOOPEE!

—Ronnie Sowards
Nashville, Davidson County

If every Tennessean were to volunteer for one day a month, we could…
help a young person do something they could be proud of. Years later, they will remember what we did for them and they will pass it on by helping others. You can become a leader by helping a child with anything he/she might attempt to do. Many times, things will not turn out right the first time, but by showing patience and a willingness to do it over, you give that child confidence and a chance to achieve, otherwise he/she might give up. You never stand as tall as when you stoop to help a child.

—B.D. and Marcella Spence
Lewisburg, Marshall County

If every Tennessean were to volunteer for one day a month, we could...

become the 100% Volunteer state and change attitudes as well as conditions.

—Gayle P. Spence
Memphis, Shelby County

If every Tennessean were to volunteer for one day a month, we could...

grow our cultural and historical heritage to heights one only dreams about. The publicity that Tennessee would garner from such a "one day a month" project would bring extremely positive value to the state's tourism economy. This would instill pride in every Tennesseean because they each had a part in it.

—Hal T. Spoden
Kingsport, Sullivan County

If every Tennessean were to volunteer for one day a month, we could...

help solve many of Tennessee's problems— homelessness, illiteracy, abuse, neglect, troubled youth, etc. In volunteering your time and talents, you gain so much personally and the recipient realizes you truly care because it's your choice to volunteer. You earn a living by what you make, but you make a life by what you give.

—Connie C. Steere
Kingsport, Sullivan County

If every Tennessean were to volunteer for one day a month, we could...

enable agencies to double their service to the community and meet many more people's needs.

—Elsie Steiner
Nashville
Davidson County

If every Tennessean were to volunteer for one day a month, we could...

assure our youth that someone cares about their needs, and assure the handicapped that someone is trying to understand their needs. We could encourage young and old to understand the system in which we live so that together we can all be achievers and assets in the communities where we live no matter how great or small the achievements.

—Debra E. Stewart
Shelbyville, Bedford County

If every Tennessean were to volunteer for one day a month, we could...

have a better community. People would learn to appreciate each other more instead of bickering and fighting. It takes a community to raise the awareness of what we need to make our school system run smoothly. We need more parent volunteers.

—Susie Stewart
Memphis, Shelby County

How to Get Connected to Volunteer in Tennessee

"Every body can be great because every body can serve," said Martin Luther King, Jr. That's especially true in the Volunteer State. This section of *Volunteer Heroes* is designed to help you think about how you would like to volunteer and to give you some resources to help you get connected if you need them.

How Do I Choose Where To Volunteer?

- Think about your interests... what do you enjoy doing?
- What special abilities do you have that you would like to share with others?
- What age group would you most like to serve?
- Do you want to serve directly with individuals or perhaps help with concrete projects?
- How much time do you want to devote to serving others?
- Do you want to volunteer with a group of other volunteers or serve individually?
- Are you ready to make a commitment?
- Above all, have fun and celebrate your gift of giving!

Where Do I Go To Volunteer?

- AIDS programs
- animal shelters
- AmeriCorps
- American Red Cross
- arts organizations
- Big Brother/Big Sister
- boards of non-profit agencies
- Boy Scouts Troops
- Boys & Girls clubs
- chambers of commerce
- child day-care centers
- churches
- civic and fraternal associations
- civil air patrol
- community action councils
- community centers/community parks
- court-appointed special advocates (CASA)
- crisis intervention hotlines
- disability programs (Easter Seals, United Cerebral Palsy)
- drug prevention programs
- environmental groups
- food banks
- foster grandparent programs
- Girl Scouts Troops
- Habitat for Humanity
- Head Start program
- highway safety groups
- historical societies
- homeless shelters
- hospitals and hospices
- immigration/refugee resettlement
- juvenile justice centers
- libraries
- literacy programs
- Little League
- local welfare departments
- meals-on-wheels
- museums
- neighborhood associations
- nursing homes
- police departments
- political groups
- prisons
- rescue squad groups
- Retired Senior Volunteer Programs (RSVP)
- Salvation Army
- senior centers
- schools
- Special Olympics
- state parks

teen centers
teen pregnancy prevention programs
Veterans Administration hospitals
VISTA programs
volunteer centers
Youth Engaged in Service program
YMCA
YWCA
Zoos

> If every Tennessean were to volunteer for one day a month, we could... straighten out the problems that still exist and we, ourselves, would be fulfilled knowing that we've done something good for somebody.
>
> —Vernon Stewart
> Memphis
> Shelby County

Can I Connect with Volunteer Opportunities On-Line?

Yes. Thanks to the world wide web, connecting with volunteer opportunities in your community is just a mouse click away! These are just a few of the many websites that will allow you to start making a difference today.

Corporation for National Service http://www.cns.gov
Since 1993, the Corporation for National Service has provided millions of Americans with the opportunity to give back through service. Connect with AmeriCorps, Learn & Serve America, Senior Corps and VISTA programs in your community.

Do Something http://www.dosomething.org/
Since its founding in 1993, Do Something has helped to inspire and empower millions of young people to be leaders who measurably strengthen their communities. Do Something has the Community Connections Campaign, which is a national effort to connect young people with civic organizations to strengthen America's communities.

Hands on Nashville http://hon.org/
Connects individuals, young people and families with volunteer opportunities in Nashville, Tennessee.

Hands on Memphis http://handsonmemphis.org/
Connects individuals, young people and families with volunteer opportunities in Memphis, Tennessee.

Generations United http://www.gu.org/
Generations United provides information about intergenerational initiatives around the country, including Learn & Serve America programs.

Idealist http://www.idealist.org/
A listing of 10,000 non-profit groups and searchable database users with volunteering opportunities in their area.

Kids Helping Kids http:/edsitewa.iinet.net.au/khk/home.html
Kids Helping Kids is an organization of children who run an annual environmental conference for children. Their site includes information on environmental issues and related organizations, details on KHK's upcoming conference, and an on-line newsletter and slide show.

Make A Difference Day http://www.usaweekend.com/diffday/ Created by USA Weekend, Make A Difference Day is the largest national day of helping others. Make A Difference Day is an annual event that takes place on the fourth Saturday of every October. The site allows volunteers to connect with Make A Difference Day service projects.

National 4-H Council http://www.4-h.org/ National 4-H is an organization that involves 5,688,461 young people in 76,572 clubs across the nation, making it the largest young service organization in the *world!* 4-H involves young people in thousands of service projects every year and is helping to better the lives of young people, their families and the communities in which they live.

The National Youth Leadership Council http://www.nylc.org/ The NYLC's mission is to engage young people in their communities and schools through innovative learning, service, leadership and public policy.

Nashville PULSE http://nashvillepulse.org/
Connects young people with opportunities to serve in Nashville, Tennessee.

President's Student Service Challenge http://www.tjhsst.edu/ysa/final/
Through the Corporation for National Service, this program includes the President's Student Service Scholarships, for which each high school in the country may select one junior or senior to receive a $1,000 scholarship for outstanding service to the community. The President's Student Service Awards recognizes students who have volunteered between 50 and 100 hours or more in their communities.

The Prudential Spirit of Community Awards
http://www.prudential.com/community/spirit/cmszz1000.html In partnership with the National Association of Secondary School Principals, Prudential sponsors a national awards program to recognize young people in grades 5-12 for outstanding community service.

Points of Light Foundation http://www.PointsofLight.org/ The Points of Light Foundation provides information on over 500 volunteer centers and is the central hub for community-based service learning initiatives across the country. The Foundation staff involve community agencies with schools, as well as develop strong community connections among and between community agencies.

SERVEnet http://www.servenet.org/ SERVEnet links volunteers to volunteer opportunities and has other resources for non-profits. Non-profits can register to be listed on the site.

UNICEF's Voices of Youth http://www.unicef.org/voy/ UNICEF's Voices of Youth program encourages children throughout the nation to learn about the conditions of their peers in developing nations and to help raise funds for those who desperately need help.

United Way http://www.unitedway.org/
Helps individuals find the nearest United Way and to connect with local volunteering opportunities.

Volunteer Tennessee http://www.volunteertennessee.org/
Volunteer Tennessee connects all of Tennessee's volunteer centers to one central website. Individuals can connect with volunteer and national service opportunities in their communities.

Youth Service America (YSA) http://ysa.ibelong.com/ YSA is a resource center and the premier alliance of 200+ organizations committed to increasing the quantity and quality of opportunities for young Americans to serve locally, nationally and globally.

If every Tennessean were to volunteer for one day a month, we could...

truly fulfill our reputation as the "Volunteer State" and raise the quality of life for every Tennessean.

—Floyd Stewart, Jr.
Nashville
Davidson County

If every Tennessean were to volunteer for one day a month, we could...

solve many problems. God has let me live this long to help others.

—Viola Tribble Street
Memphis, Shelby County

If every Tennessean were to volunteer for one day a month, we could...

have fewer lonely, isolated elderly and handicapped citizens in our state. We could relieve caretakers of the sick and elderly on a regular basis. We could help more foreign adults and children to learn English; provide transportation for seniors to doctors and hospitals, etc.

—Lottie M. Strupp
Nashville, Davidson County

If every Tennessean were to volunteer for one day a month, we could...

help our neighborhood schools, nursing homes and hospitals. Many of us just giving one day really adds up.

—Lois H. Taylor
Memphis, Shelby County

If every Tennessean were to volunteer for one day a month, we could...

help a lot of people who really need assistance in walking, feeding themselves, dressing, reading and writing.

—Lucia Thomas
Franklin, Williamson County

If every Tennessean were to volunteer for one day a month, we could...

virtually wipe out the financial demands of most taxpayer-supported social services, thereby freeing up money to concentrate on better education and health provisions (something that would benefit all). We would also increase social awareness of the extreme personal satisfaction one can glean from giving of oneself. In other words, it would be "cool" to volunteer! Tennessee could truly be representative of its heritage in a dynamic way.

—Amy Thomason
Johnson City
Washington County

If every Tennessean were to volunteer for one day a month, we could...
produce a more educated, caring community and a state that would provide our children with a future filled with hope and promise.

—Elisa Thompson
Celina, Clay County

If every Tennessean were to volunteer for one day a month, we could...
learn the needs of our communities and be more sensitive and compassionate toward others.

—Shelley Thompson
Crossville, Cumberland County

If every Tennessean were to volunteer for one day a month, we could...
have the best schools in the nation and the most beautiful and trash-free state. The arts would be overwhelmed with the support offered.

—Mrs. Ruth Thorsberg
Germantown
Shelby County

If every Tennessean were to volunteer for one day a month, we could...
make a big difference in the life of each Tennessean.

—Joyce Tidwell
Burns
Dickson County

If every Tennessean were to volunteer for one day a month, we could...
feed the hungry, clothe those in need, and provide the impetus to bridge the gap between the haves and the have-nots. Too much of what we see as violence in the streets is based on economic deprivation. Volunteerism goes a long way toward closing the economic shortfalls.

—Larry Tifverman
Memphis
Shelby County

If every Tennessean were to volunteer for one day a month, we could...
all share with great pride the truly wonderful and amazing feeling of "helping others."

—Grace Tomkins
Gallatin
Sumner County

National and Community Service Glossary

The Act The National and Community Service Trust Act of 1990, as amended by the National and Community Trust Act of 1993.

America's Promise The Alliance for America's Youth that resulted from the President's Summit for America's Future, which ensures that all children have access to caring adults; safe places; a healthy start and future; an effective education; and opportunities to give back to their community through service.

America Reads Challenge The program that engages trained reading tutors and partners working closely together to supplement the efforts of parents, teachers and schools with the goal that all children read well and independently by the end of the third grade.

AmeriCorps A national service program that engages individuals in community service that meets the education, environment, human, health and safety needs of communities. National Civilian Community Corps (NCCC) and Volunteers in Service to America (VISTA) are part of AmeriCorps.

AmeriCorps Members Individuals enrolled in AmeriCorps who commit to completing 900 to 1700 hours of service in exchange for receiving valuable professional development training and an education award that can be used to pay for college or to re-pay student loans.

Connect America A collaborative Points of Light Foundation's initiative that brings together the energies and resources of non-profit organizations, businesses and community volunteers to help build the connections that are critical to meeting the needs of communities.

Corporation for National Service Sometimes referred to as CNS, this federally established and funded corporation funds and administers AmeriCorps, Learn & Serve America and Senior Corps programs.

Ethic of Service Believing in endorsing, promoting and participating in national and community service.

Full Participation Recognition that all people have both the right and responsibility to participate in community service and volunteerism, both as providers and recipients of community and national service.

Federal Work Study A mandate from the U.S. Department of Education for colleges and universities to use five percent of their Federal award to pay students to work in the community.

Getting Things Done The motto of AmeriCorps and the Corporation for National Service, and its primary goal— means doing direct service that achieves demonstrable results in the community.

Learn & Serve America Service learning programs that are designed to enrich academic learning and promote personal growth in participants while meeting critical needs of the community. Service learning is an effective and innovative teaching methodology for K-12 and higher education.

Make A Difference Day A national day of volunteering sponsored by USA Weekend, the Points of Light Foundation and the Corporation for National Service held on the fourth Saturday in October.

Martin Luther King, Jr. Day On Service A day to honor Dr. Martin Luther King's philosophy on service. In 1994 Congress passed the King Holiday and Service Act designed to transform the observance of Martin Luther King's birthday into a day of service that reflects his life and teaching.

National Senior Service Corps National service programs designed to engage senior citizens in meeting critical education, environment, human, health and public safety needs of communities. Includes Senior Companions, Foster Grandparents, and Retired and Senior Volunteer Program. Formerly called the National Senior Volunteer Corps and before that the Older American Volunteer Program.

National Service Any community service program funded by the Corporation for National Service, including AmeriCorps, Learn & Serve America and Senior Corps.

National Volunteer Week A week designated to nationally promote and recognize the efforts of citizen volunteers of all ages. Usually the third week of April.

National Youth Service Day An annual public education campaign that occurs in April, highlighting the efforts of young people in their communities, encouraging more young people to become involved in volunteering and promoting the benefits of service to the American people.

Non-Profit Organization An organization who's primary purpose is not making a profit but meeting a community need.

Partnership Two or more entities that have entered into a written agreement specifying the partnership's goals and activities as well as the responsibilities, goals and activities of each partner.

Points of Light Foundation A non-partisan, non-profit organization established in May 1990 to engage people more effectively in volunteer community service to help meet critical community needs.

Service Learning A teaching method that integrates community service into curriculum and engages young people in community activities where academic skills are used to solve real-life problems, and develop an understanding of citizenship and their ability to help determine the quality of life in their communities.

State Commission The term used to refer to a 15 to 25 member, independent, bipartisan body appointed by the Governor to implement service programs.

VISTA See AmeriCorps

Volunteer Centers Are community organizations that promote volunteering; connect people with opportunities to serve; build the capacity for effective local volunteering; participate in strategic initiatives that mobilize community volunteers to meet local community needs.

Volunteer (n) A person who voluntarily undertakes service or duty.

Volunteer (v) To offer or give voluntarily; to offer oneself as a volunteer.

If every Tennessean were to volunteer for one day a month, we could...

improve the quality of life.

—Dawn Tomlin
Hendersonville
Sumner County

If every Tennessean were to volunteer for one day a month, we could...

make Tennessee the absolute best place in the world to live.

—Jason R. Tomlin
Franklin
Williamson County

Tennessee Volunteer Heroes 2001

Directory of Volunteer Centers in Tennessee

Volunteer centers are GREAT places! They promote volunteering, connect people with opportunities to serve, build the capacity for effective local volunteering, and participate in strategic initiatives that mobilize volunteers to meet local community needs.

Volunteer Center of Blount County
(865) 982-2251

Volunteer Center of Chattanooga
(423) 265-0514

Volunteer Center of Clarksville
(931) 552-3997

Volunteer ETSU
(423) 439-9341

Volunteer Center of Greene County
(423) 639-9341

Volunteer Center of Johnson City
(423) 282-0404

Volunteer Center of Kingsport
(423) 247-4511

Volunteer Center of Knoxville
(865) 523-9131

Volunteer Center of Memphis
(901) 458-3288

Volunteer Center of Murfreesboro
(615) 893-7303

Volunteer Center of Putnam County
(931) 520-4898

If every Tennessean were to volunteer for one day a month, we could...
reach many goals that seem impossible. To know you are helping and making a difference by giving of your time and self is such a rewarding experience. I was 39 when I started and I am now 69. I strongly believe when you volunteer for worthy causes, God remembers you in many wonderful ways.

—Luanne Townsend
Madison, Davidson County

If every Tennessean were to volunteer for one day a month, we could...

further enrich the quality of life in our communities.

—Patricia Traylor
Germantown
Shelby County

Tennessee Volunteer Heroes 2001

Other Volunteer Mobilization Organizations

Community Resource Center
(615) 781-8474

Council of Community Services
(615) 385-2221

Hands on Memphis
(901) 532-1377

Hands on Nashville
(615) 298-1108

Tennessee Commission on National and Community Service
(615) 532-9250
1-888-509-8878

> If every Tennessean were to volunteer for one day a month, we could...
>
> ### make a tremendous difference in the lives of those less fortunate.
>
> —Robert Lee Truax, Sr.
> Cordova
> Shelby County

> If every Tennessean were to volunteer for one day a month, we could...
>
> ### enhance the quality of life for everyone on the state, thus helping every Tennessean reach his or her potential.
>
> —Liz Turner
> Nashville, Davidson County

> If every Tennessean were to volunteer for one day a month, we could...
>
> ### make our schools a safe and healthy environment in which our children can grow and learn.
>
> —Mary Tuttle
> Cookeville
> Putnam County

> If every Tennessean were to volunteer for one day a month, we could...
>
> ### feel better about ourselves in serving our mission for God in helping our neighbors as we should.
>
> —Mary B. Vance
> Gatlinburg
> Sevier County

Directory of United Ways in Tennessee

United Ways are great places to explore community solutions, learn about health and human service issues, donate or volunteer, express your opinions and provide your thoughts.

United Way of Anderson County
(865) 481-8431

United Way of Bedford County
(931) 684-6685

United Way of Benton County
(931) 296-4588

United Way of Bledsoe County
See United Way of Greater Chattanooga

United Way of Blount County
(865) 982-2251

United Way of Bradley County
(423) 479-8576

United Way of Bristol/Sullivan County
(423) 968-4912

United Way of Campbell County
(423) 574-5066

United Way of Cannon County
See United Way of Rutherford County

United Way of Carroll County
See United Way of West Tennessee

United Way of Carter County/Elizabethton
(423) 543-6975

United Way of Cocke County/Newport
(423) 613-8877

United Givers Fund of Coffee County
(931) 455-5678

United Way of Clarksville/Montgomery County
(931) 647-4291

United Way of DeKalb County
(931) 526-2723

United Way of Dickson County
(615) 446-1720

United Way of Dyer County
See United Way of West Tennessee

United Way of Fayette County
See United Way of the MidSouth

United Way of Franklin County
See United Way of Greater Chattanooga

United Way of Gibson County
See United Way of West Tennessee

United Way of Greater Chattanooga
(423) 752-0300

United Way of Greater Kingsport
(423) 378 3409

United Way of Greater Knoxville
(865) 523-9131

United Way of Greene County
(423) 639 9361

United Way of Grundy County
See United Way of Greater Chattanooga

United Way of Hamblen County
(423) 581-8601

United Way of Hardeman County
See United Way of West Tennessee

United Way of Hawkins County
(865) 272-7379

United Way of Haywood County
See United Way of West Tennessee

United Way of Henderson County
See United Way of West Tennessee

United Way of Humphreys County
(931) 296-4588

United Way of Jefferson County
See United Way of Greater Knoxville

Johnson City Area United Way, Inc.
(423) 282-5682

United Way of Lauderdale County
See United Way of Mid South

United Way of Loudon County
(423) 986-4820

United Way of McMinn County
(423) 745-9606

United Way of McNairy County
See United Way of West Tennessee

United Way of Macon County
See United Way of Sumner County

United Way of Madison County
See United Way of West Tennessee

United Way of Marion County
See United Way of Greater Chattanooga

United Way of Maury County, Inc.
(931) 381-0100

United Way of Meigs County
See United Way of McMinn County

United Way of Metro Nashville
(615) 255-8501

United Way of the Mid South
(901) 543-5800

United Way of Monroe County
(423) 337-7690

United Way of Morgan County
(423) 346-3773

United Way of Obion County
(901) 885-2595

United Way of Overton County
(931) 823-8267

United Way of Polk County
See United Way of Greater Chattanooga

United Way of Putnam County
(931) 526-2723

United Way of Rhea County
See United Way of Greater Chattanooga

United Way of Roane County
(423) 882-7711

United Way of Robertson County
(615) 384-8160

United Way of Rutherford County
(615) 893-7303

United Way of Sequatchie County
See United Way of Greater Chattanooga

United Way of Sevier County
(865) 453-4261

United Way of Shelby County
See United Way of Mid South

United Way of Sumner County
(615) 451-1977

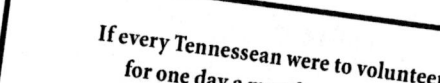

United Way of Tipton County
See United Way of Mid South

United Way of Union County
(423) 992-0512

United Way of Weakly County
See United Way of West Tennessee

United Way of West Tennessee, Inc.
(901) 422-1816

United Way of Williamson County
(615) 794-2200

If every Tennessean were to volunteer for one day a month, we could...

become someone's hero while serving God and mankind. You can't help another without being helped yourself many times over.

—Tom D. Vance
Murfreesboro, Rutherford County

If every Tennessean were to volunteer for one day a month, we could...

have a more beautiful state because litter and trash would be collected and removed from the roadsides. We could have enough adult leaders to provide the leadership and support for all boys and girls who want to become Scouts. We could have enough blood to supply all hospitals' needs and there would never be a need for an "emergency blood appeal."

—Deborah G. Varallo
Mt. Juliet
Wilson County

If every Tennessean were to volunteer for one day a month, we could...

make a difference in the lives of our elderly residents. We could put more smiles on the faces of our youth and needy families. We could make our communities better, safer places to live, and help to strengthen our schools and churches. We could provide more programs for our youth in an effort to involve them in their communities, and we could make our own lives more enjoyable by making a difference to someone or some project.

—Myra J. Vaughan
Crump
Hardin County

If every Tennessean were to volunteer for one day a month, we could...

accomplish things that help the poor and would make a good life for most of our underprivileged people. Our volunteerism would make Tennessee the greatest place to live.

—William J. Vaughn
Brentwood, Williamson County

If every Tennessean were to volunteer for one day a month, we could...

improve the living conditions of our fellow citizens. We could promote their appreciation and preservation of the natural environment, on which we all depend. We could help those adults who cannot read to do so and help vulnerable citizens to understand and apply the principles of physical, mental and emotional good health. We could do a lot!

—Grace M. Wallace
Memphis
Shelby County

If every Tennessean were to volunteer for one day a month, we could…

make a difference in the lives of many more people in our state.

—Sue Ward
Dickson, Dickson County

If every Tennessean were to volunteer for one day a month, we could…

light up the world with God's love, sharing with one another as he does with us, calling us to do for the least of our brothers.

—Doug Warner
Germantown, Shelby County

If every Tennessean were to volunteer for one day a month, we could…

all become more aware of the needs of others and thus more tolerant. Our own lives would be more fulfilled and we would set a better example for others.

—Natalie F. Watson
Germantown
Shelby County

If every Tennessean were to volunteer for one day a month, we could…

surely make Tennessee the best place in the nation to live, work, raise our families, and prosper. Volunteering will help get all our children a good education, keep down crime, and make us all better friends and neighbors. Having compassion, serving others, and practicing the golden rule will also lead to healthier and happier lives. It has worked for me in these 60 years of public service.

—Henry D. Wattenbarger
Kingston, Roane County

If every Tennessean were to volunteer for one day a month, we could…

greatly reduce many of our social problems. Our young people might be better educated and guided. Then, maybe fewer would waste their lives on drugs and crime. Our mentally ill could also be better cared for, as would our elderly. The volunteers themselves would also be enriched.

—Mary Frances Watts
Nashville
Davidson County

If every Tennessean were to volunteer for one day a month, we could…

set an example for the rest of the country to follow. We could have neighbors helping neighbors, people caring for one another. We could let the world know the Tennessee spirit is alive and well.

—Randy Wells
Harriman, Roane County

Acknowledgements

Tennessee Volunteer Heroes 2001 is a partnership between the Tennessee Commission on National & Community Service and the Council of Community Services. In addition to this book, the initiative includes a media campaign and fundraising efforts to maximize the effect of the United Nations International Year of the Volunteer in the Volunteer State, and to generate support for infrastructure to advance volunteerism in Tennessee.

The Tennessee Commission on National & Community Service is the 25 member bipartisan Commission appointed by the Governor to advance national and community service and volunteerism as a means of community problem solving in Tennessee. It was created by Executive Order in 1994 to qualify Tennessee to receive federal grant funds under the 1993 National and Community Service Trust Act.

The Commission's vision is that all Tennesseans will be inspired to assume responsibility for improving their community, state and nation through community service; will have readily available opportunities to engage their unique gifts and talents in service, no matter their age or ability; and will, by their service, improve the quality of life for us all.

The Commission's key programs are AmeriCorps and service learning. AmeriCorps is the new domestic Peace Corps in which hundreds of Tennesseans give a year of their lives to direct, measurable community service in the areas of education, environment, public safety and human needs in return for a living stipend and help with college tuition or loan repayments.

Service learning is a teaching methodology that combines academic learning with community service in schools and community-based settings. The Commission partners with the Corporation for National Service; Department of Education Learn & Serve America, Safe & Drug Free Schools and Education Edge; the Points of Light Foundation; 4-H; Lions International and Quest International; National Guard; and a variety of local schools and non-profits to provide training and grants to support service learning across Tennessee.

Following the Presidents' Summit for America's Future in 1997, the Commission was given responsibility for America's Promise — the Alliance for Youth in Tennessee. Since then, the Commission has been helping to pull the little red wagon into communities across the Volunteer State to connect kids in Tennessee with the essential resources they need to succeed.

The Commission has won national recognition for its work including the "Making of the King Holiday Award" presented by Coretta Scott King for a service project in Memphis in 1996 and the 1998 Lions Quest "most outstanding service learning state award." In 2000 the Commission brought Tennessee the distinction of being the only state of the first 18 reviewed by the Corporation for National Service Inspector General to have established effective grant management systems in all four major categories.

Commission members serve three-year terms. Most were volunteer heroes themselves before their appointments and have continued to advance service in Tennessee through quarterly business meetings, grantee site visits, and special projects like *Tennessee Volunteer Heroes 2001*.

Members of the Tennessee Commission on National & Community Service
Martha Sundquist, Honorary Chair
Fred Cole, Chair
Sara Sellers, Vice Chair
Debbie Reaves, Treasurer
Paul Clere, Secretary
Emily Beaty
Vernon Coffey
Otha Brandon
Milton Burchfield
Leighton Bush, Jr.
Jan Bushing
Katherine Darnell
Sandra Flatt
Donna Galbraith
John Harris
Jim Hughson
Austin Jennings
Pam Pfeffer
Larry Proffitt
Lynn Stewart
Martha Jo Tolley

Class of '99
Kellye Cash
Mickey Finn
Sherrie Gilchrist-Ward
Jim Jamieson
Lois Jordan
Charles Norman
Rachel Smith

Class of '98
Donna Denley
Sen. Roscoe Dixon
Susan Edwards
Sen Gene Elsea
Dee Haslam
Jerome Ryans
Sara Sellers

Class of '97
Charles Arant
Dee Ann Perkins Culbreath
Betty Haynes
Thomas Kane
Pat Lewis
Cynthia Manuel
Kim McMillan
Jane Walters
Wanda Webb

**Founding Members
 (terms expired 1996 or before)**
Sam Anderson
Jerry Anderton
Melvin Burgess
Pat Eaker
Sen. Gene Elsea
Rep. Ed Haley
Anne Helgeland
Jerry Herman
Bill Hicks
Barbara Hyde
Ben Landers
Richard Lewis
Laura Mann
Cynthia Manuel
Corniela McNeill
Martha Nan Meredith
Kim-Phuong Nguyen
Rep. Mae Ownby
Wayne Qualls
Gene Roberts
Darlene Sisco
Floyd Stewart
Sen. Danny Wallace
Randall Webb

Tennessee Volunteer Heroes 2001

In addition to the citizen members appointed by the Governor, the Commission aligns volunteerism and service with key partners though ex officio members and their designees. These currently include:

Lt. Governor John Wilder

Speaker Jimmy Naifeh

Commissioner Mike Greene
TN Department of Safety

Commissioner Milton Hamilton
Linda Tidwell
TN Department of Environment & Conservation

Commissioner George Hattaway
Joyce Day
TN Department of Children's Services

Commissioner Michael Magill
Jacqueline Cook
TN Department of Workforce Development

Commissioner Natasha Metcalf
Steven Meinbresse and Michael Dedmon
TN Department of Human Services

Commissioner C. Warren Neel, Ph.D.
Duane Hawkins
Buddy Lea and Nancy Whittemore
TN Department of Finance & Administration

Commissioner Elizabeth Ruykeyser
Jane Thompson and Larry Thompson
TN Department of Mental Health &
    Developmental Disabilities

Commissioner Fredia Wadley
Sara Smith
TN Department of Health

Adjutant General Dan Wood
Colonel Bob Murphy
TN Department of the Military

President Wade Gilley
University of Tennessee

Chancellor Charles W. Manning
Tennessee Board of Regents

TN director Jerry Herman
Corporation for National Service

Commission Staff
Carol White, Executive Director
Mary Lewis Dassinger
Chuck Gilkey
Jeanne Henry
Rayna Coe Jenkins
Tommy Royston
Jim Snell

Staff Emeritus
William Aaron
Katie Ashby
Ann Bailey
DeWayne Holman
Margaret Horn
Susie Geist
Annette Shelley
Tammy Williams
Travis Wright

> If every Tennessean were to volunteer for one day a month, we could... help education with supplies and volunteers at schools. We could help the homeless and disadvantaged, the elderly, women's shelters, and kids. We could keep Tennessee cleaner. The government would use less money. Hospitalized veterans would have an easier time.
>
> —Larry R. West
> Bon Aqua
> Hickman County

The Council of Community Services has been providing information, planning and coordination services for Nashville's health and human services community since 1923. Its goal is to research, identify and find solutions to the emerging needs of the Nashville community using the following methods:

- Research and analysis of the demographic makeup of Tennessee with attention to our underserved communities
- Coordination and leadership of innovative and collaborative efforts to respond to the emerging needs within the community
* Incubation and management for new programs and initiatives developed in response to these community needs.

The Council of Community Services is probably best known for its publications that assist the community in identifying available resources. Since 1928, CCS has published a biennial edition of the Directory of Community Services, now a two volume set detailing more than 1,100 community agencies in Davidson County and surrounding counties. Some other CCS publications include:

Salary Survey of the Tennessee Nonprofit Association
International Directory
Directory of Licensed Mental Health Providers
Nashville Area Support Group Directory
Directory of Homeless Services
Tennessee Budget Review
Stats & Stories
Directory of Services for Senior Citizens

The Council of Community Services has been the initiator, coordinator, incubator and/or mentor for many well-known Nashville agencies and initiatives in addition to the statewide *Tennessee Volunteer Heroes 2001*. Some other members of the CCS family tree include:

Family & Children's Services
Mental Health Coop
Buddies of Nashville
Senior Citizens, Inc.
Oasis Center
Senior Solutions
Book'Em
Young Leaders Council
Community Resource Center
Volunteer Center
YWCA Domestic Violence Shelter
Victim Reconciliation Program
CCS Housing Systems
Neighborhood Resource Center
The Global Center

The Council of Community Services is currently developing the Tennessee Nonprofit Association, a statewide network of agencies, to provide a strong voice for the nonprofit community. Through its Policy Center, CCS acts as a link between the nonprofit community and our local, state, and federal decision-makers.

In 1999, CCS began a joint venture with the Center for Nonprofit Management called the Innovation and Collaboration Partnership to assist nonprofit agencies in the time-consuming process of forming strategic alliances, including collaborations, affiliations and mergers.

Council of Community Services
Carol Etherington, President
Brent Poulton, Vice-President
Deborah Faulkner, Secretary
Lethia Mann, Treasurer
Susan Russell, Immediate Past President

Tennessee Volunteer Heroes 2001

Board of Directors
Honey Alexander
Kent Ballow
Cathy Bender
Al Berry
Bob Claxton
Nat Crippens
Mark Desmond
Rhonda Dunn
Carol Etherington
John Fair
Deborah Faulkner
Chris Ferrell
Mary K. Friskics-Warren
Donna Gillroy
Richard Jackson
Elizabeth Jacobs
Mark Lipsey
Lethia Mann
Mike Miller
Reavis Mitchell
Doinna Nicely
Pat Nolan
Loretta Owens
Nibal Petro
Brent Poulton
Mario Ramos
Susan Russell
Andy Shookhoff
Pearl Sims
Lottie Strupp
Debi Tate
Gif Thornton
Joyce Vise
Avon Williams

CCS Staff
Stewart Clifton, Executive Director
Tunya Bails, Fiscal Analyst
Sarah Davis, Development & Marketing Director
Mary Beth Farringer, Council on Aging Director
Deborah Manion, Receptionist
Emette Marshall, Transportation Advocacy Coordinator
Kate Monaghan, Innovation and Collaboration Partnership
Sandra Poulton, Business Manager
Nancy Wright, Global Center & Special Projects coordinator

> If every Tennessean were to volunteer for one day a month, we could... establish a community built on trust, respect and dignity for all Tennesseans. Reaching out to others requires us to get outside of our boxes, to see the world through the eyes of another, and to listen to voices of those outside our neighborhoods.
>
> —Deborah White
> Johnson City, Washington County

> If every Tennessean were to volunteer for one day a month, we could... **stamp out illiteracy, homelessness, and littering. We could provide a better place for all our citizens to live.**
>
> —Lillian White
> Celina, Clay County

> If every Tennessean were to volunteer for one day a month, we could... enable local, state and federal programs to provide many more services to more people for less money.
>
> —Lee Whitmore
> Smyrna, Rutherford County

If every Tennessean were to volunteer for one day a month, we could...
alleviate most of our poverty and make the world a much better place in which to live. I think everyone needs to give time, money and energy to those less fortunate. It makes me feel so proud to be a Tennessee Volunteer and I thank God everyday that I'm still able to serve others, at age 74.

—Lottie C. Whitmore
Smyrna
Rutherford County

If every Tennessean were to volunteer for one day a month, we could...

raise the level of literacy for our children.

— Father James Wiesner
Memphis, Shelby County

If every Tennessean were to volunteer for one day a month, we could...

serve our community and fellow man to a greater extent.

—Frances Wiley
Lewisburg
Marshall County

If every Tennessean were to volunteer for one day a month, we could...
make the lives of every veteran, hospital patient, prisoner, underprivileged child and overworked mother happier. We could help cut down crime, violence, and illiteracy— we could make this world a better place.

—Virginia Dare Williams
Friendship, Crockett County

If every Tennessean were to volunteer for one day a month, we could...
keep all charitable activities in the private sector where they can be efficiently managed by individual volunteers without involvement of government at any level.

—Louise P. Wills
Nashville, Davidson County

If every Tennessean were to volunteer for one day a month, we could...

create the idea of *giving* rather than *taking* in the next generation.

—Anne Wilson
Maryville, Blount County

Project Sponsors

This book was made possible in part by generous grants from:

BellSouth (See page 44)

JC Penney (See page 70)

Ingram Industries and Ingram Book Group (See page 67)

The Renaissance Center (See next page)

WSMV Channel 4 (See page 95)

The Tennessee Cable Telecommunications Association (See page 91)

THE RENAISSANCE CENTER

From traditional arts to state-of-the-art technology, The Renaissance Center in Dickson is a unique family learning center as well as a growing entertainment center that offers drama, music and phenomenal laser shows.

Opened in fall 1999 by The Jackson Foundation, The Renaissance Center is "a place for families to come and learn together," said Doug Jackson, executive director of The Renaissance Center.

The 110,000-square-foot facility at 855 Tenn. 46 S. contains some of the world's most advanced technology, which also is incorporated into the teaching of traditional arts.

Courses at The Renaissance Center cover a range from basic music instruction including voice, guitar, piano and violin to highly advanced computer animation and television editing that can be found in only a limited number of places in the world. There are classes in several forms of art, drama and dance, as well as courses in some of the hottest business software programs available.

The Renaissance Center offers enrichment programs through a variety of low-cost field trips available to schools in Middle Tennessee.

Field trip selections include music, art and computer classes as well as CyberSphere shows, theatrical performances and Faraday Science Theatre programs geared toward each age group.

The Renaissance Repertory Company produces age-appropriate theatrical performances such as "The Nightingale," "You're a Good Man, Charlie Brown," "The Glass Menagerie" and "The Belle of Amherst."

The Faraday Science Theatre is a re-creation of Michael Faraday's laboratory at the Royal Institution of Great Britain from the 1800s. Students participate in fun and informational science projects that cover topics such as electricity and magnetism, motion and mechanics, light and sound, chemical reactions and the elements.

But The Renaissance Center is much more than educational programs. It also is a venue for cultural and entertainment events for the public.

The Performance Hall is host to a variety of theatrical and music programs. Professional and community theater are presented throughout the year.

Musical performances include the center's own faculty in recitals, performances by the center's Children's Choir and Community Orchestra and concerts featuring acts such as David Holt, the Allison Brown Quartet, Three Dog Night with the Tennessee Symphony and more.

The Visual Arts Gallery hosts a new exhibit each month throughout the year. Exhibits feature local and internationally known artists who work in a variety of media. Most exhibits include an opening reception with the artist and several include public workshops.

The CyberSphere is a four-story domed interactive theater. It features the Digistar II digital planetarium projector and the Audio-Visual Imagineering Omniscan laser graphics projector. In addition, the theater contains a collection of high quality video projection devices, more than 20 slide and special effects projectors, 13 different speaker enclosures with 14,000 watts of amplification and a sophisticated computer control system capable of synchronizing every device.

The CyberSphere not only features programs for field trips but also hosts open planetarium and music laser shows every Friday and Saturday.

Located inside The Renaissance Center is the Virtually Unlimited Bookstore, a 3,000-sqaure-foot full-service bookstore. The store regularly hosts book signings, book discussion groups and every Saturday is the host for Children's Storytime, many featuring costumed characters.

The Renaissance Center Ambassador Program allows volunteers to assist with programs at the center and earn discounts to classes and other programs.

For more information on The Renaissance Center or any of its programs, call 615-740-5600, write to 855 Hwy. 46 South, Dickson, Tennessee, 37055, or visit the center's Website at www.rcenter.org.

If every Tennessean were to volunteer for one day a month, we could… take a giant leap forward in the quality of service provided by the non-profit community to every Tennessean in need. It would ensure that those Tennesseans in need are not left out of the chain of human support.

—Gary Wilson
Brentwood
Williamson County

If every Tennessean were to volunteer for one day a month, we could… have a more beautiful state with gardens everywhere, and our children and our seniors would benefit so much. This could be so uplifting for the one helped as well as for the volunteer who devotes her or her time!

—Judi H. Wilson
Chattanooga
Hamilton County

If every Tennessean were to volunteer for one day a month, we could… help wipe out loneliness in the elderly, help curb child abuse, alleviate hunger and other concerns as well as gaining tremendous self-satisfaction in learning new things.

—Betty Wolfe
White Bluff, Dickson County

If every Tennessean were to volunteer for one day a month, we could… make the world a better place by helping people in need, improving education by providing resources and enrichment to our existing education system, protecting and cleaning up our environment, and providing leadership opportunities for our youth to enable them to become the successful leaders and volunteers of the future.

—Laurel Wood
Germantown
Shelby County

If every Tennessean were to volunteer for one day a month, we could… help one another to achieve countless riches, from one child who can read or kick a soccer ball to whole communities that are cleaner, safer, more beautiful places to live.

—Jane Work
Germantown, Shelby County

If every Tennessean were to volunteer for one day a month, we could… make a huge impact on two causes close to my heart: cancer and spinal cord injuries/disease. As a cancer patient, I understand that the commitment of time can make a dramatic impact on not just the disease, but the individual it touches. It can be as simple as giving a little time and encouragement and, believe it or not, you would just make their day.

—Frank Wright
McEwen
Humphreys County

WRITE TOGETHER™ PUBLISHING
533 Inwood Drive
Nashville, TN 37211
615-781-1518
www.writetogether.com

We proudly support the Volunteer Tennessee Initiative and encourage all Tennesseans to make visions a reality through volunteering.

If every Tennessean were to volunteer for one day a month, we could…

all have a positive effect on the community and instill service as a responsibility for future generations to embrace.

—Rick Wyckoff
Germantown, Shelby County

If every Tennessean were to volunteer for one day a month, we could…

have clean highways.

—Howard "Posey" Young
Celina
Clay County

Volunteer Heroes 2002

To learn more about our next project, *Tennessee Volunteer Heroes 2002,* stay tuned to the Volunteer Tennessee initiative's website at:

www.volunteertennessee.com

> **If every Tennessean were to volunteer for one day a month, we could...** accomplish more than anyone could imagine. If everyone had a cause they believed in enough to spend a little time on, it would improve our families, communities, counties, state, and our nation.
>
> —William Laughlin Youree
> Readyville
> Rutherford County

Your hero's ideas here...

9 781930 142572